WILLIAMS

Other books by the same author:

DAMON HILL
From Zero to Hero

THE QUEST FOR SPEED
Modern Racing Car Design and Technology

DRIVING FORCES
Fifty Men Who Have Shaped Motor Racing

WILLIAMS
The Business of Grand Prix Racing

FIFTY FAMOUS MOTOR RACES

DEREK BELL
My Racing Life

FERRARI
The Grand Prix Cars

BRABHAM
The Grand Prix Cars

MARCH
The Grand Prix Cars

JACKIE STEWART'S PRINCIPLES OF
PERFORMANCE DRIVING

Patrick Stephens Limited, an imprint of Haynes Publishing, has published authoritative, quality books for enthusiasts for more than 25 years. During that time the company has established a reputation as one of the world's leading publishers of books on aviation, maritime, military, motor cycling, motoring, motor racing, and railway subjects. Readers or authors with suggestions for books they would like to see published are invited to write to: The Editorial Director, Patrick Stephens Limited, Sparkford, Nr Yeovil, Somerset, BA22 7JJ.

WILLIAMS

TRIUMPH out of TRAGEDY

Alan Henry

Patrick Stephens Limited

First published in July 1995

British Library Cataloguing in Publication Data:
A catalogue record for this book is
available from the British Library

ISBN 1 85260 510 3

Library of Congress catalog card no. 95-77383

Patrick Stephens Limited is an imprint of Haynes Publishing,
Sparkford, Nr Yeovil, Somerset, BA22 7JJ.

Typeset by G&M, Raunds, Northamptonshire
Printed in Great Britain by
Butler & Tanner Ltd, London and Frome

Contents

Introduction and acknowledgements

A lain Prost, Ayrton Senna and Nigel Mansell have between them won a total of 123 Grand Prix victories and take their places in the Formula 1 record books as the three most successful professional racing drivers in the history of the World Championship. It therefore speaks volumes for Williams Grand Prix Engineering that all should have driven for this highly respected British team during the course of their careers.

Mansell and Prost, of course, won World Championships at the wheel of Renault-engined Williams cars. Tragically, Senna never managed to win a single race for the team. In one of the darkest chapters of contemporary motor racing history, he was killed while leading the 1995 San Marino Grand Prix at Imola. It was a disaster that, played out live on prime-time television across the globe, stunned the entire world as well as devastating the motor racing fraternity. For Williams it was nothing less than a catastrophe at the start of what seemed set to unfold as another season of glittering achievement in the upper reaches of this dazzlingly intense, competitive sport.

Grand Prix racing isn't simply a question of designing, building and operating complex single-seater racing cars. It's also about juggling commercial pressures and striking a delicate personal balance between the drivers employed. In the 28 months covered by this volume, Williams had to do all those things and more. Mansell, Prost and Senna were dramatically different characters, yet were united by that burning desire to succeed and win – a quality that, almost by definition, made it enormously difficult to get them paired together in the same team, at the same time.

This book is intended to offer a snapshot of a period of just a little over two years during which Williams experienced every possible emotion, extending from the undiluted joy of championship success to the deep despair of that bleak day at Imola when the team's prospects, however briefly, seemed to lie in tatters. It also recounts how Williams pulled itself up by its bootstraps and, through the efforts of Damon Hill and David Coulthard, surely two of the sport's men of the future, regained its winning ways to clinch the constructors' title for the third successive season in 1994 and carried Hill to within one point of the Drivers' Championship at the last race of the year.

It is also – and inevitably – a story of personal rivalry, jealousy and intolerance stemming from the intensity of the competition between many of the extraordinarily motivated drivers concerned.

I have drawn on much taped material with many of the leading players in this drama over several years. Thanks are also due to Peter Foubister, Publisher of *Autosport* magazine, for permission to quote from various interviews, and Michael Harvey, Editor of *Autocar*, who allowed me to draw on material that I originally contributed to that magazine. Nigel Roebuck offered invaluable assistance with tapes and corroboration of certain crucial information which we have both gathered over the years. Damon Hill, David Coulthard, the late Ayrton Senna, Julian Jakobi, Sheridan Thynne, Martin Brundle and Riccardo Patrese have also been excellent sources of background information. Don McLean's lyrics at the start of Chapter One were reproduced by kind permission of MCA Music Ltd.

I have also drawn on certain interview material recorded with Nigel Mansell over the years, and while he may not accept the interpretations I have put on some of his words and deeds in this volume, I appreciate the fact that he has invariably been prepared to talk, if not always to agree.

I must also thank Frank Williams, Patrick Head, Adrian Newey, Richard West and Ann Bradshaw for their generous assistance over the years, together with various interviews and off-the-record briefings that they have kindly provided from time to time. They proved invaluable in the battle to keep abreast of developments affecting the team.

They may well find some elements missing, but I would like to think that the tone of the book comes close to mirroring their inner feelings and personal reflections on what was, by any standards, a momentous two-year period in the history of this quite remarkable motor racing team.

Alan Henry
Tillingham, Essex
February 1995

Bibliography

Books

A Decade of Continuous Challenges: A Record of Honda's Formula One Racing Activities (Honda Motor Co, 1993)

Ayrton Senna Christopher Hilton (Patrick Stephens Ltd, 1994)

Damon Hill: From Zero to Hero Alan Henry (Patrick Stephens Ltd, 1994)

Nigel Mansell's Indy Car Racing Nigel Mansell and Jeremy Shaw (Weidenfeld and Nicolson, 1993)

Williams: The Business of Grand Prix Racing Alan Henry (Patrick Stephens Ltd, 1991 and 1992)

Fangio: My Racing Life Juan Manuel Fangio with Roberto Carozzo (Patrick Stephens Ltd, 1990)

Alain Prost Nigel Roebuck (Hazleton Publishing, 1990)

Periodicals

Autocourse

Autosport

Motoring News

Chapter 1

Mansell takes his leave

'I've used my talents as I could,
I've done some bad, I've done some good.
I did a whole lot better than they thought I would . . .'

Don McLean, American singer (1971)

It was a little before 11 o'clock on the morning of Sunday 13 September 1992 that the drama began to unfold in public. For weeks there had been rumours, counter-rumours, murmurings of discontent and outright dissent swirling round the Williams Formula 1 racing team. Now it seemed as though the dream deal, which had seen Nigel Mansell clinch the World Championship only a month earlier in Budapest, was set to come unstitched at the seams.

Yet again, Mansell and his Williams-Renault FW14B had been the absolute class of the field in qualifying for the Italian Grand Prix at Monza, the 13th round of the 16-race 1992 title chase. Up to this point in the season the partnership had won no fewer than eight Grands Prix, the epitome of a world class driver squeezing every ounce out of the best car in the field. On the face of it there seemed no reason at all why the partnership couldn't continue into 1993. But there was a snag.

For months Mansell had been locked into an increasingly acrimonious row with his team chief Frank Williams over the terms of his deal for the following season. As 1992 steadily unfolded, so the championship's destiny progressively succumbed to Mansell's unyielding armlock of success. Clearly he believed he could dictate terms to Williams. Ironically, by Monza the moment at which Mansell could have struck the most advantageous deal had passed, and the two parties had apparently arrived at the point of irreconcilable impasse.

Now, with the start of the Italian Grand Prix less than four hours away, Mansell broke the impasse by playing the strongest card in the pack. Negotiation was at an end as, togged-up in his racing overalls, the musta-chioed Englishman strode towards the steps leading up to the Monza press room, a bobbing sea of journalists and television cameramen stumbling over each other in his wake as they fought to keep up.

Nigel squeezed round the end of a long table, already set out with micro-phones, and squinted slightly in the face of the arc lights. As he began to read from a prepared script, the biggest story of the Formula 1 year was at last formally revealed to the public domain.

'Due to circumstances beyond my control, I have decided to retire from Formula 1 at the end of the season,' announced Mansell. 'I have made this decision with some regret, but not without a great deal of thought.

'Any relationship between a driver and a Formula 1 team is vital for suc-cess and *partly* dependent on money – because it defines how seriously the team and its backers take the driver – but those who know me well under-stand the importance of the human side and the mutual trust and goodwill and integrity and fair play that are the basis of all human relationships. All these issues have suffered in recent weeks.

'Looking back, I feel that relationships between me and the Canon Williams Renault team started to break down at the Hungarian Grand Prix. A deal was agreed with Frank Williams before that race, in front of a witness, and I have to say that at that time I felt very good about racing again with Williams in 1993. Having won the Championship, I was looking forward to defending the title with what I believe to be a very competitive car.

'However, three days after Hungary, I was telephoned by a Williams Director who said he had been instructed to tell me that, because Senna would drive for "nothing", I, the new World Champion, had to accept a mas-sive reduction in remuneration from the figure agreed in Hungary, consider-ably less than I am receiving this year. If I did not, Senna was ready to sign "that night". I rejected this offer and said that, if these were the terms, Williams had better go ahead and sign Senna.

'Since then it is fair to say that relations with the team have not been good – and I refer here to the Directors rather than the scores of people behind the scenes at Williams. I have listened to many different opinions, some well-meaning, some not, and we heard the public statements made by Senna in Belgium. To say that I have been badly treated, I think, is a gross understate-ment. Of course a team owner – any team owner – is free to choose whomever he likes to work for him. It was the lack of information, and the sudden changes, that I have found disappointing.

'It is difficult to put into words the sort of commitment you have to make in order to succeed in Formula 1. I am aware of criticisms made of my approach to racing. But I am the way I am because I believe in total sacrifice, a total ability to withstand pain and a total belief in myself and my ability.

'To have the motivation to win a World Championship, you must in turn have those commitments back from the team. When I returned from Ferrari I did so with the belief that I had that motivation and the team had that commitment. I don't think I was wrong.

'Now things are different. I no longer feel, so far as I am concerned, that the commitment from the team towards me for next year is there. There are many reasons for this. I have tried to give some idea of how I feel – other people will no doubt draw their own conclusions. For one thing, it is clear that Alain Prost has been committed for months to drive for Williams. For another, I thought I had a deal when, clearly, I did not. Needless to say, I do not understand why these things have happened.

'Yes, in recent weeks, various key people have tried to smooth things over. I respect that and I thank them for their time. But I now realise that it is too late. To my mind, it all comes down to "fair play" – or the lack of it. Money, a trigger for the problems after Hungary, is now no longer an issue for me.

'In finishing, I would like to say, in the most sincerest [sic] of ways, that I will always be grateful to the Williams team and to Renault for the support they have given me and hopefully will still give me – in 1992. I want to win the remaining races and I am sure that the FW15, from what I know about it, will do the job in 1993.

'As for myself, I know that I am not ready to retire completely. I still love my motor racing and I still want to win. So, I may look at the Indycar World Series and see what opportunities are available, if any.

'Finally, this statement expresses all that I will say on this matter at the moment, so no one should expect any additional comments.'

There followed a scramble for phone lines as the media rushed to inform the world of this momentous development.

The deed done, Mansell and his team-mate Riccardo Patrese prepared for the race. Confirming his form in qualifying, Mansell shot away into a commanding lead from the start, leaving Patrese in third place chasing along behind Ayrton Senna's unwieldy McLaren-Honda for the first 14 laps before the Italian found a gap and dodged through to make it a Williams 1-2 at the head of the field.

Patrese had by now shrewdly appreciated that he was driving the last of his five consecutive seasons for the Williams team. Like Mansell, earlier in the season he had quickly worked out that Prost would be with the team for 1993, so, rather than be left on the sidelines, he moved quickly to accept an invitation to join the Benetton-Ford squad alongside Michael Schumacher.

Now, racing round Monza in front of his home crowd, he must have been regretting that he'd played his hand so early in the game of poker that is such a familiar feature of the end-of-season driver transfer market. With Mansell quitting, perhaps he could have stayed with Williams after all as Prost's running-mate.

Just as it seemed as though Mansell had it in the bag, the leading Williams slowed dramatically on lap 19. At a stroke he had lost 19 seconds and Patrese surged past into the lead, but any thoughts that Nigel might be in trouble were immediately dispelled. Having stamped his mastery on the race, the new World Champion had decided to defer to his team-mate on his home soil.

'I let Riccardo by, and rode shotgun for him,' he subsequently explained. 'Before the race he'd told me how much he wanted to win his home Grand Prix, and I was happy to help.'

It wasn't an easy strategy for Mansell to adopt. Senna's McLaren was still only a few seconds behind and, as the time came for the two Williams-Renaults to begin lapping slower rivals, so the Brazilian remorselessly made ground on them. Once on a clear track again, Patrese and Mansell would ease open their advantage towards the 5-second mark.

Cynics might question whether Mansell's apparent magnanimity had its roots in a genuine desire to help Patrese. Perhaps he simply couldn't have cared less as to the outcome of the race after going public on the subject of his breach with the Williams team. Conceivably he might have been attempting to demonstrate, albeit melodramatically, just what a talent Williams had allowed to slip through its fingers.

Either way, Mansell's Grand Gesture came to nothing. On lap 42 his Williams suddenly refused to change out of sixth gear due to a failure of the hydraulic pump drive that controlled, amongst many other functions, the electronically activated automatic gear-change mechanism on his Williams FW14B. At the end of that lap he came slowly in to retire.

This left Patrese nursing a 6-second lead over Senna, which he gradually extended to 10.3 seconds by the end of lap 47. With only five laps to go, Riccardo might have been forgiven for thinking his 16-year quest for a home win was at last within reach, but suddenly the Italian's Williams also fell victim to an hydraulic pump malfunction. At the end of lap 48 Senna came through into the lead and, when Patrese came into sight, the nose of his car was running unnaturally high off the ground. Not only was the gear-box stuck in fourth, but the computer-controlled active suspension system had seemingly developed a mind of its own.

By the time the chequered flag fell on the *Gran Premio d'Italia*, Senna, the Benettons of Martin Brundle and Michael Schumacher, and Gerhard Berger's Ferrari had all surged past the heartbroken Patrese. Fifth place seemed a dismal consolation prize for the popular Italian.

For Senna it may have been a fortuitous victory, but one achieved after an absolutely characteristic performance from the triple World Champion. His McLaren-Honda MP4/7 was the last, and by no means the best, car/engine combination to be produced during the five-year association between the famous British F1 constructor and its Japanese partners. Yet he drove absolutely flat out for the entire distance and was deservedly the man to inherit first place when the Williams-Renaults ran into trouble.

'I prefer to win when I have been fighting, and overtaking people,' said Senna afterwards, 'but I was pleased that I could drive with the Williams, all the way, even with inferior performance from my car.

'This year McLaren have not been able to give me a very fast car, a car to win the championship, but we have never given up, always making the best of what we had, even though we knew that, in a straight fight, we had no chance to win.'

Any pronouncement by Senna was inevitably subjected to the most rigorous and detailed scrutiny by members of the Fourth Estate. Most politicians would have envied the enigmatic Brazilian's remarkable astuteness when it came to sending discreet signals as an unspoken sub-text to his main message of the day.

Furthermore, bearing in mind Mansell's reference to Senna's apparent willingness to sign an immediate Williams contract 'for nothing', there was surely something more to his words on this occasion. Was he *really* hinting that he would join Williams in 1993? Did that mean that he and Prost would be prepared to drive as team-mates again after their bruising couple of seasons together in 1988/89? Or was he simply sending a coded message to McLaren to the effect that they had better raise the standard of their game in 1993 if they wanted to retain his services?

Who could tell? But as the media conducted a detailed post-mortem on each syllable Senna had uttered, they would have been intrigued to have been in possession of another remark, made in passing, on the winner's rostrum that sunny afternoon at Monza. As Brundle climbed to second place on the podium, he was greeted by a handshake from Senna and a chance remark that left Martin with the firm impression that there was a strong chance of them being paired together at Williams for 1993. What could Ayrton have meant?

Reflecting on this just before Christmas 1994, seven months after Senna's death, Brundle freely admitted that he couldn't quite recall the precise wording of Senna's remark. 'But I remember what he said gave me a huge boost,' he admits. In fact, in the weeks that followed Martin would indeed come close to landing the second Williams drive for the following season, only to have it snatched away virtually when the pen was poised over the contract. To this day he is not sure why the opportunity evaporated so late in the day.

Frank Williams, meanwhile, returned to his team's headquarters at Didcot and spent much of the following day, Monday 14 September, in conference with his sponsors and fellow director Patrick Head. Mansell's abrupt departure announcement had certainly not been on their personal agenda and Frank picked his words carefully as he formulated an official statement on the matter, which was released to the media the following day.

It read: 'Williams Grand Prix Engineering would like to re-emphasise its deep regret in Nigel Mansell's decision to retire from Formula 1 at Sunday's Italian Grand Prix.

'His 26 wins while driving for Williams allows him a special place in our history having won considerably more races than any other of the team's drivers.

'To ensure the team has the best chance of winning races and World Championships, fellow director Patrick Head and I have always sought to employ the best drivers and engineers.

'To allow us to express our skills as engineers we have had to raise significant funds to invest in World Championship winning technology and World Championship winning drivers. This only comes from many long hours of considered negotiations which are dependent on many variables, some known, some unknown. Our strategy for 1993 included ensuring we had Nigel in the team, a strategy we pursued right up until Nigel's announcement on Sunday.

'Without going into details of the long and protracted meetings, we have made several offers to Nigel, all of which were rejected. Some criteria for the decision-making progress have changed throughout the year, but we repeat Nigel was the focus of our efforts for the 1993 season.

'In parallel with the driver negotiations, we obviously have to ensure the team's future, which in a world recession is difficult even with our team's World Championship winning status. It is noteworthy that despite the enormous support for both the team and Nigel from many British fans, we are still unable to raise any significant sponsorship from the UK.

'Our first responsibility is to Williams Grand Prix Engineering and its 200 employees and, therefore, regrettably we could not meet Nigel's demands in the time-frame required. We are obviously aware of the disappointment that Nigel's retirement generated in the UK, but Williams Grand Prix Engineering is an international company that operates on a global basis and must continue to do so.

'In the meantime, we would like to thank Nigel for all his efforts for the team and the sponsors and wish him and his family well in America. Nigel returned to the Williams team for the sole purpose of winning the World Championship and he has now achieved this goal. In doing so he has won a further 13 races with us, and this year has equalled the record number of eight wins in one season with three races still to go.

'We know that in the early months of his second period with us he said he would retire if he won the Championship. This could have obviously been a stronger consideration than we originally thought and whatever the final reasons for Nigel's retirement we are glad he has won the Championship he richly deserved.'

Mansell had clearly seen the problems coming to the point where he had started to work on a possible back-up strategy. By timely coincidence the 1992 Italian Grand Prix also opened the door by which he could escape to one of the most competitive Indycar teams of all, in time to put together a deal for the following season.

Michael Andretti, younger son of 1978 World Champion Mario, was anxious to try his hand at Formula 1. In 1991 the young American, then barely 30 years old, had clinched the Indycar Championship at the wheel of a Ford-engined Lola fielded by the Newman/Haas team, based out of Lincolnshire, Illinois.

The team was founded on a durable business partnership between Carl Haas, one of US motor racing's most shrewd entrepreneurs, and movie star Paul Newman, himself a keen amateur racer and one of Mario Andretti's greatest fans. The team had originally been founded in 1983 as a one-car operation for Andretti Senior, but was expanded into a two-car father-and-son line-up when Michael came aboard in 1989.

Truth be told, there wasn't much anybody could tell Carl Haas about running a racing team. The son of a German immigrant family, he dabbled in sports car racing himself during the 1950s before becoming North American importer for Lola Cars. Before he even dipped his toes into the Indycar waters his team had earned itself an impeccable winning pedigree, with no fewer than three SCCA Formula 5000 and four Can-Am sports car titles to its credit through the 1970s and early '80s.

In 1984 Andretti won the PPG Indycar championship with six wins out of 16 races and scored nine more wins over the next four seasons until Michael's arrival in the second car. In 1989 Newman/Haas found itself struggling slightly as it came to terms with the challenge involved in fielding two cars, but, even so, Michael won two races.

In 1990 he won five, finishing second to Al Unser Jnr in the championship, then swept to eight victories the following year to clinch the title in a campaign that saw him lead almost 50 per cent of the season's racing laps. In 1992 he followed that up with five wins and another eight poles, but had to give best to Bobby Rahal in the battle to retain his title crown.

Michael Andretti was aggressive, highly motivated and had an apparent ability to slice through slower traffic that his father described as 'awesome'. McLaren F1 team boss Ron Dennis attended the 1992 Indianapolis 500, where Michael finished second after an epic battle with Rick Mears's Penske, and was also impressed with Andretti's relentless speed.

Having turned it all over in his mind and assessed all the options, Dennis decided to take a gamble and sign Michael to drive a full season of Grands Prix in 1992. Barely 24 hours before Mansell made public his decision to leave Formula 1, McLaren formally announced Michael Andretti's recruitment for 1993. The vacant place thus created in the Newman/Haas line-up was so obviously made to measure for Mansell that it was hard to believe such a transfer had not been worked out as a possible back-stop in the Englishman's mind ever since Prost appeared in the frame as a Williams candidate for 1993.

At the McLaren press conference Ron Dennis singled out one of the key reasons behind signing Michael Andretti as his ability to overtake other cars. 'That may seem obvious,' said Dennis, 'but I think Michael is probably in that small band of perhaps five drivers in the world who have the necessary aggression in traffic and the desire to win.' Nobody could have foreseen that this whole strategy would go disastrously wrong.

Meanwhile, back in the Williams enclave, Nigel Mansell would be proved absolutely correct in his judgement that Prost was in line for a

Williams-Renault drive in 1993. The Frenchman had taken a sabbatical in 1992 after being unceremoniously fired from the Ferrari F1 line-up just before the final race of 1991. He had, it transpired, been a little too outspoken about the Ferrari team's operational shortcomings for the management's comfort. Despite testing a Ligier-Renault early in 1992, he had correctly assessed the car to be not quite up to the competitive mark, and, despite considerable speculation that he might take a controlling stake in the Magny-Cours-based team, he eventually decided to sit out the season.

Ironically we would have to wait until the 1992 Portuguese Grand Prix before we learned that Prost had forged an agreement in principle to join Williams the following year, almost before Mansell had even embarked on his World Championship-winning campaign. However, despite plenty of leaks and extremely well-informed rumour, the question of his return was such political dynamite that it was kept under wraps for as long as possible. Once Mansell showed his hand, however, Prost was free to speak.

Alain freely admitted that the situation had developed to a point where he was beginning to have his doubts that it would ever quite come together. 'During the weeks immediately prior to this weekend [Portugal] I got close to McLaren,' he admitted. 'I didn't control the whole negotiating situation terribly well, but what I always wanted to do throughout was to drive for Williams. I just needed to detect a little more confidence on the part of the people involved in the deal.'

However, what now became clear, for all Mansell's references to Senna's willingness to drive 'for nothing', was that Alain was simply not prepared to have the Brazilian driving at Williams alongside him. This fact was addressed very forcefully by Senna at the post-race press conference in Portugal after he had finished third behind Mansell – who thereby notched up an all-time record ninth victory in a single season – and his own McLaren-Honda team-mate Gerhard Berger.

'I don't accept being vetoed by anyone in the way this has been done,' said Ayrton firmly. 'This is supposed to be the World Drivers' Championship. We had two fantastic championships this year and last. In 1989 and '90 we had two very bad ones.

'They were a consequence of unbelievable politics, and bad behaviour by some people. I think that now we are coming back to the same situation.

'If Prost wants to come back, and maybe win another title, he should be sporting. The way he is doing it, he is behaving like a coward. He must be prepared to race anybody, under any conditions, on equal terms. He now wants to win with everything laid out for him.

'It is like going for a 100-metre sprint in running shoes while everybody has lead shoes. That is the way he wants to race. [But] it is not racing.'

The extremely candid verbal assault more than anything reflected Senna's belief that the Williams-Renault package would remain technically the one to beat in 1993. Moreover, this was set against a troubled immediate future for McLaren, which was facing the end of its five-year engine supply partnership with Honda and, as yet, had no similar works deal on the horizon with which to replace the Japanese company.

Frank Williams would comment later that year that he felt both Mansell and Senna 'had done the sport a big disservice over the last 12 months in that they are such world-renowned sportsmen that, when they speak, the world listens.

'They got drunk on their own power and said things which have done Formula 1 no good at all. I think the entire Mansell affair was bad, just as I think Ayrton's remarks about not getting in at Williams were out of order. I have told Alain that he must not get involved in anything like this – and if he does, I will penalise him financially.'

By Senna's high standards the 1992 season had been extremely disappointing. It may have been a measure of McLaren's strength-in-depth that they won five Grands Prix during the course of the year, but the stark reality was that Honda's new 75-degree RA122E/B V12 engine was insufficiently competitive.

Now, to cap it all, Senna found that he no longer seemed to be completely in charge of his own personal destiny. For a professional sportsman who had controlled the direction of his own career with a seemingly relentless inevitability, this was certainly a difficult pill for the Brazilian to swallow. It was also somehow ironic that the focal point of his frustration had turned out to be the Williams team, for it was Frank who had given Ayrton his very first test at the wheel of a Formula 1 car back in 1983.

Frank freely admits that he 'kinda screwed things up' when the opportunity presented itself to sign up this enormously promising rising star. At the time Senna was mid-way through his assault on the 1983 British F3 championship, a season that would end in his just pipping Martin Brundle for the title. Yet the ascetic, serious-minded Brazilian was far from simply another bright-eyed new boy with his eye firmly trained on the bottom rung of the Formula 1 ladder.

Even at this stage of his career it was clear that he had a remarkable talent, prompting Frank's invitation for a test in the Cosworth V8-engined Williams FW08C at Donington Park. This was a sister car to that which Keke Rosberg had used to score a terrific victory in that year's Monaco Grand Prix, but at a time when Formula 1's whole emphasis was swinging away from 3-litre naturally-aspirated engines towards 1.5-litre turbos, it was not in the absolute front-line in terms of competitiveness.

'I don't think I came back to the factory thinking I'd seen a revelation,' Frank later admitted as he reflected over Senna's first F1 outing. 'But he was very quick indeed – like a second faster than our regular test driver Jonathan Palmer after only 15 laps. I knew we ought to keep an eye on him, but I didn't believe he was on today's agenda, so to speak.'

In retrospect, this failure to recognise Ayrton's natural talent reflected a remarkable lack of prescience on Frank's part. Senna signed for the Toleman F1 team at the start of 1984, served a glittering Formula 1 apprenticeship, and, next time round, Williams was naturally close to the head of the queue when bidding for his services in 1985. On balance, however, Ayrton preferred the promise offered by the Lotus-Renault package to Frank's Honda turbos, by then in their unreliable infancy after only a single season with Williams.

There was more irony here. Senna took over Nigel Mansell's place alongside Elio de Angelis at Lotus, while the Englishman was eventually signed up to run alongside Rosberg at Williams, replacing the free-wheeling Frenchman Jacques Laffite whose enormously attractive personality could no longer mask the fact that his best days in Formula 1 were now past.

It is a pretty open secret that Williams was not overwhelmed by a burning sense of conviction when he signed the man who, as things transpired, would win more races for his team than any other individual. By his own admission, Frank concedes that he was 'rather dickering around on the matter, blowing hot one day and cold the next'. It took Patrick Head to say bluntly, 'For goodness sake, Frank, make a decision and we'll live with it.' Even so, it hardly looked like the deal that would produce the most statistically successful British F1 driver in the history of the World Championship.

Nine years down the road, things were so very different. Senna now found himself in effect fighting for the scraps from Williams's table in the wake of Mansell's decision to quit Formula 1. What made it worse was the fact that he was facing seemingly overwhelming odds in the light of Prost's veto. Yet it was absolutely characteristic that Ayrton declined to adopt a conciliatory, pussy-footing approach in his efforts to gain entry to the Williams enclave. Frankly, neither he nor Prost could stand the sight of the other at this stage of their careers, and Senna aimed all his verbal shots from the hip.

Of course the Senna dimension was really only of secondary importance in Mansell's assessment of the situation. The fact that he had been told that Ayrton 'would sign for nothing' was simply another barb in the face of what he regarded as the principal assault on his authority as the newly crowned World Champion. And that, as he told the author, was the Prost factor alone.

Shortly after blasting his way to pole position on the eve of his ninth win of the season, Mansell was relaxing at his private rented villa within the exclusive *Quinta da Marina* resort, a few miles up the coast from Estoril. Any initial fury over what he regarded as his unacceptable treatment at the hands of the Williams team had now abated. He was relaxed, relatively philosophical, and clearly looking forward to his new challenge with the Newman/Haas Indycar scene.

There was no question about it. From Nigel's viewpoint, he believed that circumstances had conspired to force him out of Formula 1, although he chose a more diplomatic turn of phrase to communicate his feelings.

'Well,' he grinned, 'how do you think the situation will be remembered? At the end of the negotiations I effectively found myself last in line. What a story! What happened over these past three months was humiliating.

'I am a happy man and I didn't want a relationship with Prost. I think it is disappointing that neither of the two drivers who helped make Williams-Renault such a winning force has ended up signing a contract with the team in 1993. Prost, on the other hand, signed a long time ago – and with his contract he controls certain things. [So] I asked myself, who is running this team?'

Decisions had now been taken that ensured that this was no longer a matter of any concern to Mansell. Yet there were still three more races remaining on the 1992 Formula 1 calendar, and the new World Champion was determined to win them all.

The car used to such great effect by the Englishman throughout his Championship season at last broke the four-year stranglehold on the F1 Constructors' Championship enjoyed by the McLaren-Honda alliance. The Williams FW14B was an evolutionary development of the car used by Mansell and Patrese the previous year, but further enhanced by the addition of what was generally referred to as 'active suspension', but more precisely defined by Patrick Head as a 'rapid response, controlled ride height system'.

The decision to commit to the active suspension system was taken after an intensive pre-season test programme. The Williams FW14B came out of the starting gate like a rocket and Mansell won the first five races of the season with consummate ease before finally being beaten at Monaco, where he went down to a defeat at the hands of Ayrton Senna's McLaren-Honda after a precautionary late race pit stop prompted by a fleeting suspicion that his FW14B had developed a slow puncture. Incorrectly, as things transpired.

Yet if the Williams active suspension system had been one element in the decisive technical advantage enjoyed by Mansell in 1992, it was also an area over which the driver had harboured long-term, deep-seated concerns. Mansell had very vivid memories from his Lotus days during the early 1980s of how temperamental such systems could be.

Put simply, the principle behind active suspension was to stabilise a Formula 1 car's underbody aerodynamics by controlling the ride height – the gap between the bottom of the car and the ground – throughout a race distance. With a conventional car the business of 'setting up' its chassis adjustments was always something of a compromise.

In the early stages of a race a conventionally suspended car, heavy with fuel, would be prone to hitting undulations in the track surface. Midway through the race it would perhaps have an optimum ride-height with its tank now half empty, and in the closing stages it might well have too much ground clearance as the final portion of the fuel load was consumed. All this variation put the onus firmly on a driver not only to assess the best compromise set-up, but also to adapt his driving style to get the best out of the car in these changing operational circumstances.

Properly developed active suspension systems changed all this, allowing the driver to benefit from a consistent-handling car throughout the race, a system of hydraulic struts replacing the conventional steel springs. Responding to input from sensors on each wheel, which feed to a central computer 'brain', a complex electro-hydraulic control system kept the ride height as near unchanged as possible, irrespective of the fuel load being carried. Such systems also offered considerable benefits in terms of reducing fatigue, allowing a driver of Mansell's calibre to run faster for longer in most racing situations.

However, the downside involved in the use of such systems had been put on very graphic display during the Saturday morning free practice session at Estoril, before Mansell's storming run to pole position later in the day. The hydraulic pump on the World Champion's Williams-Renault packed up abruptly, not only shutting down the active suspension but also leaving the car jammed in fifth gear. Mansell ploughed into a sand trap, emerging a little shaken, but unscathed.

A few weeks later, before finally turning his back on Formula 1 for the moment, Mansell would criticise the pace at which F1 technology had been allowed to develop over recent years, notwithstanding the obvious benefits that had accrued to him on this front throughout his Championship year.

'I'm obviously very grateful for the role that developments like active suspension have played in helping me to win the World Championship,' he conceded, 'but I would just as soon have done without it. It makes me really happy that I am switching to Indycars, which are not as technically advanced as Formula 1 machines.

'If the Williams is reliable next year, and there is not a comparable driver in the second car, you will probably get Prost winning all 16 races. I would say there is not another engine currently in Formula 1 to compete next year with Renault. [And] there will be developments on the new FW15 with anti-lock braking, which is probably going to be used, which takes the skill away from braking. It will be an enormous advantage.'

Patrese qualified alongside Mansell on the front row of the grid for the Portuguese race, with the McLaren-Hondas of Senna and Berger side-by-side on the second row. Riccardo was moving first when the starting light blinked green, but Mansell swept across his team-mate's bows as they surged into the first tricky downhill right-hander, and flattened his rival's morale by completing the opening lap already 2.4 seconds ahead of the other Williams.

Overnight rain had washed from the track surface the protective coating of rubber progressively laid throughout two days of practice and qualifying, leaving the tarmac unpredictably abrasive. Routine stops to replace worn tyres would clearly be part of everybody's race strategy, and while Mansell made a trouble-free change on lap 29, by that point Patrese had lost his second place with a frustratingly long wheel-change six laps earlier.

At first everything seemed to go according to plan for the Italian driver, but then the rear jack supporting Riccardo's Williams suddenly collapsed, and by the time a replacement had been located in order to complete the routine, Riccardo had been at rest for 19 seconds, thus resuming the race in fourth place.

Fired up by his frustration, Patrese then got his head down and carved relentlessly into Berger's third place advantage. He was soon tight on the McLaren's tail, time and again attempting to force his Williams alongside its red and white rival only to be thwarted by the Austrian driver's energetically defensive driving.

Coming through the fast right-hander on to the Estoril pit straight at the end of the 42nd lap, Patrese was closer than ever. But Berger was coming in for tyres and, having defended his position from the Williams to the last moment before backing off, the McLaren driver saw the pit entrance lane looming on the right-hand side of the circuit.

He backed off the throttle, and the McLaren slowed abruptly. Suddenly Patrese was faced with a potentially catastrophic situation. He dried to duck left, but his Williams's right front wheel slammed into the McLaren's left-rear with a huge impact.

The instant mayhem unleashed by the collision served as a horrifying reminder of the pent-up kinetic energy developed by the contemporary breed of high-downforce Grand Prix car. The front of Patrese's car was instantly pitched skyward, rising almost vertically to the point where the tail of the FW14B appeared to be several feet off the track. The car continued to rise, the detached right front wheel bouncing away down the circuit ahead of it, until it seemed irrevocably destined to perform a backward somersault and land upside down on the track surface with a massive impact, and disastrous consequences.

During the course of these aerobatics Patrese's Williams passed by the smallest of margins *beneath* a bridge spanning the circuit. Then the tail of the car hit the deck and it crashed back onto the ground, lurching into the pit wall and ripping off its right rear wheel. Flying debris was surely set to maim many crew members. But no. Riccardo's wrecked machine slithered and banged its way to a halt and its shaken driver clambered out intact.

Patrese was understandably furious that Berger had slowed without any warning signal, but at the same time accepted that his rival had not acted with malicious intent. Nevertheless, the Williams team lodged an official protest over the episode. The stewards duly interviewed both drivers and rejected the protest, concluding that the accident had been an unfortunate misunderstanding. The fact that it had been perhaps Formula 1's closest call in recent years went unremarked.

If anybody believed that Mansell would ease up and stroke his way through to what looked like the end of his Formula 1 career, they had gravely misjudged the nature of the man. Estoril had proved just what a burningly competitive spirit still motivated the 39-year-old driver who was now approaching the end of his 12th full season in motor racing's international front line.

He kept up the relentless pressure through to the penultimate round of the title chase, the Japanese Grand Prix at Suzuka. This time Mansell was a staggering 0.9 seconds faster than Patrese as the Williams-Renault duo buttoned up the front row yet again, Senna and Berger taking the second row in their McLaren-Hondas in a re-run of the Estoril qualifying order.

Come the race, Mansell attempted to make up for Patrese's Monza disappointment. Having stamped his absolute mastery on the event, opening out a 21-second lead by lap 35, he then slowed abruptly and allowed Riccardo to power through into the lead. Thereafter Nigel made the Italian work hard for his living to the point where Patrese began to wonder what his team-mate was really doing.

'I didn't know what Nigel wanted to do,' said Patrese afterwards. 'He was pushing me hard and if he was really prepared to let me win the race, then I think he should have gone a bit slower. I thought, "My God, ten laps still to go and Nigel is still there." But, even though I realised he wasn't fighting me, at that particular moment it was difficult to know what he wanted to do.'

Either way, it didn't really matter what Nigel had in mind, for his engine expired spectacularly on lap 44, with just nine left to run. That just gave him time to change into civvies and be ready to greet the victorious Patrese with his congratulations as the Italian steered his Williams FW14B into *parc fermé* at the end of his slowing-down lap.

Twelve months earlier, Ayrton Senna had relinquished the lead of the Japanese Grand Prix in similarly abrupt circumstances on the very last lap in order to give his team-mate Gerhard Berger the opportunity to score his first McLaren-Honda victory. Like Mansell, he was criticised in some quarters for a display of largesse that was lacking in subtlety and grace. Yet, by the same token, Grand Prix victories are not something to be tossed aside lightly, least of all by such ferociously committed competitors of the calibre of these two World Champions.

All that now remained on Mansell's Formula 1 championship agenda was the final race of the season, the Australian Grand Prix in Adelaide. But while Nigel bagged pole position yet again, this time Senna joined him on the front row after a great effort with the unloved McLaren-Honda MP4/7A. 'If we can get in front at the first corner, then maybe we can make a race of it this time,' mused the Brazilian. 'But if we don't get off the line first, then it is going to be very difficult.'

As things transpired, Mansell got the jump on the McLaren off the line and although Ayrton dived down the inside to take the lead at the end of the long back straight, he immediately ran wide, allowing Nigel to nip back ahead. In the opening stages of the race Senna remained glued to the Williams's rear wing, but Mansell had opened about ten lengths on his pursuer when he was inadvertently baulked by Nicola Larini's Ferrari.

At a stroke Senna was back on his tail as they hurtled through the right-hand kink leading into the braking area for the tight right-hander before the pits. Ayrton, sensing a chance, left his braking desperately late, but the move went drastically wrong and he plunged into the back of Mansell's car.

The McLaren's left front wheel was ripped off in the impact and the Williams's rear wheels were both momentarily clear of the track surface by the force of the impact, both cars then ploughing off on to the rough on the left-hand side of the circuit.

Inevitably the recriminations started immediately. Senna accused Mansell of 'short braking', a technique sometimes employed in the heat of the battle whereby the competitor in front brakes early and abruptly, seeking to unsettle a rival following closely behind. Nigel's interpretation was less prosaic. He believed Ayrton had simply rammed him off the circuit, and went storming off to the Clerk of the Course to express this viewpoint.

The stewards examined all the video tapes of the accident and concluded it had simply been a racing incident for which neither driver was to blame. It was not a verdict that rested easily with Mansell, by now pumped up on a heady cocktail of adrenalin and indignation.

'I'm glad I'm out of it,' he glowered. 'He [Senna] just rammed me at about 40 mph more than I was going. The reason I just ran across the track like I did [after the accident] was that there would have been a big fight and I don't think that is the right way to leave Formula 1. I thought I would do the honourable thing and go and see the stewards and speak with my team.

'Certain people in Formula 1 can get away with anything they want. They [the stewards] say they have played it back and said it was just a sporting accident. That's a crock of rubbish. And I don't have any support from my team.'

Senna simply shrugged it all aside. 'He moved over on me and braked earlier than he should, as well as staying in the middle of the road,' he said calmly. 'I have no feelings about it. I think he has been complaining about it, but that is normal for him. He always complains. I would have been happy to come and shake hands and let it go.'

This was not the first occasion on which Mansell and Senna had been involved in such a controversial confrontation on the circuit. Back in 1986 Ayrton had squeezed Mansell uncompromisingly when they were battling for the lead of the Brazilian GP at Rio, contributing to the Williams driver's premature retirement from the race when he hit a guard rail. The following year they collided on the opening lap of the Belgian GP at Spa, an episode that led to Mansell having to be hauled off Senna when they later confronted each other in the Williams pit.

Even once before in 1992 – his Championship year – Mansell had found himself coming unstuck at Senna's instigation. In the Canadian GP at Montreal, Senna's McLaren-Honda MP4/7 had taken an immediate lead from the start with Mansell, Patrese, Gerhard Berger's Ferrari and Michael Schumacher's Benetton all boxed in tightly behind.

After a few laps the situation at the front of the field developed into a stalemate. Ayrton was driving well within his limits, keeping the pace of the race under control, and taking no risks, sure in the knowledge that, as long as he was not tricked into a mistake, Mansell would have his work cut out finding a way through.

Of course this theory did not take into account Mansell's aggressively self-confident belief that he could get the job done, reasoning that an over-taking manoeuvre was, in fact, feasible at one particular point on the circuit. That moment came on the 15th of the race's 69 laps.

Approaching the S-bend before the pits, Mansell dodged out from behind Senna's McLaren and attempted to outbrake the Brazilian, despite the fact that his Williams was now off-line and on the dust.

What happened next was disputed by the two drivers involved. However, close eye-witnesses say that Mansell came into the corner too fast, that Senna gave him room, but that the Williams speared dramatically across the McLaren's bows, tore across the infield gravel run-off, then hurtled back on to the track in front of the leading McLaren. Then Mansell's car, now shorn of its nose wings, spun to a halt, almost in the middle of the circuit.

Apparently dazed, Mansell sat in the cockpit for several moments as rival cars overtook his damaged machine protected by a flurry of yellow warning flags. Having lifted himself from the cockpit, Mansell immediately sought out McLaren boss Ron Dennis and gave him a piece of his mind about what he regarded as Senna's unethical driving.

'I got alongside him and he just pushed me off,' he complained. The matter was referred to the stewards of the meeting, but in the absence of any observers' report to the contrary, Senna was not found at fault.

'I think Nigel realised he was coming into the corner too quickly,' said Ayrton, 'and so he decided to open the throttle and straight-line the sand trap. The trouble was that the car landed on its nose.' Interestingly, Nigel's team-mate Riccardo Patrese sided with Senna's interpretation of events. 'Nigel decided to go for it down the inside line where the track was dusty,' observed the Italian. 'Ayrton didn't help him, but he was not unfair. They did not touch and Nigel went off.'

In many ways, the episodes at both Montreal and Adelaide were absolutely characteristic of Mansell. Seldom, if ever, did he conclude that he might be the one at fault. Some people felt this reflected an acute lack of generosity of spirit, others that his burningly competitive nature simply could not grasp the notion that he could actually be wrong. His grumbling and mumbling about the stewards' attitude towards his complaint at Adelaide was also clearly a case in point.

Thus ended Nigel Mansell's association with the Williams team, a partnership that had yielded no fewer than 26 wins over two stints extending across five seasons. He had achieved his ambition to become World Champion and, perhaps more significantly, had been a factor in just about every race in which he competed. In the car, Williams would willingly attest, Nigel Mansell never once short-changed them. In that respect, he was truly Mr 100 Per Cent.

Outside the car, however, he had proved more demanding. Put simply, the Williams team seemed glad to see the back of him at the end of 1992. The sigh of collective relief was almost tangible as the mechanics packed up for the long slog home after Adelaide.

In July 1993, having accustomed himself to a more tranquil working environment with Alain Prost, Patrick Head sought to put Mansell's persona into a well-defined perspective.

'Yes, I would say the team is more settled than last year,' he said on the eve of a Williams 1-2 in the French Grand Prix at Magny-Cours. 'In '92 Mansell was always dominant, and he's a very bullish sort of a driver – I'm not really being critical, because it's part of what makes him good.

'He's very intolerant of what he sees as failure in others, but I wouldn't say that necessarily applies to himself. If he felt he was being let down – if, say, Riccardo was 2 kph quicker through the speed trap – immediately he would assume that Renault had given Riccardo the best engine!

'So we tended to have a lot of time in the team where there was tension, for no good reason at all. Then there was tension around Riccardo's car, because he was quite determined that if there was any deficiency in the lap time between himself and Nigel, it was in the car.

'It is not breaking any new ground to say that the guy [Mansell] is *very* confrontational, *hugely* competitive, and wears that competitiveness on his sleeve – he doesn't rein it in, in any way at all. It is there the whole time.

'He also has a *very* strong persecution complex, thinks that everybody is trying to shaft him at all times. So you've got an environment of strain when Mansell is around. And Prost doesn't have those problems. On a day-to-day basis that became extremely wearing.

'But that was his way of getting the job done and that he undoubtedly did last year. But it was hard sometimes – particularly when he was sitting in front of Frank and myself, giving us a lecture. And we got a considerable number of lectures during the year, and he never had a trace of embarrassment about doing it.'

Quite clearly, if these were indeed Patrick's thoughts, he did not expect to be doing business with Nigel Mansell again.

Martin Brundle's recollection of his subsequent negotiations with Frank Williams cast an interesting light on the British team owner's apparent unpredictability when it comes to nailing down deals with his drivers. In fact, Brundle had enjoyed a one-off drive for Williams in the 1988 Belgian Grand Prix at Spa, finishing seventh in the 3.5-litre Judd-engined FW12 after being invited to understudy for Nigel Mansell who had been sidelined by a severe viral infection.

Prior to being hired for that job, Brundle remembers that he was cruising up the M11 in his Jaguar Sovereign on his way back home to Gayton, near Kings Lynn, when the carphone rang unexpectedly. It was Frank Williams ringing to offer him the drive at Spa. That season Martin had unwillingly found himself taking an enforced sabbatical from Formula 1 following a fruitless season with the German Zakspeed team. Earlier that summer he had tested the unloved Williams FW12, his willingness impressing Patrick Head at a time when both Mansell and Patrese had scorned the machine and its unreliable computer-controlled 'reactive' suspension.

Even so, Brundle's steady performance at Spa did not yield any long-term breakthrough with Williams. Another three years would pass until, following a succession of promising performances with Benetton, Martin found himself sitting across a table from Frank Williams negotiating for a full-time position in the team.

'It was a Tuesday, as I recall,' says Brundle. 'It was all systems go. The deal was agreed, the money fixed. But for some reason Frank wanted to wait until six o'clock on the Thursday before finally signing the contract. I don't know why he changed his mind. Either the information got out that we were due to sign at that time, and he came under a lot of pressure from elsewhere, or he suddenly decided he simply didn't want me.'

Williams's prevarication was not confined to Brundle. The talented Finnish driver Mika Hakkinen was also in the frame for a drive with Williams in 1993. Hakkinen, managed by the shrewd former Formula 1 racer Keke Rosberg, himself a World Champion for Williams back in 1982, was anxious to leave the Lotus team and Frank seemed anxious to have him. But yet again, the whole deal came apart at the seams.

As the curtain finally fell on Nigel Mansell's 1992 World Championship season, one of the most penetrating testaments to the Englishman's ability came in the form of a comment from Williams's Technical Director Patrick Head.

'He [Mansell] is very targeted about developments on the car,' said Head firmly. 'It is an unfair criticism to say that he is lacking in his contribution to development. OK, Nigel doesn't have a great deal of patience for, let's say, minute mapping changes on the engine [management system]. He believes that sort of thing should be sorted out before he gets into the car. But the one thing you absolutely know about Nigel is that he always gives 100 per cent when he is in the cockpit.

'I would say that it is an absolutely fundamental requirement for a test driver. If you're off the pace, then you know there is something wrong with the car. If the quick times are, say, 1 minute 20.1 seconds, and he is doing a 1 minute 20.7 seconds, you know you have to find that [deficit] in the car. It's not him.'

The relationship between the racing driver and his employer has historically proved to be a delicate and finely-balanced affair. On paper it is simply a commercial arrangement, but in reality it has to be much more than that for it to flourish. Men who have proved themselves of the calibre necessary to make it into the front line of Grand Prix action will always be burningly competitive and highly motivated operators. Understanding their psychology, and creating an atmosphere within which they can perform to their optimum, can call for a sympathetic approach that has sometimes proved beyond the ability of contemporary Grand Prix team operators.

The relationship, of course, has changed subtly over the years. During the pre-war battles between Auto Union and Mercedes-Benz, for example, the drivers were simply hired hands whose personal ambitions were, to a great degree, subjugated to the wider interests of their teams.

The two German car-makers were intent on putting their country's engineering and technical prowess on the international map. The drivers, though celebrities in their own right, fulfilled a subordinate role and fully appreciated that they could be replaced at any moment. Moreover, the danger aspect – extreme, in those wild and woolly days – was something that was accepted as part of a driver's calling. The freedom of the individual to risk his life was regarded as far more acceptable than it has become in the final decade of the 20th century.

After the war things remained substantially unchanged through the 1950s. The unlikely notion of Stirling Moss or Tony Brooks 'lecturing' Vanwall boss Tony Vandervell in the manner that Mansell employed to address Frank Williams and Patrick Head three decades later, would have been unthinkable. Without doubt, in such circumstances Vandervell would have simply shown them the door. There were plenty of other, well-qualified drivers ready to drive a Vanwall if they had no wish to continue doing so. The cult of the Grand Prix driver as a dazzling international personality whose importance transcended that of his team had simply not yet arrived.

Similarly, when Mercedes-Benz returned to Grand Prix racing in 1954, the German team was operated with a rod of iron by their portly pre-war team manager Alfred Neubauer. In 1955 Mercedes signed Stirling Moss to run alongside Juan Manuel Fangio, thereby producing a driver line-up that might have been regarded as the contemporary equivalent of Alain Prost with Ayrton Senna or Nelson Piquet alongside Nigel Mansell. Yet the manner in which these men operated reflected an inner self-confidence and, arguably, a level of sportsmanship that was to be swept away by the huge infusion of dollars into Grand Prix racing a quarter of a century later.

To this day, race fans still debate whether or not Fangio handed victory to Moss in the 1955 British Grand Prix at Aintree, such was the subtlety of the great Argentinian driver's *modus operandi*. Interestingly, however, Fangio makes reference to this question of team orders in his autobiography (*Fangio: My Racing Life*, Patrick Stephens, 1990) in which, referring to the 1955 season, he makes it clear that he was no soft touch.

'The race I had the best chance of winning in 1955 was Nurburgring,' he recalled. 'That time they could not have given orders to make it easy for their own driver [Karl Kling] because in any case someone else would have been in front of them.' His reference to 'somebody else' means Stirling Moss.

This tends to suggest that Moss and Fangio had a slightly formal professional relationship based on mutual respect, without perhaps the younger man making any over-familiar assumptions about their partnership that might have been interpreted as being presumptuous. It is strangely redolent of the way in which Ayrton Senna, at the height of his rivalry with Alain Prost in 1989, referred to the Frenchman in connection with their collision during the Japanese Grand Prix as 'somebody was there who should not have been'. Without, one must say, any trace of Senna's hostile edge.

Fangio continued: 'They certainly wouldn't have dropped any hints, as they did in England, that I should let Moss win. That hint didn't come straight from our manager, but from Herr Keser, the public relations manager for Daimler-Benz. It was clear that something had been said to him, and that's why he came to speak to me. "Let's see how things go in the race," I replied.

'It didn't matter to me that Moss won, because I was already certain of the championship when we went to Aintree. In any case, they gave me very low gear ratios for fear that I should disobey and win the race. I made a lot of headway in the last lap.'

It is, of course, almost impossible to transpose the pressures on Mercedes-Benz 40 years ago in Britain to a contemporary perspective. Only ten years after the end of Hitler's war, there was still an understandable degree of patriotic xenophobia contained in the attitude to Germany by many men and women in the street. Allowing Moss to win at Aintree would have been a shrewd piece of placatory showmanship, given the circumstances.

Contrast that, if you will, with the sledgehammer crudity demonstrated by Senna and Mansell at Suzuka, when relinquishing the lead of the 1991 and '92 Japanese Grands Prix respectively to their team-mates, and the self-serving ethos of another age is thrown into even more vivid perspective.

Twenty-five years later, when Nigel Mansell began his Formula 1 career with Team Lotus, professional motor racing had long since shrugged aside any nationalistic inclinations and now existed within what might best be described as a high-technology Global Village. Back in the 1950s and '60s, international regulations governing motor sport had required cars competing in major events to carry the prescribed racing colours of their country.

By 1980, British Racing Green, French Racing Blue and Italian Racing Red were only accommodated within the overriding parameters of commercial sponsorship liveries. The fuel, oil and tyre companies were no longer the sport's most respected paymasters, people to be reverentially deferred to. Predominantly it was now the cigarette companies that held the keys to the crock of gold at the end of the Formula 1 rainbow. The abiding philosophy was now very much Every Man For Himself.

It was against this highly competitive backdrop that Mansell entered the Grand Prix milieu. He made his GP debut in a third Lotus 81 alongside Mario Andretti and Elio de Angelis at Osterreichring in 1980, and was promoted into Chapman's full-time F1 squad the following year.

Unquestionably Chapman had a high regard for Mansell, the Lotus chief perhaps shrewdly perceiving an innate level of talent within the highly motivated driver from Birmingham that other observers may have missed. Even so, by the end of 1984, when Mansell came into the Williams orbit for the first time, it is now somehow difficult to recall just how the Englishman was regarded within the Grand Prix community at that time.

Prickly, highly motivated and with a temperament intermittently fuelled by paranoia, Mansell was admittedly extremely quick, yet frequently overdrove his machinery in his efforts to advertise his ability. On the face of it he was not the most overtly obvious choice for the Williams team to the point where the team's established number one driver, Keke Rosberg, threatened to walk away from his contract should Mansell be signed for the 1985 season.

In addition, at around this time Rosberg was also having trouble relating to Williams's Technical Director Patrick Head. 'I felt very much at home at Williams, with the exception of the 1984 season when I found Patrick impossible to deal with,' he recalls with stunning candour. 'He had been on a diet and lost about 30 pounds and, frankly, was like a bear that had been shot in the backside.

'It got to the point at Zandvoort where I said to Frank, "Look, I don't mind not being friends with Patrick, but if I can't work with him, then I'm just wasting my time here."

'So Patrick switched to the car driven by Jacques [Laffite] and I said, "Well, that's a good way of side-stepping the issue, I don't think." I ask you – moving the guy who was one of the best engineers in the F1 business, if not the very best in the business, to the team's other car.'

Rosberg attempted to negotiate a release from Williams to join the Renault works team, which had also been attempting to negotiate with Niki Lauda to switch from McLaren. Keke's general annoyance and indignation was compounded by bad reports that he had received about Mansell from the Englishman's long-time Lotus team-mate Elio de Angelis, a close friend. In an effort to force Frank into releasing him, Keke even drove around 5 seconds a lap off the pace – deliberately – at a couple of Goodyear tyre tests. But Frank steadfastly refused to budge.

In fairness, after a season working with Nigel, Keke would admit with characteristic generosity that he had been wrong about his new colleague. He got on well with Mansell, as things turned out, and grew to like the driver who would go on to become the most successful ever to be employed by Williams Grand Prix Engineering.

Even so, the whole question of signing Mansell seemed something of a footnote to the main thrust of the Williams team's priorities. Senna was unavailable, having judged that the Lotus-Renault combination offered more immediately obvious winning potential than the Honda-engined Williams, even though Head was close to completing the first of the new

FW10 machines that would dramatically raise the Anglo-Japanese partnership's level of competitiveness during the season to come.

'Sure, for 1984 we knew we would switch Jacques,' recalled Frank Williams, 'and Ayrton was our original choice, but he went to Lotus as early as August. Nigel was next on the list, but I have to confess that I was rather dickering around on the matter, blowing hot one day and cold the next. Eventually, at Zandvoort, Patrick suggested that I should get on and make a decision, for better or worse. So I went straight out of the motorhome and told Nigel, "Put it there . . ."'

It was perhaps inevitable, given the uncharitably competitive nature of Formula 1, that many others within the Grand Prix fraternity mercilessly took the rise out of Frank Williams's decision. That year's end-of-season McLaren team party included a 10-minute film clip of all Nigel's incidents. James Hunt, the by then retired 1976 World Champion, also took the opportunity to make some very critical observations about Mansell, all of which were inclined to overlook – or deliberately disregard – the very positive elements of his driving ability.

Remembers Williams: 'What we already knew was that he was exceptionally quick. On tight circuits, and in the rain, he was magic. That was pure car control, so there were obviously plus points to consider.

'To be honest, though, I thought he would produce what I had expected from Alan Jones in 1978, that he would be a good number two, always in at the end, always getting in or near to the points. No way could I ever have been said to think, "Wow, we've got a potential World Champion", but by the second half of 1985 I began to realise we'd got something a bit special on our hands.'

Sure enough, Mansell took a little time to get into the swing of things at Williams. But once he won the 1985 European Grand Prix, in front of thousands of his adoring fans at Brands Hatch, Nigel never looked back. He backed up that success by immediately winning the next race in South Africa, and finished the year with his perceived status within the Grand Prix community immeasurably enhanced.

There was, however, an unexpected knock-on effect from the apprehension displayed by Rosberg early in 1985. Long before he decided that he was, after all, quite comfortable with Mansell as a team-mate, Keke had signalled that he would leave Williams at the end of the 1985 in order to have a final Formula 1 season with McLaren prior to his retirement from front-line motor racing.

That left Frank Williams casting around for a replacement. Ascertaining that Nelson Piquet, the 1991 and '93 World Champion, simply couldn't persuade Brabham boss Bernie Ecclestone to offer him the financial terms he wanted for 1986, he moved quickly to sign the Brazilian driver for Williams-Honda. The deal was done in August 1985, weeks before Mansell began his winning streak.

In his own mind, Piquet regarded Mansell as an also-ran, a team-mate who would be something of a push-over. Yet in characteristically even-handed style, Williams did not nominate a number one driver for 1986 in the sense that the man in the cockpit of the 'second' Williams would be obliged to defer to him out on the circuit. That caused all manner of ructions further down the line, a situation that was aggravated by a road accident in which Frank Williams almost lost his life a few weeks before the start of the 1986 season.

One fateful Saturday afternoon in March, Frank's rented Ford Sierra crashed off a secondary road into a field between Le Camp and Brignoles, just inland from Bandol, in southern France. Frank and his team manager Peter Windsor had been hurrying to catch a flight home to England from Nice airport, following the final pre-season test at Paul Ricard, when tragedy intervened.

Frank Williams broke his back and, after weeks of prolonged hospitalisation, would henceforth be paralysed from the chest down. He freely blames himself for the accident and has never been burdened by self-pity or regret. Even so, the six weeks immediately after the accident were to prove a deeply traumatic experience for all those touched by the tragedy.

Windsor subsequently admitted that he grew emotionally close to Frank as he spent endless days at the team owner's bedside in the London hospital to which he had been transported in a private jet furnished by Bernie Ecclestone. Yet there was a deep-seated core of independence within Frank that eventually reasserted itself. The unruffled, slightly distant formality of the employer/employee relationship gradually re-emerged.

The fact that Frank was out of circulation for much of the 1986 season hardly helped soothe the increasingly brittle relationship that developed between Piquet and Mansell. There was no doubt that Nelson quite genuinely believed that unconditional number one status was a central tenet of the arrangement he had reached with Frank.

The Brazilian driver had no doubts that what his deal guaranteed was a repeat of the 1981 scenario when Williams attempted – with only limited success – to cast Carlos Reutemann in a supporting role to Alan Jones. This had, in the main, turned out to be something approaching a fiasco, with Reutemann ignoring the team's pit signals to beat Jones in a Williams 1-2 at the end of the rain-soaked Brazilian Grand Prix at Rio.

As in Jones's case, the uncertainties involved in this sort of situation preyed on Piquet's mind. His standpoint was not enhanced by the fact that he was infused with a sense of misplaced confidence when he won the first race of the '86 season in Rio, roundly trouncing Ayrton Senna's Lotus-Renault on a day when Mansell collided with Senna trying to take the lead on the second lap, the Englishman ending his race very firmly parked against a guard rail with a front wheel ripped off his Williams-Honda.

A commonsense view would have told Williams to nip this problem in the bud before it got out of control, but the team had its hands full in other areas. Frank's absence deeply concerned Honda, the team's engine suppliers, whose Japanese sense of order could not quite grasp how the team could continue to function in an orderly fashion with the Managing Director lying seriously ill in hospital.

The reality was that neither of these problems was addressed in a totally satisfactory manner. Piquet's indignation was left to fester away unattended as Mansell stormed to memorable victories in the Canadian, French and British Grands Prix. Then the pendulum began to swing back in Nelson's favour when he won the German and Hungarian races. Yet even though the Williams-Honda FW11 was unquestionably the class of the 1986 field, nobody doubted that there was a very real chance of the two men dividing the wins between them to the point where a third party might nip through and steal the Drivers' title from under their noses.

One man who displayed a shrewd understanding of the manner in which both Mansell and Piquet operated was Patrick Head. Very much a man's man whose concept of driver psychology was heavily influenced by four years working with the self-reliant Alan Jones, Head may have been fundamentally averse to the notion that Grand Prix drivers sometimes needed a shoulder to cry on, but he certainly grasped the difference between the way in which these two individual drivers tackled their profession.

'The fact of the matter is that with highly competitive racing drivers, you are dealing with proud, aggressive people,' he explained. 'The sort of person who will push himself to the absolute limit in order to win a race is not the sort of person who is going to say "After you, Claude; my team has told me to finish second, so that's what I'm going to do."

'There was never any conscious attempt to be anti-Piquet or overtly pro-Mansell. But when you got to a test and one driver goes round a given circuit for two days in the 1 minute 21 second bracket, then the other arrives and, on his third lap, does a 1 minute 19.9 seconds, slowly the team starts to think that this guy is more serious than the other.

'In Nelson's case I never had any doubt about his ability; he knows exactly the level he's running at on 1 minute 21 seconds, he knows he can pull out another second if need be, but that's the level he's going to test at. He knows what the car is going to do when it goes a second quicker. He is a very up-together, very confident driver, confident in his own ability, and rightly so. That's the way he wants to test.

'But you get a bloke like Mansell, who only knows one speed, and you have a problem getting the mechanics not to subconsciously fall in line with the guy who's always giving 100 per cent. Nelson doesn't really have an ego problem in terms of lap times at a test. He would run all day with a full fuel load and not worry about absolute fast times, because he knows, when it comes to the race, when that green light comes on he'll be in good shape.

'He's doing his homework and knows that the race is the only thing that counts. He's a kid in some ways, off the track, but as far as racing is concerned he knows what he's doing. In that way he is very mature.'

The Mansell/Piquet/Honda problems peaked for Williams in the 1986

Australian Grand Prix at Adelaide. A tyre failure at almost 200 mph wiped out Mansell's World Championship chances when he was running third, perfectly poised to take the title with only 18 laps of the race left to run. Prudent logic suggested that Piquet, now leading, be brought in for a precautionary tyre check, but this allowed Alain Prost to duck ahead and take the Drivers' Championship as Nelson could not make up sufficient ground to catch him when he resumed in the closing stages of the battle.

In fact, Mansell's retirement had been caused by a freak tyre failure and there had been nothing amiss with the tyres that came off Piquet's Williams in that fateful precautionary pit stop. Yet, with hindsight, Nelson could not escape from the conclusion that Williams's overall failure to control Mansell in the manner that he believed had been agreed, was the key factor behind his own failure to win the Drivers' Championship.

The trend duly continued into 1987, with Mansell and Piquet left free to race each other into the ground, and after Nigel won the British Grand Prix at Silverstone, making up over 25 seconds after an unscheduled tyre stop, and snatching the lead from him with just over two laps left in a heart-stopping manoeuvre into Stowe Corner, Nelson's patience finally ran out. He agreed a deal to move to the Lotus-Honda camp for 1988 and, with the Japanese engine-maker switching Williams's supply contract to McLaren – even though the deal still had a year to run – Williams certainly paid the price for what some people judged was a recklessly non-conformist approach to the intricacies of Formula 1 pit lane politics.

During the course of 1986 Mansell would be wooed by Ferrari, and the Englishman briefly found himself entangled in an agreement for 1987 from which he subsequently withdrew, renewing his commitment to Williams for that year and the next. During his first couple of seasons with the Williams-Honda squad he had been saddled with a retainer that didn't exceed $1 million (£660,000), and, with Piquet, Prost and Senna all making considerably in excess of this sum, clearly felt he was hard done by. The offer from Ferrari was financially flattering – and had the effect of enhancing his value to the Williams squad, which duly revised his remuneration in a suitably acceptable upward direction.

Piquet, meanwhile, would go on to win the 1987 World Championship, leaving Williams to struggle through the '88 season with 3.5-litre Judd V10 naturally-aspirated engines, in a transitional year that saw McLaren-Honda win 15 out of the 16 races, bringing the curtain down finally on the turbo era in Formula 1.

For public consumption Frank Williams picks his words carefully when it comes to articulating his feelings about the way in which Honda treated his team. Yet his diplomacy could in no way conceal the strained circumstances that surrounded this breach.

'With hindsight I suppose one could have taken a more aggressive legal stance with Honda,' he muses, 'but a settlement was duly reached, although, again with hindsight, it was grossly inadequate. Privately we thought we had a sound technical base for our switch to a Judd engine in 1988, but we were not wise enough to see that this was potentially a major disaster.

'It turned out to be the latter and, believe me, it brought the team to its knees. We were not quite on the floor, but the countdown had almost begun, if you like. The 1988 season was certainly pretty lurid thanks to Honda's clumsiness.' Off the record, Frank would not be quite so polite in his assessment of Honda's behaviour.

To this day it remains his firm conviction that, as soon as he broke his neck, Honda lost confidence in the programme. After that point nothing was conceded at all. The engine supply deal was changed to two years.

From that point it was a short step to Ron Dennis making an approach to Honda, offering them a link with Marlboro, Senna and Prost. That proved pretty well irresistible to the Japanese car-maker. Frank Williams also believes, again with hindsight, that Honda made the great mistake of bringing its founder, Soichiro Honda, to Adelaide for what turned out to be the debacle of '86. The loss of face for Honda, watching the Drivers' title slip away from both Mansell and Piquet, must have been phenomenal. If the Williams-Honda alliance was wobbly before that, it was certainly dead afterwards.

Despite losing Honda, Mansell hung on gamely through to the end of his Williams contract, then decided to succumb to the blandishments of Ferrari and join the famous Italian team alongside Gerhard Berger in 1989. In the opinion of some – including Williams's then Commercial Manager Sheridan Thynne, who would increasingly assume the role of mentor and sounding board for the English driver, as well as a close friend and admirer – Mansell was imbued with an 'over-romantic view' of the famous Italian team.

For Williams, now poised to pick up the threads of a factory-backed engine supply contract with Renault, Nigel's departure was a blow he could have done without. 'By the end of his time with us in 1988 he had developed to the point where he was much better equipped from a personal viewpoint to handle the disappointments which inevitably crop up from time to time in this business,' said Frank.

Replacing Mansell was not as easy as it might have seemed. At the start of 1988 Italian Riccardo Patrese had been signed to partner the Englishman, but Nigel's defection created another vacancy. This was duly filled by the mild-mannered Belgian Thierry Boutsen. But it wasn't the answer.

For two seasons thereafter, Williams and Mansell went their own way. Frank's team settled into its new technical partnership with Renault while Mansell, fuelled by a reputed £2.4 million retainer, donned the bright red, Marlboro-patched overalls of a Ferrari driver. On the face of it their seasons seemed pretty well-matched. Boutsen won both the Canadian and Australian Grands Prix for Williams, Mansell the Brazilian and Hungarian for Ferrari.

Yet, from an historical viewpoint, it would certainly be accurate to record that Mansell remained at the centre of Formula 1 attention whereas his former team slipped slightly from the high wire. Re-kindling the golden years of success with Honda was not going to be an easy task, and, while Patrick Head would be the first to admit that neither the 1989 Williams FW12B – a machine derived from the previous year's Judd V8 designed car – nor indeed its successor, the FW13 in 1990, were any great shakes, it could also not be denied that the team was missing the presence of a top-calibre star on the driving strength.

Mansell, meanwhile, was earning the reputation as something of a hero in the famous Maranello team. Italian motor racing fans love heroic drivers cast in a melodramatic mould, and Nigel was just what the doctor ordered. Even though he would be the first to concede that his efforts to learn Italian left him beached on the nursery slopes of this demonstrative language, he quickly became a great favourite amongst the mechanics and engineers.

The 1989 season passed well enough for Mansell until the unfortunate events that took place in the Portuguese Grand Prix at Estoril, four races from the end of the title contest. Nigel had the race in the bag when he came into the pits for a routine tyre change, overshot slightly – then reversed back by mistake. This was a breach of the rules for which he was black-flagged, although not before he had eliminated leader Ayrton Senna's McLaren from the race in a high-speed collision at the first corner.

Mansell was subsequently fined $50,000 (£33,000) and banned from the following weekend's Spanish Grand Prix at Jerez. His knee-jerk reaction was to threaten retirement, but in the end he was placated by the Ferrari management and duly picked up the threads of his career again in the Japanese Grand Prix.

Throughout 1989 Mansell's team-mate in the Ferrari squad had been the easy-going Austrian Gerhard Berger. Now he was quitting the team after a three-year stint to join Senna in the McLaren-Honda line-up. The seat that Gerhard was destined to fill had fallen vacant after Alain Prost had decided to quit the team for which he had won three World Championships. The Frenchman had been worn down by what he regarded as Senna's overtly confrontational attitude towards the business of team relationships and could take no more. In essence, the Brazilian had hounded the highly regarded sitting tenant out of the team in which Prost, quite rightly, had hitherto believed he was an integral part of the family.

Prost would now switch to Ferrari. That meant Mansell re-negotiating his existing contract – which had stipulated number one status – to accommodate the Frenchman's arrival on equal terms. Nigel was, on the face of it, willing to oblige. He made it clear that he did not fear Prost, but admired him and felt that they could work alongside each other to mutual benefit.

Speaking during a pre-season press conference at his newly acquired Ferrari dealership, at Pimperne in Dorset, Mansell was upbeat and optimistic about Ferrari's prospects for 1990.

'We've had a few set-backs, but basically I would say there was something new in the air,' he enthused. 'Ferrari is motivated like there's no tomorrow and we are moving forward. We've made a useful step forward in terms of power and we will benefit undoubtedly from the knowledge of the Honda engine which Alain will bring.'

What influence has Alain had on the team so far? 'I think it is very, very positive,' he replied firmly. 'Obviously a little bit of flexibility was required on both sides as I was number one last year and we had to re-negotiate my contract in order to put this year's deal together.

'But for the team to move forward as quickly as we have done must be good for everybody, and I've never seen Alain so motivated. It's very good, but he's going to make my job more difficult. We're moving along just that little bit faster than we would have done if it had just been myself.'

On a personal level Mansell displayed no reservations about Prost: 'I think the important thing is that one person can only do so much, one person can only be in one country at one time. We've got [test] programmes running cars in different countries and if you're the only driver in the team, you can't do that. So with Alain in the team, you can get through twice the work and make progress on the question of reliability.'

Previously Mansell had described 1989 as a 'holding season' in preparation for 1990 and '91. Did he still feel that way? 'I still stand totally by what I said a year ago,' he replied. 'I think my previous track record stands by what I said when we expected to win a few races [in 1989], get our feet under the table, so to speak, with Ferrari, consolidate, develop and work very hard to challenge for the Championship.'

Then he reaffirmed his ambitions for 1990: 'I'll stand by that to say this year I'm personally going all out for the Championship. I'm already thinking that I've got to finish 13 races, and I've got to score in every race. There's 11 that count, so I've got to have at least 11 that count towards the title.

'I might even sacrifice a race win or something to make sure I get home. Maybe, in a certain situation, where six points are guaranteed, and I'm in good shape for the Championship, I'll settle for second. But, saying that, I'll always be in there challenging. You can't change that. You don't have time to think in situations like that . . .'

In the run-up to the first race of the season, through the streets of Phoenix, Arizona, one would have had to say that the historical odds were against Mansell ever winning the title. He was now entering his 11th season of Formula 1, and nobody who had yet won a title had taken anywhere near as long. Prost, for example, took six seasons, while Jim Clark, Niki Lauda, James Hunt and Nelson Piquet had all managed it in their fourth.

Yet Mansell was too tough to be unnerved by such statistics. Like Stirling Moss, over a generation earlier, it seemed possible that he had finally reached that elusive plateau of self-confidence from where he could regard his rivals with an air of equanimity.

Gone – or so it seemed – was the anxious need to justify every action that had made him such a confused and complex individual in his long slog to the top. Like Prost and Senna, although of different character, he now radiated an air of personal tranquillity that astounded his detractors.

Nevertheless, while Mansell and Ferrari might have enjoyed a glorious romance in 1989, the honeymoon was now firmly rooted in the past. The challenge now was to live together harmoniously to avoid any hint of a divorce through the new season. In that respect, with Prost on his patch, this was easier said than done.

Six months later Mansell's dream season had all but evaporated. His Ferrari 641 seemed to be bugged by endless mechanical problems throughout the early season races. Prost, by contrast, won the Brazilian, Mexican, French and British Grands Prix before Mansell finally snapped. Stark disappointment in front of his home crowd at Silverstone seemed just too much for him to deal with.

Mansell had looked on course for a memorable home triumph in front of 100,000 adoring fans at Silverstone when another bout of transmission trouble caused him to slow, allowing Prost to surge through to the 43rd win of his career.

Grappling with gearbox problems, Mansell rolled to a halt just beyond the pits with only nine laps to go while running in a strong second place. As he erupted from the cockpit, scowling darkly, he raged, 'I was much quicker than everybody else up to that point. Obviously I'm very happy for Ferrari, but I'm bound to wonder why these problems don't seem to happen to the other guy.' The words spat out like red-hot tin-tacks.

On the face of it, this seemed to be the same knee-jerk reaction to his disappointment – and Prost's success – as he had produced a week earlier in similar circumstances at the end of the French Grand Prix. Less than half an hour later, Mansell announced his retirement. According to him, he was merely confirming a decision that he had been turning over in his mind for several months.

'I'm not making an excuse, just a straightforward statement,' he explained. 'I have been thinking about this a lot over the last four months, and it is not an emotional decision. The British Grand Prix seemed the most appropriate place to announce my retirement.

'I am looking forward to putting my family first for the first time in my life. I am looking forward to racing hard to the end of the year, and if I can help Alain to win the Championship, and perhaps win a few races myself, then all to the good.

'I have nothing else to say. As of now, the Australian Grand Prix in Adelaide will be my final race. I don't want to burst into tears in front of you, but this is the hardest decision of my life.'

Ironically, at the end of the meeting most of Mansell's fans had left the circuit ignorant of his decision to retire. Those insiders who remained in the pit lane wavered between the partially convinced and the extremely sceptical.

In fact, Ferrari's team manager, Cesare Fiorio, made the most balanced comment, calling on Nigel to think again. 'The best thing for him to do is to go home, relax and maybe reconsider before he goes through with it,' he suggested. 'He's done a fantastic job for us.'

At Monza, Mansell convened a personal press conference to reaffirm his decision to retire from Formula 1. However, less than a month later – with Jean Alesi by then firmly locked into a contract to take over his place at Ferrari for 1991 – Mansell announced that he would be returning to Williams.

The one-year deal that had been hammered out gave Mansell not only a reputed $7 million (£4.6 million) retainer, preserving his status as Britain's most highly paid sportsman, but came close to matching the $500,000 (£330,000) per race trousered by Formula 1's top earner Ayrton Senna at McLaren. According to Mansell pressure from his fans was the reason behind this not totally unexpected *volte face*.

In a self-prepared press release issued from his home in Port Erin, Isle of Man, he stated firmly that public opinion had forced him to reconsider his position.

'The response to my retirement from the fans, manufacturers, teams from many different formulae and the world's sports press was totally opposed to my decision and I have been under severe pressure to reconsider ever since,' he stated.

'I have also been touched by the fantastic encouragement from not only the British, but fans all around the world for me to continue in Formula 1.'

He added that his wife Rosanne supported the decision. He had, he claimed, been considering racing in other categories and she had said that 'the anxiety factor would still be there regardless of the type of racing cars I drive'.

However, what Mansell's statement did not address were strong rumours to the effect that he had been negotiating for a return to Williams for some time, only for talks to apparently collapse at the time of the British Grand Prix when Williams was attempting to secure Senna's services. According to some sources, only when negotiations with the Brazilian fell through – and Alesi made it clear that he was not going to drive for Williams, even though he had signed a contract to do so – did Mansell return to the head of the team's shopping list.

Mansell added: 'I felt I would be very unlikely ever to have the full weight of a team and manufacturer to give me what should be a reasonable opportunity [to win the Championship].' This observation, made at the end of a week that had seen Mansell win the Portuguese Grand Prix and finish second to Prost in the Spanish, was hardly calculated to amuse Ferrari. Moreover, you will read a very different interpretation of events during this period at Ferrari in the chapter dealing with Alain Prost, his relationship with Mansell and the events that led up to his role in the contemporary Williams story.

Williams, of course, could now offer the one thing that Nigel craved – absolute, exclusive number one status in a front line Grand Prix team. For whatever reason, Mansell had now apparently shelved his own personal uncertainties after a few months racked by confusion. Patrese would stay on as number two driver, while Thierry Boutsen moved off to join the French Ligier outfit.

For the moment, however, the Williams personnel got down to the business of reacquainting themselves with their former colleague. Whatever nagging doubts there might have been lingering beneath the surface as to Nigel's personal volatility, his first test session in a Williams-Renault reminded them just what they'd been missing over the previous couple of seasons.

At a stroke, that minuscule difference between a fine driver and a top-line ace was thrown into graphic relief before their eyes. Mansell's return instantly took the team's operation up one gear in terms of operational intensity. At Estoril, first time out in the old, unloved and now-redundant FW13, he requested detail changes to the cockpit set-up, to the adjustment of the brake pedal. But all those working with him were suddenly aware that his presence had suffused them with optimism and confidence. On only his 22nd lap, he took the Williams-Renault round Estoril on control tyres faster than it had ever gone before.

Of course it was only natural that many people doubted the depth of Mansell's motivation. After all, how could a man who made his retirement plans so clear, so frequently, suddenly regain the spark with which to remotivate his competitive edge? Was this his last shot at the Championship? Could Williams put up with the downside of a revived relationship with a man they had quite clearly been happy to see the back of when he left in 1988?

The answer to all this must be encapsulated in one word – expediency. Grand Prix motor racing is a tight, compact community, sometimes claustrophobically so. Moreover, at any one time drivers with a winning edge are few and far between. There may be several who can sustain sufficient speed to be in the right place at the right time and inherit the occasional success. But Mansell was a man with a proven record of winning from the front, a commodity that Williams urgently needed again after two seasons of performances which, at best, could be described as average.

Mansell and Patrese would go out to do battle with the all-new Williams FW14, powered by the significantly revised Renault RS3 67-degree V10-cylinder engine. The FW13 concept had been totally discarded and an enormous amount of engineering time was invested in the new machine by the Williams design team under the direction of both Head and former Leyton House F1 designer Adrian Newey, who had joined Williams midway through 1991 with a brief to work solely on the new design.

'We have one heck of a good chance of winning the World Championship in 1991,' enthused Mansell before the first race. 'I have more zest than before. I have done my apprenticeship and I've had my share of the heartache. Now I want to win the championship and I have to compliment

Williams for the fantastic job they have done in convincing me that we have
a real prospect of winning the title this year.'

To some ears this discourse sounded like another replay of a well-worn
record. Mansell had been upbeat about his prospects too many times in the
past, only to have the whole edifice come crashing down on him, for the
words to be totally convincing. Yet, this time, things just might be different.

A niggling bout of mechanical problems for Mansell and the new Williams
FW14 handed an early season advantage to Ayrton Senna's V12 Honda-
engined McLaren MP4/6, the Brazilian rattling off four successive victories
in 1991 at Phoenix, Sao Paulo, Imola and Monaco. At the season's quarter
distance point, Senna had an unblemished total of 40 points at the head of
the Drivers' Championship table, with Mansell only getting his personal
tally off the ground at Monaco, where a well-earned second place netted
him six points.

Then came the first fiasco of the year, at Montreal. Mansell utterly dominated the Canadian Grand Prix to the point where he was able to back off in
the closing stages of the race. He eased back to the point where he was lapping in the 1 minute 25 second bracket – 5 seconds away from his second
place qualifying best – but reminded everybody what the FW14 was capable
of achieving by popping in a 1 minute 22.385 second flier only four laps
from the end of the race. This stood as fastest lap of the afternoon.

On the face of it, with a lead of 47 seconds over Nelson Piquet's Benetton
B191, this could have been judged a trifle cavalier. In fact, Nigel was about
to succumb to a touch of over-confidence. Going into the last lap, he took
time off to wave to the crowd. Going into the final hairpin, barely a mile
from the chequered flag, he allowed the engine revs to drop away dramatically. As he went to select a lower gear, the semi-automatic gearbox baulked
ever so slightly and slipped into neutral instead. In the same second the
Renault V10 simply died and, deprived of the necessary electrical charge to
enable the hydraulic engagement of a gear, he was unable to bump-start the
engine back into life. Mansell and his Williams rolled to a standstill, to be
classified an eventual sixth. That last-lap error had cost him nine of the
potential ten points on offer that summer afternoon.

A fortnight later Nigel wound up taking second place to Patrese in the
Mexican Grand Prix, the Englishman seemingly beset by a mysterious
power loss in the middle of the race. Going into the French Grand Prix,
Senna now had 44 points, with Patrese second on 20, Nelson Piquet third on
16 and Nigel himself fourth on 13. But suddenly the prevailing trend of the
championship battle seemed to be reversed as Mansell stormed majestically
to three straight wins in the French, British and German Grands Prix.

Now he was only eight points behind Senna, but Ayrton bounced back to
beat the Williams driver in Hungary and score a lucky win at Spa where,

after dominating the Belgian Grand Prix, Nigel's Williams FW14 succumbed to an electrical malfunction while well in the lead.

During the summer of 1991 Frank Williams was talking to Ayrton Senna about the possibility of the Brazilian joining the team for the following year. These negotiations were effectively a re-run of the talks that had taken place 12 months earlier and, perhaps feeling rather sceptical about whether or not Senna was really serious about them, Williams took the decisive step of re-signing Mansell early in the summer.

'I am a great believer in continuity,' said Frank in announcing the deal, 'and I am sure that Nigel and Riccardo, who have worked so hard this season, will be able to achieve even more next year.'

On the face of it, Senna had seemed to want it both ways. On the one hand he seemed happy for Williams to continue courting him, while on the other he kept stressing his unwillingness to jeopardise his quest for the 1991 World Championship by entering into drawn-out contract negotiations for 1992.

Even so, Ayrton felt let down by Frank's failure to inform him in advance that he was going to conclude a deal with Mansell and Patrese for '92. 'I think it's important to respect principles and in this business it's difficult to find people who can follow these things,' he remarked acidly at Spa. What *was* he talking about?

'I didn't expect it,' continued Ayrton, 'and I had reasons not to expect it. I have some strong feelings about how to follow certain agreements, and I struggle to cope with some different attitudes.

'It is perhaps the result of the competition being so high. There is a lot at stake and people find it very difficult to stick with their commitments.'

Mansell's confidence may have been buttressed by this early deal for the following year, but there were still some disappointments waiting in the pipeline. Foremost amongst these came on the afternoon of 22 September when he found himself reliving his 1989 Portuguese Grand Prix nightmare, being black-flagged out of the Estoril race with 20 laps left to run.

However, while his previous brush with authority amounted to a self-inflicted wound after he absent-mindedly flicked his Ferrari into reverse after over-shooting his pit, this time Nigel was innocent of any blame.

While leading the race, a momentary glitch in communication amongst the Williams pit crew caused Mansell to be waved back into the fray before his car's right-rear wheel had been properly secured. It flew off and, in the heat of the moment, was then reattached while the car was standing in the outer acceleration lane in the pits, a clear breach of the rules for which Nigel was excluded.

Williams team manager Peter Windsor shouldered the entire blame for the episode in dignified style, although the management issued an official communique making it clear that no individual would be made a scapegoat for this unfortunate sequence of events. 'The car departed prematurely and that was not the driver's fault,' read the official text.

'In the sequence that occurs when the [wheel] nuts are undone, the wheels come off and the new ones go on, there is a position where the chaps on the [air] guns stand up in the air holding the guns above their heads,' explained Patrick Head.

'That is a signal to the jack men that their job is complete, the nuts are tight and the person controlling the pit stop can step away and let the car out. In that process there was a breakdown. The right rear wheel was not complete and the guys had not given the signal that they had completed their job, but the process which allowed the car to leave the pits was allowed to occur.'

This in itself need not have been a terminal disaster. The situation could have been saved if the mechanics had taken a quick-lift jack out to the stricken Williams and hauled it back into its original stopping position. This would have been totally permissible within the regulations, but in the ensuing panic instructions became slightly garbled and a wheel was rushed out and fitted to the disabled car in this prohibited area.

However, it was an unfortunate reflection on the stewards' own lack of familiarity with the rule book that Mansell was permitted to resume and complete another 20 laps at racing speeds, climbing from 17th to sixth in a sensational recovery, before he was finally given the black flag.

Patrese emerged victorious at the end of the day, but Nigel bounced back to win the Spanish Grand Prix at Barcelona's new *Circuit de Catalunya* before finally relinquishing all hopes of the title when he spun off the road in the Japanese GP at Suzuka. He rounded off the year by crashing in the rain-soaked – and prematurely terminated – Australian GP to finish the year in second place, 16 points behind Senna in the final points total.

A post-mortem on the season was a mathematically painful task for Mansell and Williams. Nine points lost at Montreal, ten points lost due to a minor electrical problem at Spa – and ten points lost due to the fumbled pit stop at Estoril. Total 29. Or, disregarding the Belgian race, 20 points lost due to a combination of over-confident driving and poor operational strategy. Even so, Frank Williams was extremely pleased with the performance of his two lads.

'I can guarantee you that they are a better couple than in most teams today,' he told *Autosport*. 'As they have both become more competitive there is a slight arm's length relationship, but there is zilch aggravation. There is trust. They swap information. They try to keep their cards close to their chests, but they know that doesn't work because the engineers talk. We try to give them both the best equipment and they just get on with it. From my point of view, life is easy.

'A lot of credit for this must go to Riccardo; he's pretty damned apolitical. Nigel is an immensely tough bastard and, if things are going wrong in the car, he will give me or – more usually – Patrick a very hard time. He's not slow in coming forward.

'That's the unpleasant side of him. It's actually a good side too, because I

bet Senna gives Ron Dennis a hard time. And Alain Prost. All these guys –
the best – are not there because they are Mr Nice. They're bastards. They're
mean.

'Riccardo is quite different. He gets on with his own life. He's very cool
and laid back. Clearly he's an extremely talented qualifier, but, to be frank,
generally speaking Nigel will drive a tougher, meaner, grittier race. When
the lights go green, he goes red!

'Nigel has come good recently in terms of results and confidence because
we have his car humming. For reasons that aren't entirely clear, Nigel had a
disproportionate amount of early season, new car aggravation compared to
Riccardo, but they both had their fair share of it. When that happens, Nigel
tends to think, 'Why is it always me?'

'What Nigel needed and Riccardo had before him was something beneath
him which could give him pretty much uninterrupted practice sessions. I
said to him one day that we might be better off trying to run just one car.

'The thing about Nigel – and I've seen the evidence time and time again –
is that he knows what he wants. He isn't always right about a softer spring,
or whatever, but he usually is. Patrick guides the drivers, but he rarely inter-
feres. Nigel knows how to make his car quick. He may wrong-slot a few
times, but he's good.'

By the end of 1991 Nigel Mansell seemed to have the world at his feet. A
consistently high earner for several seasons, he, his wife Rosanne and their
three children – Chloe, Leo and Greg – had tired of Ballaman House, their
purpose-built home on a windswept promontory of the Isle of Man. In April
of his first year back at Williams they went south to the sunshine and palm
trees of Florida's west coast, settling in a spectacular mansion with a $5 mil-
lion (£3.1 million) price tag fronting the inviting waters of the Gulf of
Mexico.

With nine bedrooms, seven bathrooms, five fireplaces, a tennis court, a
pool and a two-storey ballroom, Mansell supplemented the accommodation
by purchasing a house on the immediately adjacent property for $1.25 mil-
lion (£780,000). Joanne King Hiller, the Clearwater estate agent and owner
of Island Estates Realty – who sold Mansell the property – told *Car
magazine* that by the time he had completed all his renovation work, the
new owner had a home that could realistically be expected to fetch around
$15 million (£9.4 million).

On the face of it Britain's top Grand Prix driver had struck a good deal.
Originally the property had been on the market for $9.9 million (£6.2 mil-
lion) and had been reduced to $7.9 million (£4.9 million) by the time Nigel
submitted his successful offer. Overlooking Clearwater harbour, it had originally been built in the 1920s by a shrewd entrepreneur who apparently made
his fortune by selling black paint to Henry Ford for his Model T range.

Even so, Mansell had been a high spender over the previous few years and Ballaman House, which initially went on the market with a £3.5 million price tag in 1991, would prove more difficult to move. Over a year later he sold the property, reputedly for significantly less than it cost him to build.

Private jets, helicopters and a host of luxury cars had also become long-established markers by which his success could be outwardly judged. On the face of it, one could have been forgiven for concluding that Mansell needed to keep earning. And earning well.

For the 1992 season Mansell reputedly stayed with Williams for a retainer of $8 million (£5 million), although that figure could easily be doubled in terms of his overall earnings when one takes into account bonus payments, share of prize money, personal sponsorship and related product endorsement. More to the point, Nigel believed that the new season would offer him his best chance yet of winning the Championship that had eluded him for so long.

Just over three weeks before the start of the season he jetted in to host his traditional pre-season press conference at the Williams Conference Centre adjacent to the Didcot factory. Despite the fact that most of southern England lay beneath an impenetrable blanket of thick fog, there was a capacity turn-out from the media.

Fit, relaxed and wearing a healthy Florida suntan, Mansell radiated his usual confidence, particularly concerning his willingness to give Ayrton Senna – who by then had consolidated a reputation as the most aggressively competitive Formula 1 front-liner of his era – as good as he got.

'I am the only driver who is prepared to go down to the wire with Ayrton,' he stated firmly, 'and I think last year, towards the end of the season, I ruffled his feathers. I was the only challenger for his crown and he didn't like it. I took his attitude as a compliment because I believe he was genuinely concerned at one point about his own ability to hold on to the World Championship lead.

'Last year I appreciated that the cars were only ready a week or so before the race. I would say that we are coming out of the starting block scoring seven out of ten as far as confidence is concerned, whereas last year we were only registering about three out of ten on that score.

'This year we will be starting with basically the same car, same engine and same gearbox.'

Yet Williams had a technical ace up its sleeve that would confer a decisive advantage on both Mansell and Patrese. The new Williams-Renault FW14B would, from the start of the new season, be fitted with a traction control system to minimise wheelspin. This was to prove an enormously significant factor that served to underpin the level of domination that would be displayed by Mansell and the new car.

The new car represented the Williams team's effort to build on the solidly promising foundation laid by the original FW14. It retained the distinctive aerodynamic raised nose that had been painstakingly honed to perfection by Adrian Newey during long hours in the Williams wind tunnel. Even so, the original strategy was for the FW14B to act as something of a stop-gap, carrying the team through the first few races of the 1992 season before being supplanted by the new FW15 later in the year.

However, as things transpired the FW14B would be good enough to get the job done, and remained substantially unchanged through to the final race of the season. Another crucial element in its technical specification package was the adoption of active ride suspension, continuing a line of development the seeds of which had originally been sown as long ago as 1987 on the 1.5-litre Honda turbo-engined Williams FW11B.

Using a car equipped with such a system, Nelson Piquet won that year's Italian Grand Prix at Monza, convincing Patrick Head that the correct route for the following year would be to incorporate active ride suspension in the design of the Judd V8-engined Williams FW12 from the outset. However, this proved to be a highly disappointing exercise, the system proving so unreliable that it had to be abandoned midway through 1988, forcing Head to convert the machine back to a conventional springing system at the height of the season. It was a bruising experience that caused a great deal of aggravation, leaving Patrick understandably reluctant to race such a system again until much more development work had been focused on making it work properly.

Patrick was painfully aware of how many championship points the team had lost in 1991 due to the unreliability of the FW14's new electro-hydraulic, semi-automatic gear-change mechanism, and he was determined not to have a repeat performance with the active system. To this end a punishing 7,000-mile development programme was completed, much of which was entrusted to the team's test driver Damon Hill, and the green light was only given for the system to be raced in anger about six weeks prior to the start of the '92 season.

The other element of excellence within the overall Williams technical package was the 67-degree Renault V10 engine in its latest RS3C trim. Mansell duly dominated his opposition from the start of the first race of the season in South Africa, leading Patrese home to a commanding 1-2 finish. This was followed by repeat performances at Mexico City and Interlagos, although Riccardo led the early stages of the Brazilian race and was perhaps a little unlucky not to retain his advantage through his routine mid-race tyre stop.

In fact, Mansell admitted that the outcome of the race was only decided at this crucial juncture when, having made his own tyre stop two laps before his team-mate, he piled on the pressure as seldom before in order to get ahead when Riccardo came in.

'I was a little naughty,' he conceded. 'I switched off the rev limiter and drove two laps at qualifying speed immediately after rejoining.' That, allied to the fact that Patrese was slightly baulked by a couple of slower cars just before coming into the pits, tipped the balance decisively in Mansell's favour.

Mansell won again at Barcelona – where the symmetry of the Williams 1-2 cavalcade was spoiled when Patrese spun off in the heavy rain – but they were back to their old ways with another grand slam in the San Marino GP at Imola. With Senna hobbled by a less-than-competitive McLaren-Honda MP4/7, it seemed that nothing could stop the Mansell/Williams bandwagon. In fact, some of motor racing's most senior power brokers despaired at the level of domination exerted by the Williams-Renault partnership. It was, they suggested, bad for business.

Word began to circulate that the television ratings were suffering because of Mansell's sustained success. In fact, this was not the case and later prompted a firm denial from the Formula 1 Constructors' Association. Yet the doubts were now sown and the pit lane was buzzing with talk that the FIA was considering rule changes in order to spice up the racing.

Yet as Mansell raced full-tilt towards the 1992 World Championship, there were pressures building up behind the scenes. As early as the Mexican Grand Prix Frank Williams decided to test the water and probe Mansell as to what his reaction might be if the team let Patrese go at the end of the season and signed Alain Prost to drive alongside him in 1993.

Nigel was not in a mood to compromise. He rejected the suggestion trenchantly. In his personal demonology, he pictured Prost as the Grand Diabolarch. He was quite clear in his own mind. The Frenchman had been a troublesome stable-mate when they were paired together at Ferrari, and he did not intend willingly to be steered up the same route again. More to the point, Mansell felt that he had worked hard with Williams-Renault throughout 1991 and was now reaping the fruits of those labours. He could see no reason why Prost was needed, let alone wanted.

'Why change the team, Frank?' Mansell would ask after the first three races of the 1992 season. 'Riccardo and I have come first and second in every race. We are blowing the opposition away. Why do you need Prost?'

This was, of course, a gross over-simplification of the situation. Prost, statistically the most successful driver of all time, was sitting out the season, and Senna, Formula 1's other great player, was weighed down with an uphill struggle to compete with the new McLaren-Honda, clearly a car that was not in the same league as the new Williams-Renault.

Think about it logically, Patrese was an accomplished and very experienced F1 professional, yet by no stretch of the imagination could he be said to be approaching Senna's level of talent. Yet the Williams-Renault FW14B was sufficiently competitive to allow not only Mansell, but also this veteran Italian campaigner, to run rings round Ayrton in most circumstances. The message was overwhelmingly clear: the Williams FW14B was technically in a class of its own. To put it another way, if Mansell was sailing towards his long-cherished Championship, it could be argued that he was doing it with equipment that was, in comparative terms, significantly superior to that enjoyed by any title aspirant in the sport's history.

The negotiations that followed were complicated and exhaustive. On the face of it, Mansell was reluctant to sign for 1993 until he knew the identity of his team-mate. He really wasn't convinced that Frank had been serious about Prost and simply wanted to keep his head down, concentrating on the racing.

Even so, after five races he suggested that he might be prepared to sign for $8 million (£5 million) – the same figure as he was earning in 1992 – if Frank would guarantee that Patrese was kept on. No such guarantees were forthcoming, so Nigel changed his tack slightly, pressing for compensation if he was required to relinquish his number one status the following year in order to accommodate Prost. A figure of $2 million (£1.25 million) was mentioned in this connection.

By British Grand Prix time, where Mansell scored another dominant victory in front of a record 120,000-strong crowd, rumours that Prost had already clinched a deal with Williams resurfaced strongly. Pressed hard on the subject, Mansell says that Frank admitted that, yes, it was likely he would be signing Prost. In fact, shortly afterwards, Mansell claims he discovered that the deal was done. Williams says he simply told Mansell to bear in mind, when making his own calculations and judgements, that Alain might well come aboard for 1993.

More worryingly from his standpoint, Mansell began to assemble evidence that, he believed, pointed to the fact that Prost had been signed up with the power to veto the second driver. Perhaps understandably, that would mean that Prost could keep Senna out of the second Williams seat. But Nigel also believed that Alain, should he choose to, had also asked that Nigel be replaced!

This seemingly unlikely information was allegedly drawn to Mansell's attention by an 'unimpeachable source' within the Williams camp, but Frank Williams supposedly headed that off and persuaded Alain to change his mind. By the time of the Hungarian Grand Prix, the weekend on which Nigel would clinch his World Championship with a strong second place to Senna's McLaren-Honda, it seemed as though the storm had passed. Mansell had re-opened negotiations with Frank.

Terms were agreed for 1993. Mansell would accept $1.5 million (£937,000) compensation for accepting joint number one status alongside Prost. Nigel seemed content with the deal for the new season, although there was still one sticking point. Frank Williams was baulking at Nigel's request that he provide three hotel rooms for him and his family at each of the 16 races. Even so, Mansell jetted back to the Isle of Man on the Sunday after clinching his Championship convinced that the deal was all but done.

However, the warning lights went on for Mansell the following day when the legal documents required to finalise the contract apparently did not arrive in the Isle of Man. Frank Williams apologised for the delay, explaining that a few more details had to be checked out and approved by Elf and Renault. Mansell tried not to worry about it.

Later that day, Nigel's mobile phone rang when he was out playing golf at Ramsey. The offer had been withdrawn. In its place was a proposition for a substantial pay cut – some said as much as 50 per cent – and only a matter of hours to agree the deal. According to his message from Williams, if he did not sign then Senna was prepared to do the deal immediately – all of which was difficult to understand, as Mansell understood that Prost's contract specifically excluded Ayrton from driving the other car. It was a case of take it or leave it. Or so it seemed.

Mansell's self-absorbed attitude to the whole affair may have ignored the fact that the real world – outside Formula 1's fairy tale financial orbit – was still reeling under the effects of a global recession. Frank Williams was still waiting to see precisely what budget would be available for 1994.

In particular, Elf – one of the team's key paymasters – was uncertain as to precisely how much money would be available for Formula 1 sponsorship in 1993. The French national oil company had been buffeted by a 23 per cent drop in profits during the first six months of 1992 and, while there was no doubt that it would continue supporting Williams, it wanted to spend no more than was absolutely necessary.

So Frank Williams wanted Nigel Mansell to stay, but not at any price. The new World Champion was quick to make it clear that money was not the overriding factor in the course of these negotiations. 'We have never been motivated by money,' he claimed. 'The question of salary is only one part of the package. On a list of ten points, it probably ranks tenth . . .'

However, during August 1992 Frank Williams was rapidly concluding otherwise. Privately he had formed the opinion that money was not tenth on Mansell's list. It *was* the list. Even so, he believed that he would be able to strike a deal. True, he'd heard rumours that there might be an offer on the table for Nigel from the Newman/Haas Indycar team in the wake of Michael Andretti's impending switch to Formula 1 with McLaren.

Yet, by the same token, he knew that Andretti had been paid only $3.5 million (£2.2 million) by Newman/Haas in 1992. Huge money by Indycar standards, perhaps, but really not in Mansell's financial league. Surely Nigel would not allow his pride to get the better of him and turn his back on Formula 1 as the reigning World Champion?

Ironically, Mansell's Monza press conference had been briefly interrupted by Williams team executive Gary Crumpler, who pushed to the front of the crush and whispered a message from Frank Williams into his ear. Renault, he said, would make up the difference. A financial deal could be reached. If only this offer had been made before Nigel began reading his statement.

Frank Williams reflected on the situation with a degree of frustration. 'Put simply, it was a matter of two hard-headed idiots who couldn't communicate and then, because Nigel, as at Silverstone in 1990, made a grossly premature decision to retire, there was no turning back.

'By Monday evening, away from the circuit, it is my belief that we would have all calmed down and been able to strike a deal.'

Later still, Mansell reportedly told Williams that if Gary Crumpler had got to him before he had reached the media centre, he would have been in a position to cancel the conference. But once he had started to speak, Nigel had gone beyond the point of no return.

Meanwhile, Prost viewed things from a slightly different perspective. Comfortable with a two-year Williams-Renault deal for 1993/94 that had been in his pocket for some months, by early August he noted that Mansell was still fighting hard against his inclusion in the team. He didn't really blame him for that. From his own experience he knew that, while on paper the notion of two superstars in a team was the right way to go, what worked best was a deal like the Senna/Berger partnership at McLaren.

In his view Mansell was causing big problems. At the same time Senna was increasing his pressure on Renault, the French car company simply wanting the best two drivers. They clearly thought that, with Senna and Prost in the Williams-Renault squad, they simply could not be beaten. But there was more, much more to it than that.

Prost had thought things over carefully and realised that it would never work with him and Senna driving again for the same team. As drivers, he reasoned, they were too similar. Yet he acknowledged that Ayrton was in a different class when it came to political guile.

Alain had, quite frankly, imparted this message to Frank Williams. The team chief agreed with Prost's reasoning, as did Patrick Head. However, because Alain believed that he and Mansell were *so* different in their approach, the way in which they tackled the job and ran their races, he felt that there was no reason why they could not rub along together.

In early August Prost also took the opportunity to communicate his views to Renault. Prost and Senna would not work, he told them. If he was coming back to Formula 1, it had to be fun. He also talked to Frank Williams about the possibility of Jean Alesi joining Williams, but didn't really believe that Renault would want two French drivers.

For Mansell, however, it seemed clear that the odds were being very firmly stacked against him as August 1992 came to an end. Finally, he decided he could take no more. He was damned if he was going to take a pay cut to stay with Williams as the reigning World Champion. So he played his hand and went ahead with the Monza press conference, announcing his retirement from Formula 1.

Ironically, Mansell's decision to quit had been pre-empted by Riccardo Patrese opting to accept an offer to join Michael Schumacher in the Benetton-Ford team for 1993. Midway through August, Riccardo judged that Prost would be taking his seat in the Williams line-up alongside Mansell, so he had better make a move to secure worthwhile alternative employment while there were still some good drives going. When Nigel announced he was retiring, it naturally occurred to Patrese that – perhaps – he could have stayed with Williams after all. However, if those thoughts did in fact cross his mind, the pleasant Italian kept them firmly to himself.

At the end of the day, of course, it was inconceivable that Williams would not opt for Alain Prost in 1993. With about 45 per cent of the team's reputed £25 million operating budget provided by either Elf or Renault, in the form of free engines and technical support, there was no way in which the team was going to bite the hand that was feeding it so generously.

Renault Sport Managing Director Patrick Faure was not happy about los-ing Mansell. Yet in the aftermath of Nigel's decision to quit Formula 1, rumours began surfacing to the effect that the Englishman suddenly became less than obliging in his relations with the French car-maker. If so, then it might be easy for some to have seen Mansell's point. In his mind Renault's hand was behind the appointment of the man he hated in the team for whom he had just won the World Championship.

However, some utterly outrageous stories began to circulate just after the end of the season. Some mischief-makers hinted that Mansell had refused to take part in Renault's end-of-season Formula 1 review on French television unless they gave him the three road cars that he had been using on a loan basis during the course of the season.

This is a gross calumny, of course, untrue in every respect, and is utterly and completely rejected by Renault and all those close to the French company. Even so, it was an unfortunate reflection on the perceived state of relations between Mansell and the Williams team's engine suppliers that such outlandish stories should have been given any currency whatsoever.

By the same token, there was no concealing the fact that Renault felt pret-ty humiliated by Mansell's departure. Patrick Faure certainly expressed his displeasure to Frank on this particular subject; he wasn't impressed with the way in which the negotiations had broken down.

Mansell, however unintentionally, had embarrassed his company and also rather let himself down by his hard criticism of certain British motor sport-ing journalists in an interview with a French radio station. Coming at the end of a season in which he had accused Australian journalist Mark Fogarty of 'being on drugs' when he persisted with a particularly difficult line of questioning after the Spanish Grand Prix, it seemed as though Nigel's nerve ends were becoming more than ever so slightly frayed.

Diplomatically, Faure refrained from making any public comments on the matter, perhaps appreciating more than most the cautionary financial bottom line that fellow investors Elf had drawn in the sand. Yet other Williams team sponsors were less restrained when it came to voicing their concern.

A statement from Labatt's, the Canadian brewing company that contributed about £1.5 million (£935,000) to the overall Williams budget in addition to around £250,000 in personal sponsorship to Mansell himself, hinted that the British driver was central to their involvement with the team.

'As a company we are concerned that Nigel Mansell and Williams GPE have not been able to reach an agreement for 1993,' said John Eckmire, Managing Director of Labatt Brewing UK. 'Our sponsorship position has always assumed that Nigel Mansell would be driving for Williams next year. For the record, we greatly value our relationship with Nigel and hope it may continue in the future.

'It is our wish that Williams and Mansell should re-open discussions and the prospect of Mansell's premature retirement should vanish.'

By then, however, the rift was complete. Mansell was signed to drive the 1993 Indycar season in a Newman/Haas Lola-Ford alongside veteran campaigner Mario Andretti. Mansell's divorce from Formula 1 seemed final. There was no going back. Or so it seemed.

Chapter 2

A patchy love affair

'We should not pretend that there is anything in his long career which those who respect and admire him should wish otherwise.'

The Times, on Edward VII's accession

That Alain Prost should eventually end up in the cockpit of a Williams-Renault was no surprise to anybody in the Formula 1 business. Even before he had entered Grand Prix racing with McLaren in 1980, this chirpy, tousle-haired Charles Aznavour lookalike had been closely linked with the French car-maker throughout his time in the junior formulae.

From the very outset of his career Prost displayed a definite golden touch. He won the 1973 karting World Championship and three years later displayed a similar mastery of the European Formule Renault series. In 1979 he clinched the European F3 title, including a win in the prestigious Monaco GP supporting race, and, after McLaren offered him his first F1 test drive at the end of 1979, team director Teddy Mayer signed him on the spot.

Although 1980 proved to be one of the most disappointing seasons in McLaren's Formula 1 history, Alain scored championship points on his first two outings, sixth place on his debut in the Argentine GP at Buenos Aires, then fifth a fortnight later in the Brazilian race at Interlagos.

However, the third race of the season set Prost worrying. He had two accidents in two days with the McLaren M29, the second one leaving him with a broken wrist, no chance of a race that weekend and the harsh reality of having to miss the next Grand Prix, the street race through Long Beach, California.

'That car was always breaking,' he recalled. 'Over the season I had six or seven serious accidents. You know, if your car loses a wheel in every race, that's not good and I don't think any driver can accept that. The worst of the year was at Watkins Glen, in qualifying, when the suspension broke in a fourth gear corner. I hit the wall very hard and got a big bang on the head which knocked me out.'

At the time, McLaren was in a transitional phase with newcomers Ron Dennis and John Barnard finding their feet in a sometimes uneasy alliance with existing Director Teddy Mayer. The collaboration had been initiated by Marlboro, the team's title sponsor, who had become increasingly anxious about McLaren's fading form over the previous three seasons. The new management demonstrated its inexperience by making some remarks to the press that suggested that Alain was to blame for this accident.

'When I got back to the pits eventually, I heard people in the team telling journalists that I had made a mistake, gone too fast on cold tyres, even though I'd already done eight laps,' he remembers. 'The following day they wanted me to race, even though I knew after the warm-up that I wasn't fit. My head ached like hell and I hadn't been able to sleep all night.

'After their remarks to the press after the accident, I made up my mind to leave. I said, "If you want to say things like that, it's finished. I have a three-year contract with you, but I won't drive for you any more. If you won't release me, OK, I stop racing Formula 1."'

However, although he finished his first stint at McLaren under something of a cloud, he has fond memories of his partnership with John Watson, with whom had a cordial and supportive relationship. Watson's career was beginning to edge downwards when Alain joined the team, and the Frenchman admits he found himself slightly annoyed about the way in which Watson was criticised, even from people within the team.

'John was under no real obligation to be helpful with me or be forthcoming with technical information,' he says. 'But I have a great affection for him. He was always available to give me helpful advice and, of course, knew every circuit in the Championship. He did all this despite the fact that I was making life pretty difficult for him in all manner of ways.

'In all honesty, I was much better than John when it came to setting up the cars, and I was faster. This caused a lot of gossip within the team and I didn't appreciate some of the facetious remarks which were made about him. But John was very long-suffering and gentlemanly about all this. I wouldn't have put up with it in the way he did.'

The McLaren management was understandably bitter. They accused Renault, who immediately offered Prost a drive for 1981, of poaching him. He would join his compatriot René Arnoux in the Renault turbo squad for that year, during which season he won the French, Dutch and Italian Grands Prix and finished the year with fifth place in the Drivers' World Championship, having accumulated 43 points.

Prost had joined Renault as equal number one with Arnoux, but his superior performances in 1981 ensured that he was promoted to de facto number one status in the team management's mind, even though there was, officially, no number one/number two concept in the team's way of doing things.

In many ways Prost was a simple and straightforward individual. Later in his career both Senna and Mansell in particular would accuse him of being a highly politicised operator, capable of manipulating intra-team situations behind the scenes to his own advantage. Yet no firm evidence of such alleged duplicity was ever offered – it was all very much 'nudge, nudge, wink, wink' gossip – and most of the evidence available to journalists, in particular, suggested that Alain played things a good deal straighter than many of his contemporaries.

An early example of what might be described as his innocent naïvety came at the 1982 French Grand Prix. Prost was better placed for the championship in terms of the number of points he had accumulated at this stage of the season, so Renault team manager Gerard Larrousse asked Arnoux if he would let Alain win. René agreed – then reneged on his word, refusing to slow up and let his team-mate overtake.

Inevitably, Prost was cast in the role of complaining villain when he voiced some complaints about this situation. Nevertheless, he was furious with indignation. 'For a few days after that race, I decided absolutely to retire from Formula 1 at the end of the season,' he fumed, 'and I told Larrousse that I would leave Renault if Arnoux stayed. You must trust your team-mate. I remembered what happened with Villeneuve, after Pironi duped him at Imola, and I learned a lesson from that – which later came back to me again in 1989, with Senna.'

However, by the end of 1984 Alain admitted that he had put those problems behind him: 'All I will say now is that I am happy that René and I have long since forgotten that episode and get along fine today.'

At the start of the 1983 season Arnoux duly left to join Ferrari. His place in the Renault squad alongside Prost was taken by the American driver Eddie Cheever, and there was no doubt that Alain was now clearly the team's number one driver. Armed with the new Renault RE40, Prost now got down to the serious business of challenging for the World Championship.

The turbo era was steadily gathering its high-technology momentum. Renault and Ferrari were both highly competitive with their twin-turbo V6 engines, but the most potent challenge of all was brewing from BMW's single-turbo, four-cylinder engine used in the works Brabhams.

Prost won the French, Belgian, British and Austrian Grands Prix. After that fourth success he was 14 points clear of Brabham team leader Nelson Piquet. There were only four races left to run, yet Alain brought Renault's engine department up with something of a shock when he predicted that more power was needed if they were not to lose the title to Nelson.

'Renault didn't respond,' he recalls. '"Look," I said, "we can't get pole position anyway, because our engine won't accept a lot of boost, so Piquet will always be ahead of us on the grid – and with his horsepower he will be impossible to pass in the race."'

Alain's anxiety brimmed over in the Dutch GP at Zandvoort where he tangled with Piquet. Under the circumstances he had to take a chance. But it hadn't paid off. Piquet then won easily at both Monza and Brands Hatch, ensuring that the title battle would go down to the wire in the final race, the South African Grand Prix at Kyalami.

As an aside to these problems, Alain had very real difficulties on the personal front. There was a faction that regarded him as the key obstacle standing between the Ferrari-mounted Arnoux and the World Championship. René, mounting a late mathematical challenge, had a lot of support, both in France and Switzerland. Alain received death threats and, as a result, was accompanied by a bodyguard at Monza. He moved his family to Switzerland and, at the height of this turmoil, signed for Renault in 1984. Against his better judgement.

He was almost resigned to defeat, going to Kyalami believing that only luck could win him the World Championship. He was right. The Brabham-BMWs were on another planet, Riccardo Patrese winning the race after Piquet had slowed to finish third, thus making sure he was Champion a second time. Prost retired from a distant third place when his Renault V6 suffered another turbo failure.

Renault, who had flown out dozens of French journalists to witness what was planned to be its Day of Glory, was humiliated. Under the circumstances it was all too easy to shift the blame onto Prost. He never forgot the aftermath of that disagreeable race.

'Every week there is a house newspaper in the Renault factories, and after Kyalami it said I had stopped, not because there was a problem with the car, but because I was only running third and didn't want to look bad,' he recalls in a voice tinged with disbelief.

'There were also some French journalists who wrote the same sort of thing. Renault pushed too much. If they wanted to invite journalists to the race, OK. But journalists should always write what they truly think, which wasn't easy in the circumstances.'

Quite clearly, France's honour had been impugned. Somebody had to be made the scapegoat and it turned out to be Prost. Incomprehensibly, the team's biggest single asset was fired a couple of days later at a meeting in Paris, even though Renault briefly considered challenging BMW's World Championship in the courts on the basis of the legality of the fuel in Piquet's car at Kyalami.

Yet making Prost carry the can was an unwarranted and disreputable decision on Renault's part. The French works team never won another Grand Prix after Prost left, withdrawing from Formula 1 in disarray two years later. Alain, as history relates, fared rather better.

Over in the McLaren camp, Ron Dennis was bogged down in contract negotiations with John Watson. Once he heard that Prost was on the market, he ceased worrying about the Ulsterman. The new TAG-Porsche V6 turbo engine was just coming on-line for the British team and Dennis knew enough about Prost's ability to snap him up for 1984. More to the point, he got his services for financial peanuts. It was the bargain of the decade.

'As it turned out, the Renault people did me a big favour,' said Prost, reflecting on the breach several years later. 'The situation had become impossible. I was very tired with the ridiculous amount of PR work I had to do for them. The guys who worked for the team were always good, but the organisation was so bad that I despaired.

'There were too many bosses, and it was impossible to get anything done quickly because there were too many people to convince and persuade. And if you can't react quickly, you [will] never beat people like Ferrari and Brabham. It made me sad to realise just how much hypocrisy there was in Formula 1. By the time I left Renault I was on my guard the whole time, always wondering if the hand slapping me on the back had a dagger in it.'

Ironically, a few weeks before the breach with Renault, Prost had spoken with Ron Dennis about the possibility of rejoining McLaren. Now the threads of that debate were taken up once more. But Dennis was setting the agenda. He knew that Alain had nothing.

'It embarrasses me now that I signed for so little,' grins Prost, 'but at that time I didn't care. I was away from Renault. That was all that mattered.' Prost's Days of Glory were now only a short distance away, just over the horizon.

The new Porsche-made TAG turbo V6 had made its Formula 1 debut installed in a McLaren MP4/2 test car at the 1983 Dutch GP in the hands of Niki Lauda. This engine, designed to strict dimensional and performance parameters by the team's highly demanding Chief Designer John Barnard, would now power Prost and Lauda into the '84 season. At a stroke it re-wrote the parameters of contemporary Grand Prix car performance.

Prost won at Rio on his maiden outing in the McLaren-TAG. He remembers it as a delicious moment, laying the ghosts of his relationship with Renault. Ironically, Alain only inherited the lead when Derek Warwick – who had replaced him in the Renault squad – spun out with a broken suspension. Warwick was never to get as close to winning a Grand Prix again, but Prost surged through 1984 with a total of seven wins.

'You just can't imagine the importance of that win in Brazil,' recalls Prost with delight. 'Some of the French press, you know, gave me a very hard time when I left Renault, and if Warwick had won and I had not finished, it would have been very bad for me. But the problem disappeared after that.'

Lauda, though, won five races to pip his French team-mate to the title by half a point, this closest winning margin in the history of the World Championship coming about due to the rain-soaked Monaco GP being flagged to a halt at half distance in torrential rain, leaving Prost with four and a half points for the victory, rather than the customary full helping of nine.

Prost quickly made himself as comfortable within the McLaren enclave as he had been ill at ease during that last season with Renault. He soon formed a reputation for being undemanding, easy on the equipment and mechanically very astute. Ironically, these were the same qualities for which Niki Lauda had been noted over the past decade. Niki, who had been wooed out of retirement by Ron Dennis at the start of 1982, was a little cautious about Prost at first.

To be frank, Lauda always felt that he could get the upper hand over John Watson. Now things were slightly different. But he soon realised that Alain was a totally dependable team-mate who played things absolutely fair. 'He was extremely quick,' he acknowledged, 'and having him as a team-mate certainly stimulated me, but it also haunted me. There was no break from the pressure. He was always right there, always on form. In qualifying, he was simply unbelievable.

'It is true that I was never in this position with a team-mate before. Sometimes one of them would beat me, but inwardly I always believed that I would be in front next time. With Prost it was different. I had to drive faster and faster, better and better, all the time. It was the most satisfying season I ever experienced.'

Prost admitted that Lauda had been his hero during his karting apprenticeship: 'He was my idol. I used to model myself on him, dream of achieving success like him. And now I was in the same team, with the same equipment, the same chances. It was something fantastic for me, as I was now free of all the tension and responsibility at Renault.

'I did not know Niki very well when I came back to McLaren. In fact, it wasn't easy to know him well. But I believed he was completely honest – the most important thing – and after a year racing with him I knew this fact for sure.

'I was very glad to hear he would be staying in the team for 1985. OK, he won the '84 World Championship, but it was the mutual trust between us which was the important thing. When we agreed a joint strategy together for an individual race, we both kept to it and there was never a cross word.'

More significantly, Lauda would teach Prost a great deal about tactics and the technique of getting the most out of a Formula 1 car with the minimum physical effort. Niki later admitted that he only won the '84 Championship by drawing on all the accumulated experience at his disposal. In 1985 he simply couldn't compete. Prost raised the standard of his game yet another notch and became the first French World Champion in the sport's history.

Interestingly, this nationalistic aspect of his success did not significantly move him. Since moving to Switzerland, Prost counted himself as a Citizen of the World. French by nationality he might still have been, but he never lost sight of the fact that he won the World Championship in a British car, powered by a German engine and using American tyres. The day of the national racing team, as defined by the standards of the 1930s and '50s, had long been consigned to the history books.

Prost had scored nine wins for Renault. He then added another seven in his first season at McLaren, another five in 1985, four in 1986 (clinching his second Championship) and three in 1987. That took his personal tally to an all-time record of 28 wins, beating the 13-year-old record established by Jackie Stewart, who had retired at the end of 1973.

Stewart felt that Prost was a worthy successor, the Scot being particularly impressed with his relentless competitive edge and the fact that he retained the Drivers' Championship in 1986. 'Undoubtedly there is an infectious disease which afflicts every World Champion and his team,' noted Jackie, 'and it's been going on for years. It's not quite right to say that the guy who is champion loses his edge, or that the designer relaxes, or the mechanics lose interest or whatever.

'Yet somewhere along the line, these things occur. I'm talking about decimal points, yet they all add up. The record book shows that hardly ever have a driver and team won back-to-back titles. Fangio previously did it with Mercedes, and Brabham with Cooper, and that's it.

'So that aspect of Prost and McLaren is the thing that so impresses me. As for Alain, I used to think he and [Nelson] Piquet were on a par, but not any more. Nelson's car in 1986 was undoubtedly quicker, but he made a lot of mistakes. On the other hand, Prost makes incredibly few errors. For me, he is the best driver in the world. No argument.'

After Lauda's retirement from Formula 1 at the end of 1985, throughout 1986 and '87 Prost continued to enjoy himself enormously at McLaren, partnered respectively by Keke Rosberg and Stefan Johansson.

'I must say I was taken aback with his [Rosberg's] confidence at the first test at Rio,' he laughs. 'Keke just brushed aside advice from John Barnard, put his foot down hard and flew off the road midway round his second flying lap. The car was very badly damaged and I don't think Keke and John ever saw eye-to-eye again.

'Keke was very skilful, motivated and hungry. Perhaps he didn't quite have the necessary finesse to get the best out of the sort of turbo, fuel consumption racing we had at the time. But he was certainly a great competitor. And a great friend.'

Then everything changed for 1988 when Ayrton Senna came aboard, bringing with him a Honda turbo engine deal. There was to be nothing cosy about this relationship.

Prost won three out of the first four races. But then Senna came into his own and, throughout the summer of '88, the complexities of the relationship between the two men came to monopolise the headlines far more than the technical domination of the McLaren-Honda alliance. If that seemed unfair, it was simply a reflection of an inevitable trend. Media interest in Formula 1 was running at fever pitch, so it was personalities rather than machines that guaranteed the column inches.

At the end of the day Senna won eight races to Prost's seven, and clinched his first Championship during his maiden season with McLaren. Alain unquestionably felt marginalised by the force of Senna's dominant personality and the fact that he seemed to have Honda's ear in terms of engine development. Also there is no doubt that the McLaren management went out of its way to cosset Senna, who had signed a three-year contract at the start of 1988, with the result that Alain found that the 'special relationship' with what he had come to regard as an extension of his own family was suddenly under threat.

'At Monaco, I was angry with Ron [Dennis],' recalled Prost. 'Ayrton crashed and I won the race. At the gala dinner that evening I made a small speech, and thought I was very nice about Ayrton, but there was only so far I could go.

'Then Ron came on the podium . . . He wanted to help Senna too much. He said I was behind, and Ayrton was fantastic, and for sure he had a problem with the car because he couldn't have crashed because of a mistake, and things like that.

'It wasn't necessary for him to have done that. What I had said was enough, that Senna had pole position, that it was his race, but it was part of the game, and I was very happy to win. But no, Ron had to go further than that. Afterwards he admitted he had been wrong. But . . .'

In 1989 the Formula 1 regulations called for 3.5-litre naturally-aspirated engines, and the new Honda V10-propelled McLaren MP4/5s continued to be the cars to beat. Prost was already wary of Senna's driving tactics after the Brazilian had almost pushed him into the pit wall at 190 mph as they battled for the lead of the '88 Portuguese GP at Estoril, but he was prepared to give Ayrton the benefit of the doubt as they went into the new season together. But their relationship fell apart for good after the 1989 San Marino race at Imola.

Before the start Senna suggested to Prost that they should not fight over the lead going into the first corner on the opening lap. Whichever of them got the best start and led into the corner should not be challenged by the other. Prost agreed, led down to the first turn – and was overtaken by Senna. However, Ayrton viewed it differently, believing that he had surged past Alain on the straight, well before the braking area. Prost dismissed this as duplicitous nonsense.

From then on he decided to work with Senna only on a technical basis. Dennis forced Ayrton to apologise in an effort to keep the peace, but only a superficial armistice resulted. Before the French GP Alain announced that he would be leaving McLaren at the end of the season. Dennis and the team's patron, TAG boss Mansour Ojjeh, attempted to talk him out of it. It was even suggested that McLaren would finance a paid sabbatical in 1990 for the Frenchman. It was a shrewd move. To borrow from Lyndon Johnson, 'Better to have him on the inside pissing out, rather than on the outside pissing in'.

However, at Monza, on the weekend when he won the Italian Grand Prix, Prost announced that he would be driving for Ferrari in 1990. His battle for the '89 title, meanwhile, seemed destined to go down to the wire with Senna. In fact the two McLaren drivers arrived at the Japanese GP, the penultimate round of the series, with Ayrton needing a win if he was to have a chance of retaining his '88 crown.

Prost led from the start at Suzuka, but Senna gradually whittled away his early advantage and closed in onto his tail. With six laps to go Ayrton attempted a do-or-die overtaking manoeuvre into the braking area for the tight chicane before the pits. Such a strategy relied totally on Prost giving way, but such a compliant attitude on the Frenchman's part was now consigned to history. He closed the door on Senna and the two McLarens slithered to an inelegant halt, locked together in the middle of the circuit.

Senna resumed, rejoining the race through the chicane. He won on the road – and was then disqualified. Prost was World Champion and the breach between the two men was, apparently, sealed for good. Neither ever wanted anything to do with the other again.

'I've learned a big lesson this year,' admitted Prost. 'It's the first time I've ever been in a weak position in a team, and I've seen things I've never realised before. I never knew what John Watson was going through in 1980, for example, or how bad it must have been for Niki in '85, even for Keke the year after. I never realised how a team can control everything.' From now on, he vowed, things would be different.

Prost would have two seasons with Ferrari, ending up when he was fired one race before the end of 1991 for being too overt in his criticism of the team for the management's comfort. In 1990, of course, he won five races, the first of which was an enormously satisfying success in the Brazilian GP at Interlagos where Senna could only finish third after damaging the nose of his McLaren lapping Satoru Nakajima's Tyrrell.

Most significantly, after Mansell's decision to retire following his disappointment in the British Grand Prix, Prost seemed set fair for priority treatment for the team in an effort to win the Championship. In fact, according to the Frenchman, after Mansell's two lacklustre outings at Hockenheim and Spa – where, in both cases, he retired after complaining about the car – the Englishman was poised on the verge of premature dismissal.

These electrifying allegations were made in an Elf-produced video produced for internal circulation only within the French petroleum company. In it Prost firmly states that Mansell was to be fired before the Italian Grand Prix at Monza and replaced by Italian Gianni Morbidelli. Yet, suddenly, according to Alain, the decision was reversed and 'Mansell was allowed to act in his own interest'.

This was followed by an extraordinary incident at the start of the 1990 Portuguese Grand Prix where Mansell almost pushed Prost into the pit wall at the start, the two Ferraris coming within an ace of colliding as they accelerated away from the line. To this day Prost believes that Mansell had connived with Ayrton Senna – the two spent a long time sitting together in a hire car in the paddock after final qualifying – to ensure that the McLaren driver had the best chance of winning the Championship. In the event Mansell won the race from Senna with Prost a distant, delayed and fuming third.

A year later the circumstances surrounding Prost's departure from Ferrari were manifestly absurd. The notion that a triple World Champion should not be permitted to venture any public criticism of his team is simply not valid. In the past neither Senna nor Mansell had stinted on this front when things went wrong. Like it or not, brazen candour seems to be as much a quality of the contemporary Formula 1 star as the raw ability to conduct a racing car at competitive speed out on a circuit.

Yet the bottom line was even more serious than that. Ferrari had effectively sacrificed its most valuable single asset on the altar of nationalistic pride. Prost had taken them closer to a World Championship than any driver since Jody Scheckter had won the title for Maranello in 1979. On the face of it Ferrari seemed to be cutting off its nose to spite its face. It also proved an expensive luxury. Lawyers negotiated a substantial financial settlement to prevent Prost from suing the team for breach of contract, leaving the Frenchman wealthier to the tune of a sum rumoured to be in the region of $10 million.

However, the first signs that Alain was not yet ready to retire came on Sunday 19 January 1992. Wearing white overalls with no sponsorship identification, and using a helmet borrowed from regular team driver Erik Comas, Prost drove one of the brand new Ligier-Renault JS37s in a 49-lap test at Paul Ricard. He recorded a best lap of 1 minute 4.78 seconds on the short circuit, refused to speak to the press and left the track without any comment.

However, Ligier Technical Director Frank Dernie was undeniably impressed. 'He's remarkable,' he enthused. 'He certainly knows what he wants. We spent the test concentrating on making the drivers comfortable. The windscreen was causing a bit of buffeting for both Alain and Thierry Boutsen [the team's other regular driver].

'Really, I'm disappointed that we were not a second quicker, but the car was amazingly reliable straight out of the box. It also proved easy to work on. Alain quite liked driving it. He said there were no vicious characteristics, but at the moment it's nothing to get excited about.'

In fact, testing the JS37 was designed as the first step in preparation to see whether Prost would take a financial stake in the Magny-Cours-based Ligier team. Early in March 1992 Elf's Minitel operation – the French telephone information network – actually circulated a story that the deal was done, but the information was almost immediately withdrawn after a matter of minutes.

It seems that the basis of the deal was that Guy Ligier, who had founded the F1 operation back in 1976, would gradually to transfer his shareholding to Prost in an operation that would see the three-times Champion controlling the team by the start of 1994. Sources suggested that Alain and Guy would become 50 per cent owners during the spring of 1992, followed by Prost taking a further 20 per cent in '93 before becoming the sole owner after another 12 months.

At the end of the day, however, Prost could not satisfy himself that long-term sponsorship funding would be feasible to develop the team into a front-line operation. Sadly, the deal collapsed amidst a degree of frustration, with Ligier thwarted in his efforts to lay the foundations for what he hoped would effectively become *Ecurie France*, in essence a French national Grand Prix team.

Prost was hard pressed to conceal his indignation over the way in which events had panned out. 'We started with a plan to have a French team cap-able of taking on the best, but it has ended up in such a shabby way, as if I was the one who capsized it because I wanted too much money,' he told *Autosport*.

'Remember one thing: when Guy [Ligier] came to see me in November [1991], it was not me who was asking. I had to be the foundation of the pro-ject. At that time my motivation was split between taking a year's sabbatical or working on the development of a French team capable of becoming Champion one day.

'I would not want to be just the driver. I brought along people who would have been responsible for the organisation and technical management. They would have enabled the team to climb to the highest levels, but it would have been expensive.

'[Money] was the unworkable condition. I wanted 70 per cent of the shares at the end of 1992. If not it would have been impossible to take any decisions. In every company you have to have one sole boss.

'I was looking for a security of funding, but no one would make a com-mitment. From a budget of FF500 million [$50 million/£32 million], we managed to get together FF410-420 million which is the absolute minimum to play in the big league. If you cannot get that together in France, you can stop talking about a national team.'

However, as we have seen elsewhere in this volume, Renault was not going to allow Prost to slip through its corporate fingers for a second time. A lot of water had flowed under the bridge since the French car company had clumsily engineered Alain's dismissal at the end of the 1983 season. More to the point, in that time Prost had grown from being a promising lad to three-times World Champion. Now, early in his unscheduled sabbatical year, he negotiated a firm two-year deal to drive a Williams-Renault in 1993 and '94. From May onwards he could sit back and regard his future with equanimity.

Interestingly, this was not the first time that Prost had negotiated with Williams. At Monaco in the early summer of 1989, at the height of his dejection over his deteriorating situation with Senna at McLaren, Alain had asked Frank whether it would be possible to talk seriously about a deal for 1990.

'Negotiations ran step by step,' recalls Frank, 'first in general terms, later getting down to more specific matters. He came to Didcot after the 1989 British Grand Prix and spent three hours talking with Patrick Head and me in the conference centre.'

Although the negotiations seemed to be promising in Frank's mind, Patrick Head had some private reservations. Although he had no doubts about Prost's quality as a driver, he wondered about his mental attitude. 'He seemed consumed by his dislike for Senna in a way that rather took me aback,' says Head. 'It was as if he couldn't talk about anything else.'

However, Marlboro, who sponsored both McLaren and Ferrari, brought their Big Guns to bear on the problem. If Prost was going to throw in the towel at McLaren, they wanted him to switch to Ferrari. Frank suddenly detected that Alain was going cold on the deal.

'To be honest, I think Alain strung us out a bit unfairly,' says Frank. 'It wasn't until the Monday before that year's Italian Grand Prix he told me he was going to Ferrari. We'd been outmanoeuvred and, in retrospect, we should have gone straight back into the market with an even bigger offer.'

In fact, Alain's return to the Formula 1 fold for 1993 was not destined to be as straightforward as one might have reasonably expected. Powerful forces began to be marshalled against not only him, but also the Williams team, towards the end of the 1992 season. There was mounting pressure amongst some of the competing teams for a change in technical regulations in order to close up the racing in Formula 1, a need that seemed to be somehow more pressing than usual set against the level of domination achieved by Williams, Renault and Mansell throughout that year.

Rightly, Frank Williams wasn't interested in accommodating such requests. Not a man to complain when his team's fortunes were down, he saw no reason why others should offer any objections when Williams was on a high. Patrick Head, the design team and the Renault engineers had produced a car/engine combination head and shoulders above the rest, but that was the others' bad luck. This was motor racing, not a staged peep-show.

Even so, Frank inadvertently offered not only the FIA, but also all his rivals, a stick to beat him with when his team's entries for the 1993 World Championship were submitted a couple of days beyond the designated closing date. The entries were due to be lodged a week after the final race of 1992 – the memorable Senna/Mansell tangle at Adelaide – but team manager Peter Windsor stayed on in Australia for a few days after the final round of the Championship, most unfortunately still with the entry forms in his briefcase. By the time the forms were eventually lodged, they were technically two days late.

As a result, in late January 1993 yet another bruising political storm threatened to envelop Grand Prix racing when the World Championship-winning Williams team found its name was left off the official published list of entries for the new World Championship.

The absence of the entries for Prost and Damon Hill were officially attributed to that failure to submit the entries on time. As a result, only 13 two-car teams were confirmed in the entry list, with 18 of the 26 drivers named at this stage.

Frank Williams was trenchant in his defence of the situation. 'I submitted these entries to the Formula 1 Constructors' Association office as I have done for the past 12 years,' he stated. But by now he was firmly in the hands of others. The rules stipulated that late entries must receive the unanimous approval of the other teams and, according to Frank, two teams – Benetton and Minardi – refused to sign 'in order to obtain concessions from us'.

However, he declined to further inflame a very delicate situation. 'The knives are out for me at the moment,' he conceded. 'I think that the governing body may try to make me sweat.'

Flavio Briatore, the Benetton team chief, denied that he was attempting to force Williams out of the title chase. 'We do not wish to see Williams out of the championship,' he warned, 'but if that is the price we have to pay for some sensible changes to the Concorde Agreement, then so be it. We cannot compromise, but as I have always said, we can be flexible.'

However, as one insider within his team remarked, 'This is a very delicate situation. Frank feels he has been publicly humiliated and his sponsors are up in arms. But he has no need to do anything but just sit it out. Everybody knows that the cars will be on the grid come South Africa.'

Taking a less charitable view, one might well have also observed that if the Williams team had been a little less casual about its paperwork, the issue would not have arisen in the first place. Off the record, Frank has since acknowledged the validity of such an observation.

From the touchlines the desire to spice up Grand Prix racing as a televised spectacle had been given added impetus by Nigel Mansell's defection to Indycar racing, a development that threatened a loss of television viewers to the rival US series. There was also a degree of nervousness over Ayrton Senna's decision to test a Penske Indycar at Willow Springs just before Christmas – long before he was firmly committed to continue driving for McLaren.

Bernie Ecclestone, in his role as FIA Vice-President Public Affairs, and the driving force behind the global television exposure now enjoyed by Formula 1, tended to play down the threat posed by Mansell's plans, characterising the American series as somehow second division. Yet the zeal that he would later apply to the task of luring the 1992 World Champion back across the Atlantic in the wake of Senna's tragic death in 1994 tended to suggest that his concerns were more deep-rooted than he conceded at the time.

As always in these sorts of situations, some wayward suggestions were advanced in an effort to spice up the racing. These included variable weight

Day of decision: on the morning of the 1992 Italian Grand Prix Nigel Mansell leaves the Monza press centre accompanied by Williams PR Ann Bradshaw and Commercial Director Sheridan Thynne, after announcing his intention to quit Williams.

Last F1 race, for now. Mansell's Williams FW14B leads Ayrton Senna's McLaren-Honda MP4/7 in the opening stages of the '92 Australian GP at Adelaide. Later, Senna would plunge into the back of the Williams as they braked for a tight corner, eliminating both cars.

Left *Damon's debut. Hill at the wheel of the Williams FW15C in the 1993 South African GP, seconds before Alessandro Zanardi's Lotus (following) rammed him off the track.*

Below left *First corner of the '93 Brazilian GP at Interlagos, with Alain Prost's Williams just getting the jump on Ayrton Senna's McLaren MP4/8, Hill's Williams and Gerhard Berger's Ferrari.*

Right *Learning the art of front-line F1: Damon at speed with the Williams-Renault FW15C.*

Below *Hill leads Prost in the opening stages of the '93 Canadian GP at Montreal, but Alain would eventually go through to win the race.*

Flying the flag: Damon's Williams FW15C goes through the pit-stop routine.

End of an era. Senna celebrates his '93 Australian GP victory with Prost (second) and Hill (third). It was Alain's final Grand Prix outing and Senna's last for McLaren before making his ill-fated switch to Williams.

Damon Hill's maiden Grand Prix victory came with an unchallenged flag-to-flag run at Hungaroring in 1993.

Prost's first test with the Williams FW15. He could hardly have imagined that his spell with the team would last only a single season.

Above left *New recruit: Dame Edna Everage (aka Barry Humphries), broadcaster Clive James, Hill and obligatory gladioli, Adelaide, '93.*

Above right *Weighing it up: Damon gets down to some serious physical training.*

Below left *Hill, ready for action in 1993 . . .*

Below right *. . . and en route for that season's historic Hungaroring victory.*

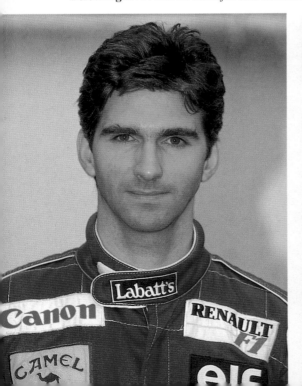

Damon's race number coincidentally mimicked his father's double zero, which he carried in the 1963 Le Mans 24-hour race in the Rover-BRM turbine car.

Above *Hill led the '93 British Grand Prix at Silverstone until a sudden engine failure intervened.*

Below *Ayrton Senna and Damon Hill pose for the cameras during the official launch of their 1994 F1 partnership at Estoril.*

Right *Through the '93 season Damon matured from a slightly tentative front-runner to a confident, proven race-winner.*

The great man: Ayrton Senna finally joined Williams at the start of the '94 season, but the partnership would end in the depths of tragedy.

First corner of the first '94 race; Senna leads Alesi and Schumacher at Interlagos.

Ayrton Senna's Williams FW16 leads Michael Schumacher's Benetton B194 during the opening stages of the '94 Brazilian Grand Prix.

Senna's Williams plunges off the track at the first corner of the '94 Pacific GP, to be rammed by Nicola Larini's Ferrari.

The blackest day. Ayrton Senna leads Michael Schumacher's Benetton on the opening lap of the ill-starred '94 San Marino GP at Imola.

Frustration: Damon Hill during qualifying for the '94 Monaco Grand Prix, the first race to take place after Senna's death. He was out on the opening lap after a collision with Mika Hakkinen's McLaren.

Restoration: a fortnight after the Monaco debacle, Damon wins the '94 Spanish GP to give Williams team morale a timely boost.

Damon gradually got to grips with the Williams FW16's handling during the course of the '94 season.

New boy lights up. David Coulthard testing at Jerez just prior to his Grand Prix debut at Barcelona, 1994.

Powerful men: Renault Sport Technical Director Bernard Dudot (left) with colleague Christian Contzen and one of the 3.5-litre V10s used by the Williams team.

The power behind the '94 Constructors' World Championship.

Opening lap scramble in the '94 Canadian GP, with David Coulthard just getting the jump on Damon Hill.

Above left *Hill wrestles with Berger's Ferrari in the opening stages of the Canadian GP.*

Above right *Picking up the threads. Nigel Mansell talks with Patrick Head on a visit to the Williams team's Didcot headquarters prior to his F1 return in the '94 French GP.*

Below *Teacher and pupil: Hill and Mansell in conference. Damon raised his game to meet Nige's challenge.*

Ready to go: Coulthard monitors the progress of his rivals on a portable timing screen.

On the grid: Mansell climbs aboard his Williams FW16 at the French GP, Magny-Cours, 1994.

Schumacher's Benetton gets the jump on Hill's Williams at the start of the '94 French GP as Mansell falls back to third place.

Red Five becomes Red Two. Mansell revives old times with his personalised race number on the FW16.

Andrea Murray, Coulthard's girlfriend, shares time with Damon Hill's wife Georgie (right).

Glorious moment: Damon Hill leads into Copse at the start of the '94 British GP at Silverstone, which he would go on to win.

Coulthard swings his Williams FW16 into Spa's La Source hairpin during the '94 Belgian GP, where he ran confidently ahead of Hill for much of the race.

Star car: Sylvester Stallone tries a Williams FW16 cockpit for size at Monza, 1994.

Gerhard Berger's Ferrari leads the pack into the first corner of the '94 Portuguese GP at Estoril, pursued by Coulthard, Hill and Alesi.

Hill leads Coulthard into the La Source hairpin at Spa during their battle in the '94 Belgian GP.

The Old 1–2: Hill and Coulthard celebrate their '94 Portuguese GP grand slam together with third-placed Mika Hakkinen.

Coulthard ahead of Hill in the opening stages of the race. Damon would reverse the order with a slick overtaking manoeuvre.

Start of the '94 Japanese GP with Schumacher surfing ahead of Heinz-Harald Frentzen's Sauber, Hill, and Johnny Herbert's Benetton.

Mansell's Williams challenges Alesi's Ferrari during the rain-soaked '94 Japanese GP. Their wheel-to-wheel battle for third place lasted all the way to the chequered flag.

Left *Keeping the battle open. Damon Hill on the rostrum at Suzuka after his crucial victory, which ensured that the title would go down to the wire in Adelaide the following weekend.*

Above *Shoot-out: Mansell, Schumacher and Hill sprint for the first corner in the '94 Australian GP.*

Below *Schumacher's Benetton under pressure from Hill's Williams at Adelaide. The destiny of the Championship would be resolved in a controversial collision between the two contenders.*

Mansell en route and taking the chequered flag for his '94 Adelaide victory with the Williams FW16. It would turn out to be his final drive for Williams.

Immediately after his win Mansell is congratulated by second-placeman Gerhard Berger. The Austrian ran ahead of the Englishman until losing the lead when his Ferrari slid wide over a kerb.

The way they were: end-of-term photograph of the '94 F1 field prior to the Australian GP.

Renault Sport's headquarters at Viry-Chatillon near Paris; home of the Williams team's engines.

In 1995 Renault would expand its engine supply contract to include Benetton. Here at the '95 Brazil GP Frank Williams confers with his arch-rival, Benetton boss Flavio Briatore.

Now bound by the same engine supplier, Benetton and Williams personnel join up for a pre-season photographic cease-fire.

Above left *Damon Hill samples a Russian winter during his off-season promotional world tour for Rothmans, the Williams team's title sponsor.*

Above right *Mansell, on the rostrum at Adelaide, celebrates his last Grand Prix victory for Williams.*

Below *Second race, first win of '95. Hill in wet practice for the Argentine GP at Buenos Aires, a race he went on to win in decisive style.*

Man of the future: David Coulthard got the Williams drive for 1995 in preference to Mansell.

The 1995 team. From the left, test-driver Jean-Christophe Boullion with Hill and Coulthard.

Hill and Coulthard meet the press at the 1995 team launch.

Schumacher together with Coulthard and Berger on the rostrum after the 1995 Brazilian GP. The Renault-propelled duo would be disqualified due to a discrepancy over fuel specification – then reinstated on appeal.

Coulthard leads off his first pole position at the start of the '95 Argentine GP, Buenos Aires.

Hill chats to Carlos Reutemann at Buenos Aires, 1995. The Argentine driver had finished second for Williams in the previous Argentine GP held in 1981.

Coulthard refuels during the '95 Spanish GP at Barcelona. He retired in the closing stages with gearbox hydraulic failure.

Williams's current two lads – heading for the 1995 World Championship?

limits and the possible intervention of a pace car in the event of any competitor building up a lead in excess of a certain level, thus artificially closing up the field.

However, the terms of the Concorde Agreement, the complex legal protocol by means of which Formula 1 racing's rules are framed and implemented, required unanimous agreement amongst the competing teams before any short-term rule changes could be made. As a result Frank Williams was able to hold out against changes that might have eroded the domination of his cars, which won ten out of the 16 races in 1992.

There were further problems relating to Prost's recruitment to the Williams team, which left some observers with the strong suspicion that those in authority within the Formula 1 world had taken very firmly against him. These concerns surfaced when Frank Williams received a letter on the subject of his team's new driver from the FIA President, Max Mosley. Dated 21 January 1993, it read:

'Dear Frank.

'Attached is an interview with Alain Prost from last week's *Auto Plus*. I had hoped this week's edition would contain a correction or denial but this is not the case. Indeed, he seems to have given a further interview in similar terms to *Le Figaro*, also attached.

I do not need to tell you how much damage this sort of thing does.

'A top Formula 1 driver has a great responsibility to the sport. The more prominent he is, the greater the damage he can do and thus the greater the responsibility. He is like an ambassador. An ambassador may say very harsh things to his government (indeed, sometimes it is his duty to do so), but he never says them to the press. Prost knows this perfectly well but has nevertheless repeatedly attacked the whole structure of Formula 1 and, what is worse, done so without ascertaining the facts.

'During November, I read in the French press that he had complained he had no contact with the President of the FISA. Although he has never made the slightest effort to contact me, I thought it polite (although not really appropriate) to take the initiative. I telephoned his home number in Switzerland and had a 22-minute discussion with him during which I said he could ring me any time if anything was worrying him, as could any of the other drivers. I made no complaint about the numerous damaging and inaccurate remarks he had made during his year as a TV reporter but suggested we resolve any problems privately, not in the media. Since then I have heard nothing. It seems that not only does he not know what is really happening but he does not want to know.

'Let me give you a few examples of his technique of attacking the sport and the governing body without making any attempts first to discover the facts.

1. Commentating on the German Grand Prix last year [1993] he said

"Cars will be much more difficult to drive and, of course, very danger-ous" on the new narrow tyres. I think this was based on a paddock rumour that cars which spin on narrow tyres take longer to stop. Any engineering student knows why this is a fallacy, but the public believed Prost. In the event, of course, the tyres work perfectly well, even too well.

2. In the same commentary he said, "Nobody knows for the moment what will be the result of the sum of narrower tyres together with less ground effect. Cars may go up to 350–360 kph and be practically undriveable." He may not have known, but we did. Any interested dri-ver would have asked us (several did). Even more so a responsible TV commentator. Again, he did not know, he did not want to know and he made a damaging and wholly inaccurate public pronouncement which was believed because of who he is.

3. Again, in the same commentary, he accused me of making "totally arbitrary decisions without an exchange of views and without know-ing that on the technical aspects there are some obligations". You, Frank, know well how utterly ludicrous, indeed offensive, this sugges-tion is. You yourself were present at most of the interminable exchanges of views which took place.

4. At the end of the Hungarian Grand Prix, Prost and the rest of the French television commentary team assured their viewers that the cap-tions were wrong and Mansell had not won the World Championship. Seemingly, none of them, including Prost, knew the rules. This did not matter to FISA, but is yet another example of him talking without knowing the facts.

5. In the *Auto Plus* interview he claims that Donington is unsuitable. He has made this allegation without any knowledge of the work which the FISA inspectors have required and which Donington are carrying out. Again, he has made no attempt to discover the facts. [This was a refer-ence to differences of opinion, widely voiced within the F1 fraternity, over whether or not Donington Park was a suitable venue for the forthcoming European Grand Prix that the British circuit was sched-uled to host on Easter Sunday 1993.]

6. In the *Auto Plus* article he speaks of the need for a commission of interested parties to run Formula 1. Apparently he does not know that such a commission has been in existence for 12 years, and he has not bothered to find out.

7. Before condemning the efforts of Bernie Ecclestone in Formula 1, he might perhaps have sought the views of some of the team managers and older drivers who have shared Bernie's 20 years of work. The consensus is, I think, that Bernie has done more to make Formula 1 a leading world sport than any other individual.

'All of this (and there is much more on file) seems to be a systematic attempt to damage the reputation of Formula 1 and to undermine its credibility. If, as a driver, Prost were genuinely worried or concerned, would he not pick up the telephone and find out the facts? Would he not seek meetings to discuss matters rather than attack the organisation from which he lives? What would we think of an ambassador who never contacted his government either to find out what was going on or to express his concerns, but simply attacked them in the press at every opportunity and without regard for the truth?

'Frank, we really have to ask ourselves if the best interests of Formula 1 and the FIA World Championship are served by allowing a man like this to participate. He clearly thinks he should be running everything. He pontificates about things he does not understand and he describes the entire governing body in contemptuous and offensive terms, eg "les sous-fifres de la FISA sont incompétents" ("the underlings of the FISA are incompetent"). He even attacks Formula 1 for being too concerned with money when he has probably taken a bigger share than anyone, certainly more than the members of the FISA World Council, who earn nothing. Can you think of anything more calculated to persuade the head of a major corporation not to take his company into Formula 1 than constant attacks and abuse from a triple World Champion whom the public respect and admire? Don't forget, sponsors and heads of companies, indeed all the decision makers on whom we depend, read this stuff. And because he is a three-times World Champion, they think he knows what he is talking about.

'You know that I support free speech and believe everyone should be at liberty to express an opinion even if they don't know the facts or understand the subject. Certainly Prost should be free to express an opinion, but I question whether we should give weight and authority to his attacks by making him, again, a top driver.

'If he held a Super Licence there would, I think, be a strong case for the World Council taking it away under Article 151 of the International Sporting Code. As he does not, it might be better not to give him one.

'I do not believe you or your sponsors can control him. Indeed, I am sure you have clauses in your contract which cover this situation, but have had no effect. And even if he cannot be quoted directly, he will probably find a way to poison the atmosphere just at the time we most need to improve it.

'I do not subscribe to the view that Formula 1 is a public convenience which anyone can use or abuse whenever they like. It is the property of the FIA and it is the duty of the FISA to preserve it and protect it. It is the duty of the competing teams to help in this – see Article 5 of the Concorde Agreement [the regulatory protocol governing the manner in which Formula 1 World Championship rules can be framed and implemented]. I feel the question of Alain Prost is one which warrants full discussion at the next Formula 1 Commission meeting and I am therefore sending a copy of this letter, in confidence, to the other members. I should be grateful for your views.

'Yours sincerely, Max Mosley.'

This matter would subsequently be defused when Prost appeared in front of the FISA and satisfied Mosley he had been seriously misquoted. In any event, since at the time he made the alleged remarks, he was not an FIA competition licence holder it was difficult to see how disciplinary sanctions could be made to stick had the governing body been of a mind to impose any penalty.

Meanwhile, Mosley drove a coach and horses through the Concorde Agreement by eventually accepting the Williams team's entry for the 1993 World Championship, irrespective of the feelings of the dissenting teams. But this strategy had a sting in its tail. He also unilaterally imposed changes in the technical regulations that would see all the highly sophisticated electronic driver aids, developed by top teams at enormous cost, swept away from the start of 1994.

Teams such as Williams and McLaren were aghast, yet Mosley remained unabashed. 'Politics is the art of the possible and, like finance, it is all to do with timing,' he insisted. 'Although what we are doing this year may be seen as a breach of the Concorde Agreement, I do not regard this as a moral breach. In the final analysis, if adhering to the Concorde Agreement meant inflicting serious damage on motor racing, then I believe it was right for us to think again.

'These rule changes will only affect control systems operated by the driver. Whereas the man in the road car should benefit from such systems, to minimise the risk of his having an accident, that is not what motor racing is all about. These computer systems have taken away many of the driver's tasks, and that we have to stop.

'I believe that, had I not acted in the way I did, the alternative we were facing was a large number of the teams going out of business, no Williams in the 1993 Championship and no overall clear direction for the future.'

Immediate changes for 1993 included a reduction in the length of practice and qualifying sessions, a ban on the use of spare cars, a maximum of seven sets of tyres per car per weekend, and new fuel regulations restricting the development of so-called 'exotic brews'. Further down the line, for 1994, electronic driver aids were to be prohibited. Mosley sprung this news on the teams at a stormy meeting of the Formula 1 Commission at Heathrow on 14 February – one month to the day before the first race of the season.

Williams and McLaren naturally bridled at this development, pointing out that the governing body was well out of order. Nobody had ever offered a helping hand to Williams during his fight through the Formula 1 ranks during the 1970s. Furthermore, as McLaren chief Ron Dennis was quick to point out, no artificial tinkering with the rules could magically transform technically less competent teams into potential front-runners.

For the moment, however, it was time for Prost to settle into his new role as Williams-Renault team leader. After weeks of careful consideration, Frank and Patrick had opted to promote the team's test driver Damon Hill to the full-time race team as Alain's partner. This was an enormously popular move with the British media, going some way to quell their disappointment over Mansell's departure. Yet, as Hill would quickly demonstrate, he was certainly no makeweight. He would carve out his own reputation in a distinctive, unflustered and slightly reticent manner.

As far as the Williams team's equipment for 1993 was concerned, the old FW14 chassis was retired after two seasons, leaving Prost and Hill to go into battle with the evolutionary FW15C, powered from the outset by the latest Renault RS5 V10 engine. After the 1992 season had ended, Williams ran a few tests with the original FW15 chassis, using the wide tyres and aerodynamic specification that it would have used had it raced during Mansell's title-winning campaign. This was developed into the FW15B, a development car fitted with a narrow-track front suspension, raised nose and wing end plates to conform with the new 1993 technical regulations. This was followed by the FW15C, which would serve as the definitive race car for the season.

The active suspension system employed on the new car was a derivation of that employed the previous season, but some of the components were repackaged. Slight changes to the weight distribution of this latest Williams produced a car that was slightly more responsive than its immediate predecessor, if rather more nervous when driven at the limit. In particular, this trait manifested itself in slight rear-end instability under braking, most notably on fast circuits such as Hockenheim, when the car was being operated in low-downforce aerodynamic trim.

There were also significant changes incorporated in the hydraulic activation system of the semi-automatic gear-change. This included a press-button starting device, which, although attracting unreserved praise from the drivers during testing, was not used in the races. Prost and Hill seemed to prefer the mental reassurance of controlling the clutch pedal on their own. There was also a fully automatic change facility, which could be overridden if the drivers called for a gear before the computer decided it was time to make the change.

Against Prost and Hill was ranged, most ominously, Ayrton Senna in the compact new Ford HB V8-engined McLaren MP4/8. The Brazilian started the new season bristling with indignation over the fact that McLaren had lost its Honda engine deal, that it was now being obliged to stand in line for 'customer' Ford engines one specification behind those used by the works-backed Benetton team – and the fact that Prost had kept him out of the second Williams.

In fact, over the winter months there had been some very real doubt as to whether Senna would take part at all. Eventually he agreed a race-by-race deal with Ron Dennis – at a figure of $1 million a weekend. Ayrton was calling the shots, pushing the McLaren sponsors to all reasonable limits, but he knew he held the strongest hand. Although Mika Hakkinen had been signed as test driver, Indycar refugee Michael Andretti was Senna's nominated team-mate from the outset, so all McLaren's eggs had, for all practical purposes, been placed in a single basket.

Prost qualified on pole at Kyalami, but Senna and Michael Schumacher's Benetton B193A got the jump on him at the start, the Brazilian leading for the first 23 laps. Prost quickly got into the swing of things, moving into second place on lap 14, but Senna controlled the pace of the race magnificently, and it took the new Williams team leader another nine laps to get ahead.

Prost's ensuing victory, coming after a year's sabbatical, not only sustained the Williams team's position of ascendancy after its stormy 1992 season with Mansell, but also re-emphasised the Frenchman's brilliant tactical acuity. By any standards it was a measured and convincing performance, earning Prost his first victory since he triumphed in the 1990 Spanish Grand Prix for Ferrari.

Hill, meanwhile, had a hesitant start to his season. Having spun wildly while holding second place going through the first sequence of S-bends, seconds after the start, he resumed 11th only to be shunted out of the race by Alessandro Zanardi's Lotus. 'But it was my fault for having spun and being that far back in the first place,' shrugged Damon.

It was a good start for Prost, but disappointment quickly followed. The second and third rounds of the Championship were conducted, at least in part, in conditions of torrential rain. In the Brazilian GP at Interlagos, Prost misheard a radio message from his engineer David Brown aborting a planned tyre stop at the last moment and aquaplaned into retirement after colliding with Christian Fittipaldi's pirouetting Minardi. Then, in the saturated European GP at Donington, Prost came home a disappointed third after a less than convincing performance from driver and team.

What made it worse was that Senna won both these races in magnificent style. And Hill, driving with an expert precision for a man who had only two GP starts under his belt before the start of the year, managed second place in both. Three races done, and Senna led the Championship with 26 points to Prost's 14 and Hill's 12.

Frank Williams unfortunately chose the aftermath of the Donington race to venture some mild, if tactless, criticism of his new number one driver, saying that Alain had misjudged the timing of his tyre stops in the chaotic conditions, which changed from wet to damp to soaking almost from lap to lap.

'It is obvious that Alain made a very tactical [first] change onto dry tyres, but threw it away with a vastly premature switch back to wets, and that was the end of the race,' he observed. 'It surprised me that a driver of Alain's ability should make those mistakes, but he doesn't like the wet and is cautious.'

Prost wasn't having that. He prodded the Renault management with the

result that, two days after the event, an absurdly self-conscious press statement was issued over the signatures of Frank Williams and Renault Sport
MD Christian Contzen. It read:

'Certain press reports have suggested that differences in opinion exist
between Williams, Renault and Alain Prost following the European GP at
Donington. Such suggestions are not founded. The solidarity uniting
Williams, Renault and its drivers, Alain Prost and Damon Hill, is as real in
defeat as it is in victory and responsibilities for the actions of the team are
shared, not individually apportioned.' The farcical document had all the
credibility of a Party Political Broadcast.

Williams's spontaneous throw-away observation had overlooked the logic
of Prost's avowed caution in the rain. Back in 1982 he had been groping
along at the wheel of his Renault in impossible conditions of torrential rain
during practice at Hockenheim when Didier Pironi's Ferrari ran full-tilt into
the back of him. The other Frenchman never saw the Renault in the ball of
spray – and paid for it with multiple leg injuries that ended a brilliant career.

Prost had seen the consequences of what he regarded as the folly of racing in zero visibility, and never forgot the lesson. In 1989 he pulled out of
the Australian GP for the same reason after only a lap. Some people labelled
him a coward. But as Gerhard Berger remarked, 'Alain was the only one
brave enough to do what many of us wanted to – but hadn't got the guts.'
Going with the flow had not always been part of Prost's *modus operandi*.

Alain admitted that he first started to think in terms of retirement after all
the criticism following that third place at Donington Park. 'The following
day I just stayed at home in Switzerland,' he remembers. 'I didn't move.
Even though I had a lot of support from the team and from Renault, I really
seriously thought that I would stop, perhaps even immediately. I didn't, of
course, but the more the season went on, the more convinced I was that I
would retire at the end of the year.'

Prost could not rid himself of the notion that the Formula 1 rule-makers
positively discriminated against him during his final season. 'Look at the
start at Estoril,' he said. 'Hakkinen nearly put me off on the run to the first
corner. After five or six laps he was weaving around in front of me. For him
the rule was different, and I didn't want to stay in such an environment.

'This is all symptomatic of a basic problem in Formula 1 which is that the
sport has been taken over by business. My sort of driving etiquette has gone
and the sport is not going in that direction. If you are a driver, it seems that
the way to do things is to take more risk, to do stupid things on the track.
That's what people want to see, so for sure those like Bernie Ecclestone
don't want to see a guy like me racing because I'm not stupid about my driving, and every time I think something is wrong, I say so. That has not made
me popular.

'The problem is, increasingly, that you cannot – you are not *allowed* to –
speak against anything in this business. That upsets me a great deal.'

The fourth round of the Championship yielded a better result for Alain.

The Williams FW15Cs were fitted with power throttle systems for the San Marino Grand Prix at Imola, eliminating a tendency for the cars momentarily to lock their rear wheels during downchanges, which had so frustrated Prost and Hill in the wet conditions. The adoption of this system ensured that the revs could be perfectly matched when the clutch was engaged, and Alain salvaged his wet weather reputation with a fine run to victory at Imola, despite nursing an intermittently sticking throttle. In this race Senna's McLaren retired and Hill slid into a sand trap on the greasy track surface after leading in the early stages.

Senna still led the Drivers' Championship, but with his advantage reduced to two points over Alain, who then won in Spain, battling against Hill in a hard-to-drive car that was particularly difficult to handle on the bumpy surface. Had Damon not retired with a rare Renault engine failure, Alain believed he would have been obliged to give best to his team-mate. Still, he now led the Championship again, Senna's two-point advantage now translated into a similar deficit.

'Alain was getting thrown around [at Barcelona] and the problem was air in the active system which causes all sorts of problems,' explained Patrick Head. 'It's like having a broken damper, or a soft spring on one side and not on the other. That's one of the problems for Alain – he likes to know his car, and by that I mean he likes to know that when you change this, that happens.

'He likes a consistent behaviour, so that he knows what changes he wants. The problem with an active system is getting it to be consistent all the time. Generally, if it's not behaving consistently, it's because we've got air in the system. Active suspension is like a tiger in a cage, not a kindly thing if you don't treat it right. You can't afford to leave the hatch off – or it'll get you!'

By now, Patrick had confirmed his initial conclusions about Prost and expressed himself extremely impressed with his whole approach to the business of Formula 1. 'He is *immensely* talented, but one never gets the impression with Alain that he lets anger or any of the more direct emotions overpower the intellect,' noted the Williams Technical Director after final qualifying for the 1993 French GP at Magny-Cours.

'One of the reasons Mansell was *so* quick at the British Grand Prix was that his adrenalin was pumped up by emotion. His overtaking manoeuvres – particularly during the turbo days – involved, I thought, enormous risks. But on the other hand he seemed to get away with it, so you had to conclude that he was making good judgements – although, from the outside, it didn't always look that way.

'I don't think Alain ever lets himself veer into that area, which is why his winning always comes across a bit clinically. He's been sitting over there with David Brown [his race engineer] for two hours, and they're going carefully through every item on the car, trying to understand everything that's happened on it relative to this track and to previous experiences, and through an intellectual process they will arrive at an optimum set-up for the race.

'Nigel would do it more on an emotional basis, in that he'd just say, "I want this, this, this and this", and if you asked why, he wouldn't really be prepared to discuss it.

'Mansell seemed to be very good at building up a datafile in his mind, and if he went to a circuit and the set-up wasn't very good, he would have something that would tell him that if he set the car up as it had been at some previous circuit, which he'd decided was similar, then the car would go well.

'Generally I would say he was right. But it was never brought into the conscious – it was never shared with us, in terms of how he arrived at it. So, on the one hand, one is not necessarily achieving greater results with the car this year, but certainly we now know why the driver prefers this or that.'

At Monaco, where Prost qualified on pole, a marginal jump start saw him hauled into the pits for what some people regarded as an unnecessarily harsh 10-second stop-go penalty. He finished a lapped fourth, leaving Senna to win from Hill.

'I think I did the perfect start,' said Prost. 'Sure, the car moved a little bit on the grid, but plenty of cars do that. It's difficult not to, with the carbon-fibre clutches we have at the moment – as soon as they get hot, it's difficult to stop the car from creeping.

'When the team called me in, I had started to lap some of the slower cars and thought maybe I'd passed somebody under the yellow flag, or something. I just couldn't believe that the penalty was for the start.'

Hill, meanwhile, saved the day for Williams with a plucky performance, chasing Senna for all he was worth before being pitched into a spin at the Loews hairpin after being rammed from behind by Gerhard Berger's Ferrari. 'He hit me and spun me round,' explained Damon. 'I was fuming, I must say, and then there was the situation that my car was parked across the track so that nobody else could get through.

'I managed to continue, but I was a bit worried about the car, as for a few laps it felt slightly unusual. But it proved to be OK. It had been handling well up to about 20 laps from the end.'

Prost won in Canada, but that was the race at which more serious problems began to beset the Formula 1 fraternity. At a time when Williams and McLaren, in particular, were standing firm against the FISA plans to impose a ban on electronic driver aids, everybody was astounded when Charlie Whiting, the FISA F1 Technical Delegate, submitted a report to the stewards expressing the view that Williams, Tyrrell, Benetton, McLaren, Ferrari, Lotus and Minardi all infringed the Formula 1 technical regulations by virtue of the fact that their cars were fitted with active suspension or ride height controls.

In the same report Whiting concluded that Jordan, Footwork, Larrousse, Ligier and Sauber had traction control systems that breached the rule stating that drivers should be in control of their cars at all times.

This report was shrugged aside as a cynical attempt by the governing body to manipulate its own rules. 'You might just as well screw up those releases and throw them into the wastepaper basket,' said Patrick Head trenchantly. 'On this basis, I suppose that FISA is going to go back and exclude us from the 1992 World Championship. This is just complete nonsense and doesn't mean anything.' The transparent nature of FISA's efforts to impose its iron will on the teams could be judged from the fact that Williams had been using the same suspension system for the previous 22 races. Nobody had objected. Up until now.

Back to Europe for the French Grand Prix at Magny-Cours, and Prost led Hill across the line to score the Williams team's first 1-2 of the season, the two FW15Cs separated by less than a second at the chequered flag. This understandably buoyed Hill's hopes for the British GP at Silverstone a week later, where an army of motorsport fans was hoping against hope that Williams team orders would be such as to permit Damon a win in front of his home crowd.

Yet there were problems with such a strategy. 'I must think of the championship,' said Prost. However, Patrick Head sent a slightly different coded message: 'I think it's fairly clear that we were asking Damon to support Alain in this race [at Magny-Cours] and I think it will be slightly different at Silverstone.'

In fact, there was another problem lurking in the back of the Williams team's mind. On the Friday after the British GP, the FISA World Council was due to adjudicate on the legality of certain fuel samples collected from various cars earlier in the season. Such was the mood of suspicion with which Williams now regarded the sport's governing body, that the British team began to feel distinctly sceptical as to whether it would receive a favourable judgement in respect of the fuel sample taken from Prost's car after his Barcelona victory.

With that in mind, the Williams team went into the Silverstone race privately feeling that it would be nice if Hill could be given the chance of winning, but worried that, should they lose the Barcelona win, Alain's points situation would be adversely affected. Put simply, could they afford the risk of allowing Prost to defer to Hill in the British Grand Prix?

As things transpired, the dilemma was resolved by force of circumstance. Hill led decisively in the opening stages of the race as Senna kept Prost boxed into third place behind his McLaren, the Brazilian staying ahead by means of some pretty ruthless and marginal driving tactics that were criticised even by his most enthusiastic fans. By the time Prost got through into second place, Damon was 8.1 seconds ahead and Alain had it all to do. He pulled up on to Hill's tail and resumed his assault on the Englishman's advantage after the field had a brief spell behind the Safety Car to enable Luca Badoer's abandoned Lola-Ferrari to be removed from a vulnerable position on the outside of Woodcote corner.

But with 17 laps to go, it was all over. Hill's engine expired spectacularly, an exhaust valve having shattered, allowing Prost through to an easy win.

But Alain fully understood from the crowd's politely muted applause that this hadn't quite been the result it was looking for.

'I don't really like winning in this ambience,' he acknowledged. 'I think Damon deserved to win here at home, but I also think I did a good job here today. I caught him without too much difficulty, but it might have been a different matter getting past him because he was going really well.'

Prost and Williams breathed again the following week after FISA announced that the fuel sample taken at Barcelona had not in any way infringed the rules. Alain's Spanish GP win stood, but he was in for another weekend of mixed emotions at Hockenheim where he only won the German Grand Prix after Hill suffered a tyre deflation while leading with just over a lap to go.

Earlier, however, Prost had been signalled to come in for another 10-second stop-go penalty at the end of the ninth lap, this time for 'straight-lining' the Ostkurve chicane on the opening lap. But he had only done so after a glance in his mirrors revealed that Martin Brundle's Ligier was in the process of spinning right behind him and, had he attempted to take the conventional line through the corner, the Englishman would have surely piled straight into his Williams. Under the circumstances he was furious to be hit with another penalty.

'I think it was a scandal, because we were talking about that chicane at the drivers' briefing and Senna, in particular, was anxious to get the position clarified as Mansell had gone straight through it last year, wasn't penalised and gained sufficient momentum on the following straight to overtake Ayrton,' he explained.

'But I did not get any advantage. Really, I don't think these people are capable of judging these things properly. I think they really called me in to make the race more interesting.'

Prior to the German Grand Prix, a marathon seven-hour meeting of the Formula 1 Constructors' Association had been convened in the Hotel Weiksershof at nearby Reilingen. The FISA World Council had previously met to consider Charlie Whiting's report to the stewards at Canada and, after initially threatening to ban active suspension, traction control and other electronic aids from the Hungarian GP (a fortnight after Hockenheim), retreated from this extreme standpoint and agreed to the constructors' request that a ban on such systems should be deferred to the start of 1994.

A selection of other technical rules were provisionally introduced for 1994, some of which were eventually adopted, some not. But to cut a long story short, active suspension, traction control and all other electronic aids would be banned from the end of the 1993 season. More ominously the competing teams – who by this time had been worn down by the onslaught from the governing body – found themselves agreeing that in-race refuelling would be re-introduced for the following season.

The Williams team had now firmly concluded that Charlie Whiting was acting at Max Mosley's behest in these matters. Six months later Frank

Williams would describe bitterly the whole issue of refuelling and the banning of electronic driver aids.

Three months later, at the Portuguese Grand Prix, the constructors had a change of heart about refuelling. But they were blocked by Ferrari when it came to changing the rules. Suddenly the roof seemed to be falling in on the Formula 1 teams who believed that the rules were clearly mapped out into the foreseeable future.

Moreover, the ban on electronic driver aids from the start of 1994 also extended to such high-technology developments as Continuously Variable Transmission (CVT). Williams was close to being in a position to race such a system, but suddenly it was wiped from the agenda. 'Ten years work down the pan,' remarked Williams crisply.

The season ground on. Prost stalled in pole position at the Hungaroring before the parade lap prior to the Hungarian Grand Prix. As it transpired this did not affect the outcome of his afternoon, as he retired from the race with a broken rear wing mounting, a rare Williams failure. Hill celebrated the day by scoring his first Grand Prix victory, thereby becoming the first second-generation World Championship GP winner in the sport's history.

Behind the scenes, although Frank Williams was certainly musing over how he could introduce Ayrton Senna alongside Prost to form his own personal 'super team' for 1994, there could be no concealing his admiration for Alain, whom he clearly regarded as a straightforward, very mentally organised F1 operator. Prost and Hill represented a very different sort of driver pairing from Mansell and Patrese; yet it seemed to be working just as well.

'The team is different because its two focal points – Mansell and Patrese – have gone, and Alain and Damon are here,' he reflected at Magny-Cours. 'That's the future. Riccardo was a lovely man, very popular. There are lots of photographs of him on the walls at the factory. Nigel was terrific in the car, but a tough man out of it – he knew what he wanted, and pushed to get it.

'Sometimes that could be unpleasant. But he did the job, and he was certainly . . . *interesting* . . . to deal with. Alain is a different human being, has a different approach, character, temperament. He clearly has an enormous talent. You know, I say to him to give me a shout on the radio when he's going to do the quick lap, because he's unbelievably smooth. I don't think any driver ever made it look so easy.

'He's very easy to get on with, very straightforward, and has a very good relationship with the team, and with Renault.'

It was quite clear that the Williams team garage radiated a much calmer, less confrontational atmosphere in 1993 than it had done the previous year. Yet for all Prost's skill, some observers wondered whether the team missed Mansell's sparky approach to the business of operating an F1 car. Did Frank worry that the team might have lost the fine edge of its hunger in this more tranquil environment?

'No,' he replied firmly. 'There's an immense respect for Alain and his talents. And the guys on Damon's car have got their tails up too. Alain's a charming individual, never makes waves. His approach to life – and to racing – is different from Nigel's.

'At this point last year Nigel had won six races, whereas Alain's total is five. But you've got to look at the whole year – and Nigel won only one out of the last six. As I point out to people, Prost has won 49 Grands Prix and I'm not aware of any that were by accident. Three World Championships, none of them by accident. I'm a very happy team director!'

Prost was becoming less so. After the debacle at Budapest, he finished a disappointed third behind Hill and Michael Schumacher's Benetton at Spa, frustrated by his car's poor handling after his second tyre stop. 'I was two laps late making my second stop, during which there was some confusion,' he explained. 'When I returned to the circuit, the handling didn't seem to be as good. Earlier in the race I was getting through Eau Rouge flat in sixth with a full fuel load. Now I found I couldn't get through in fifth gear without lifting from the throttle.'

More disappointment was waiting at Monza in the Italian GP. Only five laps away from a victory that would have clinched his fourth Drivers' Championship, Prost suffered a major engine failure. This allowed Damon to complete a hat trick of wins. Alain would now have to wait until the Portuguese Grand Prix at Estoril before he could finally nail down the title.

By now, though, he was disillusioned and had set his mind on retirement. After Friday's first qualifying session for the Portuguese GP, Alain convened a joint press conference with Frank Williams to announce his decision.

'The sport has given me a lot,' he admitted, 'but I decided that the game wasn't worth it any more. I have taken too many blows. I will not drive for Williams nor anyone else. That goes for Formula 1 and all the other formulae. There will be no comeback.'

A few hours before Prost's press conference, Ayrton Senna had formally announced that he would be leaving McLaren at the end of the season. It did not take a genius to work out that Ayrton was on course to join Williams. As Prost's successor.

Senna was reportedly first contacted by Williams at the start of September when Prost had indicated his decision to retire. Even so, rumours persisted that Prost really retired because he was not prepared to drive alongside Senna in 1994. And Frank Williams was hell-bent on having Ayrton in the team at last.

Challenged on the point and specifically asked whether it was not true that, in reality, he had first spoken to Ayrton about a possible deal in July 1993, Frank replied, 'This is grossly untrue. I am astonished that you should believe that.' Maybe so. Perhaps no deal had been arranged, but there had certainly been a considerable amount of contact with the brilliant Brazilian.

'Ever since Ayrton had volunteered to drive for Williams for nothing at Budapest in 1992, there had been non-stop contact between the two of them,' said Julian Jakobi, the former International Management Group executive who went to work as Senna's full-time business manager at the end of that season.

'But I don't think there was ever any way in which Ayrton and Alain would have driven together again. Having said that, it didn't bother Ayrton – as far as he was concerned, he would never veto a team-mate. He was happy to be partnered with anybody – and felt confident that he could beat them.'

Yet Prost simply could not rid his mind of the fact that Ayrton had cheated him during their days at McLaren, and could never quite bring himself to forgive the Brazilian for ramming him off the circuit at Suzuka in 1990. So with Senna poised to take over his seat in the Williams-Renault squad, Alain clinched his Championship with mixed feelings. Second place to Michael Schumacher's Benetton at Estoril was enough to finish the job.

The person who best understood Frank Williams's personal ambition was Ron Dennis, the McLaren chief who had worked with Prost and Senna when they were together at McLaren in 1988/89. He could also see the futility of trying to pair them together again.

'There were suggestions that Frank was trying to create a super team again, to have Prost and Senna together,' he observed. 'But I knew there was never a chance of that. In what they achieve, they are extremely similar, but that's about it.

'Ayrton and Alain have very different attitudes towards their team-mates, for example. Alain's philosophy of motor racing is a very simple one: he is there to win and it doesn't matter if it's by a second or a minute.

'That is why, in 1992, victories that could have been more spectacular – lapping the field and so on – were not there. Prost would see that as superfluous, and I think that reflected positively on Damon Hill and probably helped him. He felt stronger and more motivated and therefore *was* a stronger driver.

'If you crush someone, he can't even do what he is capable of doing, and that's one of Ayrton's strategies; he destroys them psychologically. Whoever his team-mate is, he will always work on the psychology of the process. Motor racing makes up an incredibly big percentage of Ayrton's life, much bigger than most. However, I believe that he is much more of a team player now than he was five years ago.'

Prost rounded off the season by finishing second to Senna's McLaren-Ford in both the Japanese and Australian GPs, two of Ayrton's most outstanding victories. They made a brave effort at reconciliation on the winner's rostrum at Adelaide, but it appeared almost anxiously contrived and unconvincing to all those who had witnessed their earlier rivalry at close quarters.

In talking about Senna, Prost's mind would always go back to Suzuka. Did Alain feel that driving standards in Formula 1 had deteriorated during his time in the sport? 'Absolutely,' he insisted. 'I have always said that. Can you imagine Niki Lauda behaving like that? No way. Absolutely no way. Or

Emerson Fittipaldi? Or Keke Rosberg? I mean, I ask just one question – is this kind of thing [the way Senna behaved at Suzuka] the right way to give a positive example to the people racing Formula Ford?'

Thus Prost finished the season reflecting on his fourth World Championship in a somewhat dejected frame of mind. 'Psychologically, winning my fourth Championship left me with quite a strange feeling,' he confessed. 'This is especially from the media point of view because, in the opinion of many journalists, it seemed almost as if the result of the season was known even before it started. Everybody somehow expected me to win.

'That made my job more difficult and also gave me less fun. It is obvious that when one is subjected to such comments you won't get the same satisfaction from winning a race, because it just looks as though it is simple. But when you lose, on the same basis it becomes a disaster.'

For all that, life with the Williams team amounted to a very special experience for him. Prost admits that he was very happy with that aspect of the year: 'On the working side, the team was bloody good. I was impressed with its ambience and the willingness with which they solved the minor problems we experienced with the car early in the season.

'I am quite pleased, for sure, to have won the Championship – but even more important for me was to have been working with a team which provided such a good atmosphere in what proved to be my final year in Formula 1.'

Yet, by the same token, Alain acknowledged that his year off in 1992 had lost him some ground, costing him a season during which there had been a great deal of technical development in connection with electronic driver aids. With that in mind, did he regret not racing for Ligier after all?

'No,' he replied firmly. 'I had the chance to drive for them, but although I tested the JS37 – and it felt pretty good – I quickly realised that it was not capable of challenging for race victories. In my estimation it was a car quite capable of scoring points quite regularly, but this wasn't what I was looking for at that stage of my career.

'So the 1993 season was difficult at the beginning, a little like when I started Formula 1 for the first time in 1980. I was again in a position where I had to learn not only the car, but also how a new team operated. If I had been coming directly from McLaren or Ferrari, for example, straight into Williams, then I am sure it would have been much easier.

'But because it was immediately after a sabbatical year, I am sure there were a lot of people, even within the team itself, asking some questions as to whether I could still do it. I suppose this was a normal situation, but I had to take things steadily when it came to learning how the car worked. I must say it was steadily getting better and better, and I only found my best potential in the second half of the season.

'There is also the point that if the regulations had still called for passive suspension cars, then my experience with this sort of machine would have counted for a little bit more. With the active suspension, I had to rely much more on the input and experience of the team because I had no previous knowledge of these systems. This made things quite hard as the present active Williams, which we used in 1993, while not being a difficult car to drive, was not really one which suited my type of driving style.

'I think that an active suspension car with traction control needs to be thrown around quite a lot, whereas I like to drive a little more quietly, perhaps using the throttle more sensitively, which perhaps is not needed quite so much with an active car.'

Prost quit Formula 1 having achieved an all-time record of 51 Grand Prix victories. In the main he had enjoyed his time at Williams, although there could be no concealing that he probably looked back on his years with McLaren with the greatest affection. It was a point that Frank Williams found it in him to concede.

'He may well have been happier with McLaren,' said Frank, 'but we had a fabulous season with Alain who is a very great guy. He always went just as fast as he did to get the job done. I suppose I was furious, in a way, that he didn't pass Schumacher to win at Estoril, but he came to Williams to win a World Championship, do a job and that's what he did.'

In fact, behind the scenes Prost was paid a substantial fee for relinquishing his seat in the Williams-Renault line-up. He was prepared to drive for Williams through to the end of 1994, as contracted. 'We had a two-year deal with Alain and it was totally his choice to stop driving,' insisted Williams.

Yet the evidence is at odds with such an assurance. The firm implication is that, yes, Prost chose to stop driving. But only because Williams put him in an impossible position by indicating that Senna would probably be coming aboard in 1994. For once in his life, Alain must have appreciated how Mansell felt when confronted with his impending arrival for 1993.

Moreover, when it looked as if Prost might return to drive a McLaren-Peugeot in 1994, Senna was asked what he thought about it. 'It will be good for my bank balance,' he replied, with a twinkle in his eye.

Frank Williams dismissed this observation as 'macho talk', but others assumed Senna to mean that if Prost drove for McLaren, he would have to reimburse Williams with the severance fee. In turn, that would leave more money available for Senna. Simplistic perhaps, but we shall never quite know the truth of it all. Frank Williams makes it his rule not to discuss details of his driver's contracts. And he wasn't about to make an exception on this issue.

McLaren boss Ron Dennis added a thought-provoking footnote. 'What you have to remember is that Alain had a two-year contract with Williams,' he reflected. 'He had just won his fourth World Championship, had a car that could have won him his fifth, and a lot of money.

'More than anything, all that says to me is that neither I, nor anybody else, realised how unhappy Alain actually was.' And the only thing that could have made Prost so unhappy was the thought that he was being backed into a corner to accept Ayrton Senna as a team-mate. He regarded this as totally untenable.

Chapter 3

Romance and tragedy

'He never wants anything but what's right and fair; only when you come to settle what's right and fair, it's everything that he wants and nothing that you want. And that's his idea of a compromise.'

Thomas Hughes, *Tom Brown's Schooldays*

Ayrton Senna's career developed in parallel with Mansell's, albeit outside the Williams orbit. Both men won their first two Grands Prix by the end of 1985, but another two years down the line Senna only managed to accumulate a total of six wins, whereas Mansell had no fewer than 13. In reality, of course, this simply mirrored Nigel's glorious two seasons with the superbly competitive Williams-Honda FW11 and FW11B in 1986/87.

Of course nobody doubted for a moment Senna's sheer class, and the Formula 1 landscape changed quite dramatically at the start of 1988 when, armed with Honda engines that the Japanese company had switched from Williams in highly acrimonious circumstances, Ayrton embarked on a three-year contract with McLaren.

As far as Frank's relationship with Senna was concerned, Ayrton had got into the habit of chatting with him on the telephone regularly ever since he entered Formula 1 with Toleman, a year after Frank gave him his first test at the wheel of a Grand Prix car in the Cosworth DFV-engined Williams FW08C. There is no question about it, Frank Williams absolutely worshipped Ayrton Senna, and the lingering, very genuine friendship was fuelled in part by a realisation that, at some time in the future, they wanted to do business together.

'We always stayed in touch down the years,' said Frank. 'Sometimes [we talked] twice a week, sometimes not for a couple of months, but we never lost touch. The basic thing was that he just loved to talk motor racing. Get

him on the phone and you couldn't get him off it; he'd talk all day about so-
and-so's tyres, or whatever. It's pretty unusual for a driver and the owner of
another team to talk as we did, I would say.'

Senna had enjoyed a glittering freshman year in Formula 1 with the
Toleman-Hart team in 1984, the high points of which were a brilliant second
place to Prost's McLaren in the rain-soaked Monaco Grand Prix followed up
by third places in the British and Portuguese races. Yet that the Brazilian driver quickly outgrew Toleman in terms of competency is beyond dispute. At
the end of August 1984 he signed a deal to drive for the Lotus-Renault team
for 1985/86, for the first year as joint number one to Elio de Angelis, but
with the proviso that he should be team leader the following season.

In 1987 Honda expanded its engine supply deal to encompass the Lotus
team, primarily to secure Senna's services. From the outset Senna proved
himself extremely adept at the business of engine development and quickly
made himself an indispensable component of the Honda F1 equation. Even
so, it was clear that the Lotus-Honda 99T was not sufficiently competitive a
car to guarantee his continued tenure with the Norfolk-based team and, after
winning what would be Lotus's last-ever GP victory in Detroit, he switched
to McLaren for 1988.

The opportunity for Ayrton to join the Williams team as early as 1988 had
even been discussed. Had he done so, then it is probable that Frank's team
would have retained its supply of Honda engines, for the Japanese company
had forged a warm relationship with Ayrton during his season driving the
Lotus-Honda in 1987. No question about it, he was Honda's number one man.

However, with characteristic candour Ayrton put his cards on the table
and admitted that he was wary about Frank Williams's lack of personal
mobility. In fact this was a bigger problem in terms of perception than of
reality.

'When he [Ayrton] was here in 1987, discussing the possibility of joining
us, he eventually admitted that one of the reasons he decided against us was
that he wanted a team boss rushing about, overseeing everything like the
good old days,' recalls Frank. 'For certain, those words also reflected the
Honda view, but we had a board meeting and decided that we were prepared
to invest the sort of money he wanted. He took the offer seriously, but
McLaren remained ahead.'

By the middle of 1990 Williams was still bogged down attempting to sign
an absolute front-line driver for the following season. Initially French star
Jean Alesi was considered. He was midway through his second year with the
Tyrrell team and clearly had a promising future. Williams succeeded in getting his signature on a conditional contract quite early in the year, but he
eventually decided that he really wanted to go to Ferrari. Williams exacted a
high price on Maranello for releasing him from his commitment, as evi-
denced by the scarlet Ferrari 641 that now stands out dramatically amidst a
sea of Frank's own F1 cars in the collection within the Williams Conference
Centre at Didcot.

Just to complicate the situation further, at around this time Senna was approaching the end of his first three-year contract with McLaren. With characteristic shrewdness he was keen to examine every serious option available. Moreover, he now had fewer reservations about Frank's handicap.

'When we talked this time round, my lack of personal mobility was not a problem with him,' says Williams, 'because he'd had a couple of years seeing me around the place, knowing that I was in touch with what was going on. I think he had a better appreciation of our management structure.'

At this time Senna's negotiations for a renewal of his McLaren contract seemed deadlocked. However, although he talked to Frank with apparently increased enthusiasm, there were those at Williams who believed that he was doing nothing more than using the negotiations as a bargaining counter with Ron Dennis.

Ayrton Senna had been introduced to the world of karting by his father Milton when he was only four years old, but another ten years would pass before he began to think in terms of a professional career in motor racing.

'Karting was my hobby, my fun only, and the idea was that I would continue what my father had started,' he recalled. 'I was mentally directed towards that. But as I got more and more involved with karting, and got to the age of about 14 or 15, then I started to think about it a bit. But it was only when I was about 18 that I seriously began to think in terms of a professional career.'

In 1977 and '78 he won the South American kart championship and was Brazilian national champion four times in a row from 1978 to 1981. In 1977 he also had his first attempt at the karting World Championship – a one-race contest at Le Mans – when he finished sixth. Two years later he would contest the same event at Estoril, finishing second to Dutchman Peter Koene. He was second again in 1980 and fourth in 1981, by which time he was competing in Formula Ford 1600 on the British national scene.

Even before that first season of FF1600, Senna had started to develop a finely tuned business mind. On his first visit to Van Diemen, the Norfolk-based maker of Formula Ford cars, he quite took owner Ralph Firman's breath away when he made it clear that he expected to be paid to race his cars.

This was not exactly the way in which Britain's motor racing infrastructure functioned. Anybody struggling to get a foot on the lowest rung of the single-seater ladder could expect to invest many thousands of pounds in an effort to make a name for themselves. Moreover, the odds were firmly stacked against them. Nevertheless, Firman was impressed with Senna's confidence.

'He'd been paid to drive karts, so he thought that was the natural thing,' Firman told the author in 1994. 'I eventually steered him round to a realistic

deal and he began racing with us from the start of that season. He was clearly very good, that was obvious from the start. But he was never satisfied.
Not in the sense of not being gracious, you understand, but in his continual
search for ways to improve. He was totally dedicated, obviously a man who
was destined for the top. He had great style, great ability. The rest speaks for
itself.'

Ayrton won his third ever car race, at Brands Hatch, on 15 March 1981.
By the end of that season he was firmly established as the man to beat, having won two of the prestigious British national Formula Ford championships. Commercial reality had suddenly dawned on him. If he was going
to go any further up the ladder, then he would have to raise more finance.
With a compelling naïvety, Ayrton had believed that success alone should
have been the factor that earned him promotion.

'I left England before the end of the season, before doing the Formula
Ford Festival for which I had a good car,' he remembered. 'I was in a good
position to compete strongly for that, but I just didn't bother.

'Luckily my father has always been in a position to finance me – if I
needed it – but, as I was trying to be a professional, I thought I should go my
own way and not be dependent on him. When I realised it was difficult to do
this, my father also had some difficulties in Brazil, and I understood it
would be very valuable for him for me to be close to him at that time.

'I tried hard, but after five months, although I could do what I was supposed to there [the job], I realised I couldn't be without racing.' This period
also coincided with his divorce from his childhood sweetheart Liliane whom
he had married when both were barely out of their teens. In 1982 he would
return to Europe without her.

Ayrton's second season in Europe would see him dominate the Formula
Ford 2000 scene before he moved up into Formula 3 to contest the 1983
British Championship. This contest turned out to be a relentless head-to-
head with Norfolk garage-owner's son Martin Brundle. The title was eventually resolved in Ayrton's favour in the last round of the 20-race season, a
year in which Brundle's status had also been immeasurably enhanced by his
performance against the young Brazilian star.

Admittedly there was a lot of aggravation spicing the competition
between the two men. Ayrton, displaying a touch of the paranoia that would
dog him to a greater or lesser extent throughout his entire racing career, concluded that the British motor racing world was somehow ranged against
him. Yet on the rostrum after the final race of the year, Brundle recalls the
Brazilian being extremely generous.

'After all the nonsense and rivalry we went through – and, believe me, I
sometimes got the impression that Ayrton thought the British motor racing
establishment was ganging up on him – he was truly magnanimous,' says
Martin. 'On the rostrum he was quite emotional. He told me I was the best
British driver since Jim Clark!'

Senna's commercial confidence had surfaced again even prior to his F3 season. McLaren boss Ron Dennis offered to finance his season in exchange for an option on his services. Ayrton wasn't having that. With remarkable precocity, he declined the offer on the basis that, if he won races, the F1 teams would have no choice but to court him for the future. In this respect, Senna was remarkably astute.

It was obvious to anybody with even a superficial knowledge of motor racing that Senna would go all the way to the top. His three seasons with Lotus yielded six Grand Prix victories; impressive enough, but certainly not what the Brazilian had in mind. He wanted a situation where he could dominate his chosen game, reel off win after Grand Prix win and dominate the upper reaches of Formula 1. To do this he had to forge a deal with a team that had the capability, drive and technical resources to remain in the forefront of competitiveness for a consistently long period of time. After toying with Williams, he eventually decided that this meant McLaren, with whom he duly signed to drive on a three-year contract from the start of 1988.

Ron Dennis understood from the outset that Senna would be a demanding man to work with. In the Brazilian's order of things, compromise was something other people did. Usually to accommodate his own wishes. From the start of his partnership with McLaren, he set out to crush Alain Prost, determining that he would beat the Frenchman consistently, psychologically and physically.

Equipped with the McLaren-Honda MP4/4s in 1988, the final year that the use of the 1.5-litre F1 turbocharged engine was permitted, Senna and Prost ran riot across the circuits of the world. Together they won 15 of the season's 16 races, Senna taking eight victories to Prost's seven and winning the first of his three World Championships. On many occasions the McLaren duo was left to race amongst itself and Prost suddenly found himself, almost involuntarily, assuming a role similar to that played out by Niki Lauda three years earlier.

Just as Lauda found himself unable any longer to shoulder the apparent risks he saw Prost taking in heavy traffic, so Alain had now matured into a more calculating driver. Now he found himself paired with Senna, a man who had no qualms about making a total commitment to passing every car in front of him the very moment he pulled up onto its tail.

The first real confrontation between these two highly motivated men came during the 1988 Portuguese Grand Prix at Estoril. At the start of the race Senna felt that Prost had edged him out on an unnecessarily wide line as the two McLaren-Hondas sprinted for the first corner. The event was subsequently stopped and later restarted due to a multiple collision further back in the pack. This time Ayrton got away cleanly to lead into the opening lap, but Alain came swooping alongside him as they came out of the final corner and hurtled past the pits for the first time.

Ayrton simply wasn't having it. He squeezed Prost so tightly against the pit wall that rival teams had to lift their signalling boards violently out of the way, lest they be struck by the Frenchman's McLaren as it rocketed by at

180 mph. Prost won the race, but as we have seen the episode left him absolutely bristling with indignation. Behind closed doors he would tell Senna that he hadn't realised that he was prepared to die to win the World Championship, and if it meant so much to him, then, for all Alain cared, he could have it.

It was the first crack in their relationship. The fissures would erupt again the following spring at the San Marino GP, then again after their collision at Suzuka. Senna's manipulative power behind the scenes was quite remarkable. At Jerez, in 1989, the author heard Ayrton lecturing the Honda engineers as to how 'Prost should be fired now, before the end of the season. We are haemorrhaging technical information which he will take with him to Ferrari.' Informed of this outburst, Alain said he wasn't really surprised at Senna's attitude. By this stage in the relationship he believed that Ayrton was capable of doing anything to destabilise his racing future.

Not that Prost was slow in coming forward in the political stakes, of course. With his Ferrari contract for 1990 now firmly tucked away in his back pocket, at the '89 Italian Grand Prix he had voiced the opinion that Honda was favouring Senna with better engines. The Japanese company was aghast at such an allegation, forcing Prost to involve himself in an absurdly self-conscious retraction that was circulated in Portugal prior to the next race on the calendar. Prost shrewdly chose to bite his tongue in the interests of sustaining his World Championship challenge. Years later he would claim that Ron Dennis had admitted to him that his accusations had been closer to the truth than Honda would have liked to concede at the time.

Of course, the real breach between Prost and Senna came at the 1990 Japanese Grand Prix at the end of Alain's maiden season with Ferrari. Having qualified on pole position, Senna was furious when he discovered that the sport's governing body blocked an effort to move his starting position from the dusty right-hand side of the circuit to the cleaner racing line on the left. Prost, who had qualified second, was, in his mind, therefore better positioned for a good, clean start.

Senna's agitation spilled over on race morning. 'If Prost gets the best start, then I'm warning him he'd better not turn in on me, because he isn't going to make it,' he noted ominously. And sure enough, the potential disaster unfolded.

Prost got a better start and nosed ahead of Senna's McLaren as they went into the first turn. But Ayrton kept on coming, ramming into the back of the Italian car at undiminished speed. The Ferrari's rear wing was ripped off in the ensuing impact, together with the McLaren's right front wheel. The two mortally damaged cars slithered to a stop in the gravel trap on the outside of the corner. Mercifully, neither driver was hurt.

The incident resolved the 1990 World Championship in Ayrton's favour, leaving the motor racing fraternity deeply split as to where the responsibility for the incident really lay. Prost could hardly believe what had happened. 'Losing this way is disgusting,' he fumed. 'If you accept Senna's behaviour, then perhaps we will get to a situation in which people will start entering a team with one car specifically intended to push off the opposition to enable the other man to win. This man [Senna] has no value.'

Ayrton trenchantly rejected Prost's viewpoint. As far as he was concerned, the Frenchman had taken a risk by turning in as he did at the first corner, when he could not afford to jeopardise his car. In Senna's view Prost knew that he would come down the inside and he should have borne that in mind when he closed the door on his McLaren.

Senna's rationale was truly frightening in its strategic objectivity. Clearly he had given no consideration to his own personal safety and security – and precious little to the 24 cars making up the rest of the field, which were accelerating hard close behind. Had the McLaren and Ferrari ended up in the middle of the corner – or, worse still, bounced back into the middle of the pack – then who knows how disastrous the consequences might have been?

More depressing still was the number of highly respected names within the Grand Prix fraternity who sided with Senna. It was almost as if they had been hypnotised by the Brazilian's perception that those who did not support him 100 per cent were totally against him. They ran to offer support to a man who, by the standards of most objective observers, had been guilty of a grossly irresponsible piece of driving. The most incomprehensible standpoint was adopted by those who said that they 'understood how annoyed Senna felt.' Yet offering sympathy for a perceived injustice is one thing; lending support to the supposition that two wrongs make a right is quite something else. Particularly on this sort of scale. The reality was that the Suzuka episode left an indelible blemish on Ayrton Senna's professional reputation until the day he died, and the fact that he got away with it unpenalised on the day indicates a degree of pusillanimity on behalf of the sport's governing body that can only be regarded as shameful.

Twelve months later, in an astonishing attack on outgoing FISA President Jean-Marie Balestre, Senna would admit that, indeed, he had deliberately taken Prost out of the race. This confession came during the course of a stormy outburst that Senna would have to recant before being issued with an F1 Super Licence in 1992. But that was not the point. The governing body may have eventually acted against him, but their response was prompted by his uncomfortably offensive criticism rather than his unethical driving.

Yet in the dust and debris of that first-corner collision lay a tangle of contradictions. Ayrton was a deeply religious man. He had a close bond with his family and his enormous wealth enabled him to indulge in many anonymous acts of charity in his native Brazil. He particularly identified with children and could be moved to tears when confronted with what he identified as the deep injustices of day-to-day life outside the motor racing environment.

'It is a question of the way I was educated,' he explained, 'along with the warm and healthy atmosphere at home. I just feel good to be with them. And I owe to my family and friends everything I have achieved as a man and as a professional. We are very close.

'They worried a lot at the beginning when I was thinking about going motor racing professionally. I discussed it with them a lot, showing them that I needed it so much – that it was part of me – and once they realised that, they were totally supportive. They then looked at it in a more positive way; how to make it more enjoyable and more successful.'

He also admitted to being an introspective, private character: 'It is a way of protecting yourself in an environment like this, which can be quite heavy sometimes. This is the best way I have found to minimise the difficulties within the Formula 1 business.

'If I am in Europe I do a lot of running before a race and am totally committed to my profession, dealing with my future plans and commitments, programming my mind and generally trying to go forward for the future. But when I go back to Brazil, I don't have to do any of this, so I can completely cut off and take my life-style completely away from racing.'

Williams was obviously delighted to have got Senna's signature on a contract at last. After all those years of waiting, of mis-timed negotiations, of hoping and, eventually, of being disappointed, Frank had achieved an ambition. Ayrton shared his sense of satisfaction.

'I feel comfortable saying this is a dream come true,' said Ayrton. 'Frank Williams is the man who gave me my first opportunity to drive a Formula 1 car and, with a Renault engine, I won my first Grand Prix. We have been so close to doing the deal in the past. This year we finally made it.

'I'm really looking forward to driving a Williams-Renault in what I consider the beginning of a new life in motor racing for me. I have been waiting for this move for so long, from the moment I decided to change direction. A new team; new people to work with and get to know. It's a big challenge for me because I am the newcomer here; I am the one who had to adjust. I've been waiting impatiently for this. I need it for motivation.'

Senna's departure from McLaren represented a major blow for team chief Ron Dennis. Although the McLaren MD was sufficiently seasoned in the way of the Formula 1 world to realise that nothing necessarily lasts for ever, his signing both Senna and Honda together at the start of 1988 had represented one of the high spots of his professional career.

Dennis had believed that he could make the Prost/Senna partnership work and, long after the explosive relationship had fallen apart, admitted that his failure to keep them together represented one of the biggest disappointments of his professional life. But there was worse to come. The commitment with Honda, which Dennis had described as 'open-ended' during the halcyon days of 1988/89, was now coming apart at the seams.

Honda was finding that the sheer expense of Grand Prix racing was getting out of hand; the Japanese company's 1992 V12 engine was insufficiently competitive and the cost of helping McLaren to retain Senna's services was another key factor which seemed in danger of running out of financial control.

By the middle of 1992 Senna was also uncertain about his own future. Kept out of Williams for the following season thanks to Prost's veto, he knew that McLaren was set to lose the Honda engine deal and had no works-backed alternative arranged. He hinted that he might well take a sabbatical, stringing his decision out until a matter of weeks prior to the start of the '93 season before finally agreeing to drive on a race-to-race basis.

McLaren was now reduced to the role of a customer using the Cosworth-built Ford HB V8 engines. Yet the combination of Senna, the team's customary impeccable standards of race preparation and a willingness to continue investing in active suspension technology right up to the end of the season, after which it would be banned, ensured that McLaren emerged from 1993 with five race victories.

Examined in detail, Ayrton's wins at Interlagos, Donington Park, Monaco, Suzuka and Adelaide were all absolute top-drawer performances. Yet by the time he scored those last two triumphs at the wheel of the McLaren, Senna's future already lay with Williams. The closing months of his tenure with his long-time employers had, furthermore, been tarnished by some off-the-record remarks made by Dennis to the effect that Ayrton was 'unemployable', which were subsequently leaked to the Brazilian press.

The differences were patched up. You had to have some sympathy with Dennis. Senna *was* an extremely difficult man to deal with. A ruthless, totally inflexible negotiator, he never shied away from using any advantage at his disposal to maximise his position. In many ways Ron and Ayrton were very alike; supremely competitive, intolerant of failure and committed to strive for excellence. Dennis would freely admit that he felt almost physical pain if he woke up on a Monday morning and realised that his team hadn't won the previous day's race. Senna was much the same.

Signing Senna for 1994 was a major coup for Williams as his team started a two-year sponsorship deal with Rothmans worth in the region of $20 million (£12.5 million) per season. Frank makes no bones about the fact that he was nervous about what Ayrton's reaction might be to the demands that would obviously be placed on his time for promotional glad-handing and so on by this major cigarette corporation.

'When he came here I thought, "Gawd, here we are with Ayrton and we've got this major cigarette company who are going to want him to do this, this and this – it's going to be wall-to-wall aggravation from start to finish",' he admitted. 'I never thought he would agree to their demands, but he came out here with Julian Jakobi one Saturday morning before the media launch at Estoril and we told him what we wanted.'

'We kicked it around, honed it a bit, and then, to my surprise, he said, "Yep, I'll do that. Part of the deal." And he did every little bit of it without a murmur. OK, you wouldn't get him to do anything else that he hadn't agreed to, but that meeting astonished me. I'd been dreading that day!'

For the 1994 season Senna would be paired alongside Damon Hill driving the all-new Williams-Renault FW16, the first car from the Patrick Head/Adrian Newey partnership since 1991 not to incorporate active suspension. The Williams design team had attempted to tackle the aerodynamic packaging of the new car in a manner that would tidy up the air flow over the rear of the car in an effort to claw back some of the grip lost by the ban on traction control systems.

The new configuration included a distinctive anhedral rear wing, the effectiveness of which depended on a low outboard tail section, which was achieved by totally enclosing the drive-shafts within wing-section carbon-fibre composite shrouds that doubled as the upper wishbones.

The car was powered by the latest variation on Renault's superbly reliable 67-degree V10 engine, now in RS6 specification. Its power was transmitted by means of a revised and lightened version of the six-speed transverse gearbox used the previous year, but now restricted to semi-automatic control in place of the 'fully automatic' system used in 1993. The FW16 also featured power-assisted steering, hydraulically driven and reacting to input from electronic sensors, a system that drew heavily from the knowledge gained from the team's active suspension technology.

Damon Hill, for one, appreciated that Senna would be a truly formidable contender to have cast in the role of team-mate. He admitted that it was possible that driving with Ayrton would mean a less-easy relationship than he had enjoyed with Prost.

'It may well be, but I don't want to pre-judge it,' he admitted. 'I don't really know Ayrton terribly well. I've spoken to him a few times and raced him very little, really. But put it this way; I'm looking forward to it. I know it's going to be a very exciting year.

'I think he is by far and away the most complete and fastest driver currently racing, or will be when Alain retires. He's head and shoulders above everyone else.

'But I'm not easily demoralised or crushed, so I'm well prepared for that. I'm still on an upward climb in my Formula 1 career and I still have a lot to learn. Having someone like Ayrton as a team-mate will only add to my development.'

Senna began the 1994 season under the cloud of a two-race suspended ban, imposed on him after he had jostled Jordan driver Eddie Irvine in a post-race row following the previous year's Japanese Grand Prix. Ayrton had accused Irvine of reckless stupidity in holding up his leading McLaren when he came up to lap the British driver. Irvine replied that he was simply getting on with his own race, battling with Hill's Williams over fifth place, and Senna was just being unreasonably provocative.

The bottom line was that Senna swung a punch at his rival – and Irvine fell backwards over a table as he ducked out of the way. There clearly seemed to be something about Senna and Suzuka that spelled trouble. But this time, for once, he was taken to task by the sport's governing body over his behaviour.

The first race of the season took place in front of Senna's adoring home crowd at Sao Paulo's Interlagos circuit, and Ayrton knew full well that he could expect a pretty stiff level of competition from the new Benetton-Ford B194 driven by Michael Schumacher. As things transpired, Ayrton check-mated his young German rival with a brilliant run to take pole position in second qualifying, seconds before a torrential rainstorm wiped out any prospect of Schumacher launching a counter-attack. But Senna was not taking anything for granted.

'Our car in particular would perform better on a smooth track surface,' he said thoughtfully. In Friday qualifying he had already expressed himself unhappy with the FW16's handling and the Williams crew had worked almost until midnight checking over the car and changing its suspension settings.

Schumacher was happy with second on the grid, but Damon Hill had a nightmarish first day's qualifying for the 1994 season. It seemed that all he shared with the Benetton driver was a streaming cold, and lost crucial time when his car's on-board fire extinguisher accidentally discharged into the cockpit, then found himself stopped out on the circuit by an obscure electrical fault at the start of the first timed session.

'I don't think I've ever sweated so much in a short space of time in my life,' said Hill glumly. 'It was very stressful.' Thereafter he was reduced to playing catch-up, effectively a day behind Ayrton in the Brazilian's personal playground. He wound up a disappointing 1.6 seconds slower to take fourth place on the grid behind Jean Alesi's Ferrari 412T1.

Senna got cleanly away from pole position to take an immediate lead as Alesi nipped ahead of Schumacher to such good effect that the Benetton star was 4.0 seconds adrift by the time he forced his way past the Ferrari to take second place on lap three. Thereafter Schumacher chiselled away to pull up onto Senna's tail, leapfrogging ahead of the Williams when the two cars came together for their first refuelling stops with 22 of the race's 71 laps completed. Thereafter Schumacher opened a 6.5-second advantage before the second spate of refuelling stops. On lap 44 Senna made an 8.5-second pit visit followed by Schumacher next time round, the Benetton being stationary for only 7.4 seconds.

On the face of it the Brazilian GP was all over bar the shouting, Sao Paulo's most famous son poised to go down to a rare defeat at the hands of the German outsider. Yet Ayrton was confident. With 20 laps to go, he began to steady the gap, then reduce the deficit. But just as he seemed poised on the verge of a counter-attack, on lap 56 Senna spun and stalled on the climbing uphill left-hander leading on to the start/finish straight. The crowds immediately made for the exit gates.

Ayrton remained philosophical in the face of this disappointment, inwardly knowing that much work still needed to be done before the Williams FW16 realised its full potential. 'It was a good race, fast and very quick,' he agreed. 'Michael was a little bit quicker than us and only at the end was I able to push a little more and go with him. I was driving right on my limit when I got caught out on the exit of that third-gear corner. It was my own mistake as I was pushing a bit too hard.'

The only consolation for the Williams team was that Hill finished second after a steady run, his race performance compromised by a gamble to make only a single refuelling stop. In retrospect it was not the most competitive option.

The second round of the '94 title chase was a new addition to the Formula 1 schedule. The Pacific Grand Prix took place at Japan's Tanaka International circuit located at Aida, some 100 miles from Osaka, which had been purpose-built by millionaire businessman Hajime Tanaka, who had previously made a fortune from exclusive golfing resorts.

Williams arrived in Japan guardedly confident that an intensive test session at Jerez might have gone some way to eliminating the FW16's distinctly nervous handling characteristics. As things transpired it was a forlorn hope – for this race, at least.

On paper it looked good. Senna took pole position after a characteristically feisty performance on the low-grip track surface. The reality, however, was different. Schumacher only lost the pole by making an incorrect chassis adjustment in Friday's crucial qualifying session, which, held in cooler conditions than those on Saturday, also proved to be the fastest.

From the touchlines Schumacher seemed to be having a much easier time of it. His Benetton B194 looked more secure and significantly sharper through the corners. By contrast the Williams FW16s seemed to wash out towards the kerbs on a ponderous understeering slide, then suddenly snap into ragged oversteer.

Some indication of the dilemma facing the Williams drivers could be judged from the fact that Senna and Hill both spun off at the same corner on the Saturday. 'It seems more than a coincidence that we both spun at the same place, in the same way, using the same chassis settings,' said Hill thoughtfully. As late as the race-morning warm-up session the Williams drivers were experimenting by slightly raising their cars' ride heights, feeling perhaps that they had been running them too low during qualifying, and were duly rewarded with first and second fastest times in this half-hour stint.

In the race Schumacher made the best start, just reaching the first corner ahead of Senna with Mika Hakkinen's McLaren-Peugeot coming up fast in third place. 'I had too much wheelspin, so Michael took the lead,' said Ayrton. 'At the first corner we were close together and it would have been possible [for me] to try an overtaking manoeuvre, but that would have been very risky, so I decided to stay second and be safe.'

Unfortunately, as Senna eased off slightly so Hakkinen kept coming. The result was that the Brazilian's Williams received a light tap from behind, pitching it into a spin that ended in the gravel trap on the outside of the turn, after which it was gently T-boned by Nicola Larini, the Ferrari test driver who was deputising for Jean Alesi at this race after the Frenchman had damaged his back in a testing accident at Mugello.

Senna later expressed the view to the Brazilian media that it was about time the FIA reined in some of the more over-exuberant young members of the present Formula 1 generation. By any standards that sounded a bit rich coming from the man who, more than any other, had legitimised over-aggressive driving standards across the preceding decade. Senna also sought out Hakkinen to read him the Riot Act. 'I won't tell you what he said,' said Mika, 'but it wasn't complimentary or positive.'

So that was Senna out of the equation for the second straight race. Hill, meanwhile, was left to complete the opening lap third behind Schumacher and Hakkinen; in his anxiety to get ahead of the McLaren, he attempted to overtake on the outside at a particularly tricky turn midway round lap four. But Mika resolutely stuck to his line, forcing the Williams up the kerb and into a quick spin.

Damon resumed eighth and spent the next 28 laps muscling through the traffic to regain second place. But his efforts came to nothing when transmission failure claimed his FW16 after 42 laps. That left Schumacher to win again from Gerhard Berger's Ferrari 412T1 and the Jordan-Hart 194 of Rubens Barrichello. The German driver now had 20 championship points to Barrichello's seven and the six apiece for Berger and Hill. Senna had none, and was pretty fed up about things.

'The World Championship starts at Imola.' Those words encapsulated Senna's attitude towards the San Marino Grand Prix, the race that would open the European leg of the 1994 title chase on 1 May. Moreover, despite winning those first two races Schumacher had come to Imola expecting Senna's ostensibly more powerful Williams-Renault to seize the initiative.

Williams had worked hard to incorporate significant changes to the FW16 in time for the Imola race, most significantly including a revised nose profile with the wings positioned slightly higher, new aerodynamic end-plates, a revised wheelbase and a re-shaped cockpit surround. Some of these cockpit changes were designed to accommodate Ayrton's desire to be made more comfortable in the FW16 and, perhaps crucially in the light of what was to follow, they included changes to the steering column design to adjust the steering wheel position in line with Senna's personal preference.

'To be honest we made a bloody awful cock-up,' reflected Williams Chief Designer Adrian Newey in connection with the FW16's early season form. 'The rear-end grip problem was purely a set-up problem. We were learning about springs and dampers all over again after concentrating on active suspension for two years, whereas most people had been away for only one.

'We also had a rather silly aerodynamic problem – basically the front wing was too low – but that was raised for Imola, by which time we were looking in pretty good shape.'

Senna duly qualified on pole position ahead of Schumacher, but the number-crunching detail of the race and its qualifying sessions were lost amidst a whirlwind of stark tragedy. The tone for the weekend had unknowingly been set by Rubens Barrichello whose Jordan somersaulted after clipping the kerb at 140 mph entering the tricky *Variante Bassa* S-bend just before the pits during Friday qualifying.

The young Brazilian was fortunate enough to get away with superficial injuries and was back in the paddock the following afternoon, although he was sidelined from the race. Then, in Saturday qualifying, Austrian novice Roland Ratzenberger crashed at over 190 mph when the nose section of his Simtek-Ford loosened in an early off-track moment and it flew off on the flat-out section immediately beyond the Tamburello left-hander.

The car was immediately pitched out of control and slammed into the left-hand barrier on the following Villeneuve right-hander before slithering to a halt in the middle of the Tosa hairpin. Ratzenberger succumbed to multiple injuries shortly afterwards.

The 31-year old from Salzburg was the first driver to be killed at the wheel of a Formula 1 car since Italy's Elio de Angelis crashed his Brabham-BMW during testing at Paul Ricard in 1985, three years after his compatriot Ricardo Paletti had been the most recent fatality in an actual race meeting, when his Osella ploughed into the back of Didier Pironi's Ferrari, which had stalled on pole position seconds before the start of the Canadian GP at Montreal.

The entire paddock was stunned by this sudden tragedy. At a stroke everybody was forced to re-calibrate their perception of Grand Prix racing's dangers. In their heart of hearts every driver fully understood the inherent hazards of their chosen profession. Yet in the decade that had passed since Paletti's accident at Montreal, there was an unspoken undercurrent that tempted people towards the dangerous belief that the sport had become too safe, too secure, for such a tragedy to be repeated. At a stroke Ratzenberger's death had swept away such comfortable assumptions.

Senna took the opportunity to go out to the scene of the Simtek accident and was deeply moved by the whole disaster. But he duly took up his place on pole position for the following day's race and accelerated straight into the lead at the green light. Unbelievably there was more mayhem unfolding in his wake.

J. J. Lehto, the Finnish driver who had done an excellent job qualifying his Benetton fifth for what was his first race of the season, taking over from Jos Verstappen after recovering from neck injuries sustained in pre-season testing, stalled his car only seconds before the start was given. For a couple of seconds it looked as though the rest of the pack would get through safely, but then Pedro Lamy's Lotus-Mugen, which was accelerating hard from 22nd place on the grid, slammed over the stationary Benetton's left rear wheel.

The two cars were momentarily locked together before Lamy's Lotus catapulted into the left-hand wall, shedding components in all directions. Debris flew into the crowded grandstand opposite the pits, injuring several onlookers. With wreckage scattered all over the start line, the Safety Car was deployed to slow the field and give marshals a chance to clean up the debris. For three laps the field was kept down to a cruising pace before the pace car pulled off as Senna led the pack round to complete its fifth lap of the afternoon.

As the Safety Car pulled into the pits Ayrton calmly acknowledged a radio signal from his engineer David Brown and, timing his restart to perfection, slammed into the next lap about ten lengths clear of Schumacher. Through Tamburello the Williams kicked up a shower of sparks as its titanium skid plates bottomed out over the undulations on the track surface, but Senna seemed safe and secure in the lead as he braked for the Tosa hairpin and headed back up the hill through an avenue of fans cheering for the rival Ferrari team.

At the end of lap six Senna was 0.6 seconds ahead of Schumacher as he hurtled into Tamburello. Then, suddenly, the Williams FW16 twitched slightly, lurched to the right and slammed off the road into the concrete retaining wall lining the right-hand side of the circuit. The car bounced back on to the run-off area, spinning down the edge of the circuit as wheels and suspension components scattered in all directions. One piece of debris lodged under Berger's Ferrari. After the race had been immediately redflagged to a halt, Gerhard was shaken to find that his car's right front suspension had almost been severed by the impact.

Professor Sid Watkins, the FIA Medical Delegate and one of the world's most eminent neuro-surgeons, was on the scene in a matter of minutes. A close friend of Senna, his emotions were immediately subjugated to the medical needs of the moment. From the moment he arrived Watkins could see that the situation was extremely serious.

Ayrton had clearly suffered a major injury to his right forehead and a medical helicopter was despatched to land on the circuit alongside the badly damaged Williams. Within 15 minutes Senna was loaded aboard and flown directly to Bologna's Maggiore Hospital.

The race was restarted, almost as a footnote, to be won by Schumacher's Benetton from Larini's Ferrari and Hakkinen's McLaren. Berger withdrew after leading valiantly, his Ferrari's handling having deteriorated due to a malfunctioning rear shock absorber.

As the howl of the racing engines was stilled, the paddock at Imola became enveloped in a mood of bleak communal desperation. Rumours ran wild, but many who had seen the television shots of Senna being lifted from the car feared the worst. When the initial reports filtered back from Bologna, it was clearly only a matter of time.

Ayrton was in a deep coma, suffering with severe brain injuries. In the early evening he died, shortly after being visited by his dear friend Gerhard Berger. The Formula 1 fraternity was immediately overwhelmed by a flood-tide of tangled emotions. Only a sense of acute disbelief and feelings of immense sadness were left to round off the sport's blackest weekend in living memory.

For Frank Williams the 1994 season would always be regarded with enormous sadness. In some ways it was a re-run of his 1970 tragedy in the Dutch Grand Prix at Zandvoort when Piers Courage, the upper-crust scion of the famous brewing dynasty, was killed in Frank's de Tomaso. Yet, by the same token, those distant days were somehow different. Frank was young and resilient, clawing his way up the lower reaches of the Formula 1 ladder. Death and disaster were still regarded as an integral part of the motor racing equation. Not so a generation later.

'If you want a summary of Ayrton Senna, he was actually a greater man out of the car than in it,' said Frank. 'The adoration they felt for him in Brazil reminded you this was no ordinary person. He was very clever, shrewd, focused, tough . . . All the things I admired.'

To this day a photograph of Senna remains on Frank Williams's table in his first-floor corner office at the team's Didcot factory. There is another one in the team's motorhome that travels from race to race. How did the team cope with his death?

'Everyone in the company was truly shattered by what happened,' continued Williams. 'They all felt a certain responsibility, and it's still on the minds of many people here. At the end of the day the fact is that Ayrton died in a Williams car, and that's an enormously important responsibility. I feel very embarrassed that he never got a fair crack of the whip at Williams. He wanted to come here, and he'd wanted to for some time. He drove a good race in Brazil in a difficult car and got nowhere in Aida.

'Julian Jakobi, who was very close to him, told me the other day that Ayrton remained pretty certain he'd be World Champion. And, with hindsight, he would have been, I think. He'd have got the car sorted very quickly. I mean, Damon clearly, at that time, certainly wasn't in the same league as Ayrton in terms of getting to a problem, analysing it and presenting it to the engineers for solution.

'It [the FW16] was a difficult car at the beginning of the year, and yet he was on pole position at each of his three races. Quite remarkable. He never bitched publicly about the car, but he gave us a hard time in terms of making clear what the problems were.'

Despite all the stories about Ayrton's frame of mind in the aftermath of the Ratzenberger accident, and the feeling that he may somehow have had a premonition of impending disaster, Frank recalls that Senna appeared remarkably relaxed back at the hotel in the evening before the race. Last thing, he padded down barefoot in his pyjamas to his employer's room for an informal chat. 'Don't worry Frank, I'm alright now,' he said.

On race morning he seemed fine. He chatted to his old adversary Alain Prost and, during the warm-up, TF1, the French television station that now employed the former champion as a commentator, was patched into Senna's radio link for a few laps. 'Welcome back, Alain, we've missed you,' said Ayrton.

With hindsight they did not appear as empty words. In the last few months of his life there had been signs that Ayrton was at last lightening up slightly, relaxing and realising that perhaps there was more to his existence than simply Formula 1. The last words Senna said to Frank Williams were, 'I've got to go and see Gerhard.' The former McLaren-Honda team-mates were very close buddies. Berger was always totally honest with Ayrton, and that mattered to him more than anything else. He felt he could trust Gerhard absolutely.

What would the future have held for Ayrton Senna? Certainly there is no doubt that he would have served out his two-year partnership with the Williams-Renault squad through to the end of 1995. Almost certainly, in the estimation of Michael Schumacher, he would have won the 1994 World Championship. Probably by Monza.

Yet he was still tantalised by the possibility of working with Ferrari. Like Niki Lauda two decades before, Ayrton's intensely logical mind told him that Ferrari had the resources, ability and engineering potential to get the job done. All it required was for the famous Italian team to be properly focused and directed. Clearly, Ayrton believed he could bring the very qualities that Niki – and indeed Alain Prost as recently as 1990 – had brought to bear on the challenge.

Many people believed that part of his motivation for switching from McLaren to Williams was a burning need to emphasise his driving superiority with a fresh team. He had driven for McLaren for six years and won 35 of his 41 Grands Prix victories with the 'red and whites'.

Now was the time to break free and prove that, while McLaren might not be able to do without Senna, he could weave his own special magic to equal effect in a fresh environment. And the signs were that Williams was only another port of call on Ayrton's journey of achievement through Formula 1.

He clearly regarded driving for Ferrari as unfinished business. On 27 April 1994 – only four days before he died – Ayrton reportedly had a two-hour phone conversation with Luca di Montezemolo, the President of Ferrari. During the course of their talk Senna strongly hinted that he would complete his two years with Williams then come to Maranello. The indications were that Ayrton Senna wanted to complete his active career with the team that, more than any other, symbolises the very essence of Grand Prix motor racing.

Chapter 4

The consequences
of the accident

'And if I laugh at any mortal thing,
'Tis that I may not weep.'

George Gordon, 6th Baron Byron

The Williams team returned to Didcot to find dozens of fans mounting a vigil outside the factory gates where a mass of floral tributes lay next to the perimeter fence. Brazil, meanwhile, was thrown into a state of national grief. President Itamar Franco declared that there would be three days of national mourning leading up to a state funeral for the country's national hero.

For the European racing fans Senna's loss was a body-blow, but as nothing to the sheer sense of desperation felt by his native land. In an environment racked by economic problems, corruption in public life and a gaping chasm separating the glitteringly rich from the miserably poor, Ayrton represented an anchor for public self-esteem. *He* gave Brazilians a sense of self-respect and dignity on the international scene, offering a sliver of dignity and national recognition on the global sporting stage in a manner perhaps only previously achieved by the legendary Pele two decades before.

For the downtrodden masses, to see Senna proudly waving aloft their national flag as he completed the slowing-down lap after another victory was nothing short of a morale-boosting tonic. To them, he was The Greatest. But now the dream was over.

On Wednesday 4 May 1994 Varig flight RG271 from Paris touched down in the early morning at Sao Paulo's Guarulhos international airport carrying Senna's coffin, which was immediately transported to the state legislature building for a ceremonial lying in state. More than a quarter of a million Brazilians lined the route to witness the homecoming of their national champion.

On Thursday 5 May Senna was buried at Sao Paulo's Morumbi cemetery amidst scenes usually reserved for Heads of State, and then only rarely. A 21-gun salute and a flypast of airforce jets, two of which scribed a giant heart and an 'S' in the sky over the city, added to the deep sense of emotion as Ayrton's coffin was carried to his final resting place by pall-bearers Gerhard Berger, Emerson Fittipaldi – Brazil's very first World Champion – Alain Prost, Rubens Barrichello, Christian Fittipaldi, Damon Hill, Roberto Moreno, Thierry Boutsen, Derek Warwick and Maurizio Sandro Sala.

Also present were Frank Williams and his team's Commercial Manager Richard West, Julian Jakobi and McLaren team chief Ron Dennis. Bernie Ecclestone made the trip but was barred from attending the funeral by Ayrton's younger brother Leonardo who, the previous day, had attacked the sport's governing body.

'If there had been some sort of protection, maybe tyres or something, Ayrton would be alive and intact today,' he told the Reuters press agency. 'Unfortunately in Formula 1 all people think about is money.'

Ecclestone was deeply hurt to be turned away from the church, but deferred graciously and returned to his hotel. Gerhard Berger noted the military precision with which the whole funeral had been planned, admiring the quiet dignity of Ayrton's parents and family. He found himself thinking that it must have been planned by Senna in advance, and comforted himself with the image of his old friend looking down on the proceedings with a characteristically critical eye.

In motor racing terms the Imola weekend went down in the history books alongside the Le Mans disaster of 1955, Fon de Portago's fatal accident in the 1957 Mille Miglia, the 1960 Belgian GP, which claimed the lives of both Alan Stacey and Chris Bristow, and the death of the great Jim Clark at Hockenheim in the spring of 1968.

On a broader canvas it was to the Williams team what the loss of the 'Busby Babes' in the 1958 Munich air disaster had been to Manchester United and to the world of international football in general. The death of Senna was a disaster on an almost incomprehensible scale, such as strikes any sport perhaps once in a generation.

Personal tragedy aside, there were three other key dimensions to the disaster. What caused the accident? How would Williams now pick up the pieces? And what would the sport's governing body do in terms of uprating Formula 1 safety standards?

Senna's damaged Williams FW16 was immediately impounded by the Italian authorities, leaving Patrick Head and his colleagues to piece together what information they could from the telemetry traces available to them. What became clear very quickly was that Ayrton was travelling at just over 193 mph when his car began to deviate from the racing line just beyond the second apex of the Tamburello left-hander.

Instantly he had come off the throttle and applied the brakes, scrubbing off almost 60 mph of his momentum in 0.9 seconds before impacting the vertical concrete wall at just over 135 mph. Two thick black lines of rubber were left for almost the entire 18 metres from the point where he left the racing line to the point where he left the circuit, indications suggesting that the Williams was skimming the run-off area like a pebble across the surface of a lake just prior to hitting the wall.

Whether Senna initially backed off the throttle simply to steady the car, or he suddenly appreciated he was the victim of a cataclysmic technical failure, was more difficult to ascertain. The frenzy of speculation was hardly calmed when the Brazilian press quoted Leonardo Senna as saying: 'Frank Williams told me that the car was hitting the ground more than normal – only a mechanical problem could have caused such a crash.'

This remark came a few days after Patrick Head had been quoted, badly out of context, as saying that driver error seemed the most likely cause of the accident. This brought a prompt response from the Williams Technical Director.

'We are still studying the data, still gathering the information, and at this stage we have reached no conclusions,' he said firmly. 'All the relevant information is not available yet. At no time did I ever say Ayrton Senna was to blame.'

Goodyear quickly ruled out the likelihood of tyre failure and the mystery deepened when former Formula 1 drivers Keke Rosberg and Jonathan Palmer, who examined the TV footage in frame-by-frame detail, concluded that Ayrton's final lurch to the right was not consistent with driver error. Rosberg crisply made the point that Tamburello, fast though it certainly may be, was easily taken flat-out with no problem in the current breed of Grand Prix car.

Head and Adrian Newey obviously wanted to make a detailed examination of the FW16 at the first possible opportunity, but with the car impounded under the jurisdiction of the legal authorities, they were obliged to try putting together the complex technical jigsaw with many crucial pieces missing. The matter was further complicated by newspaper photographs showing the FW16's steering wheel, attached to a section of its column, *outside* the car amidst the debris of the accident.

This caused warning lights to flash on in the minds of many expert observers, raising speculation that the steering column itself might have suffered a pre-impact failure. More crucially, notices were served on the Williams team by the magistrate charged with investigating the Senna affair warning representatives of the team that they might be investigated on suspicion of culpable homicide.

From the Williams team's standpoint, there was the question of replacing Senna, a task that was hardly the work of the moment. Initially it was decided to run just a single car in the Monaco Grand Prix, the next race on the calendar, but speculation that Prost might be persuaded to reverse his retirement decision were quashed after the Frenchman's comments at Senna's funeral.

'I was proud to compete against him,' said Alain. 'Professionally, he was the only driver I respected. In Senna's honour, I will never sit in a Formula 1 car again.'

It was also rumoured that Riccardo Patrese might consider a return to Formula 1. Out of work since being dropped by Benetton, the popular Italian made a courtesy call on Frank Williams during the Monaco GP weekend. But they both knew it wasn't the answer. Aside from the fact that Riccardo wasn't really quick enough to fill the breach, he admitted that something inside him had finally died with Senna. After 17 happy years in Formula 1 Patrese was content to acknowledge that his Grand Prix career had run its course.

FIA President Max Mosley had an even trickier agenda to control. The sport's governing body immediately pledged itself to improve the long-term safety of Formula 1, as one would have expected it to do in such trying circumstances. But Mosley was nervous about being seen to produce a knee-jerk response to the disaster, appreciating full well that such a strategy might not work to best effect.

For the moment the FIA had a meeting in Paris on the Wednesday following the Imola tragedy where it was confirmed that serious consideration would be given to measures to enhance head and neck protection for Formula 1 drivers, including the question of head restraints and additional side protection.

Even though Mosley wanted to tread carefully, he suddenly found himself facing melodramatic threats that the Italian Grand Prix at Monza might be cancelled unless some instant fix was applied. He responded robustly on this point.

'The modern Formula 1 car cannot safely be regulated by snap judgements or panic measure,' he insisted. 'However, it is right that recent events reinforce the research into increased safety for Formula 1 which continues all the time at the FIA as part of a wide-ranging programme to improve safety standards in motor sport.' He also emphasised the point that the five major incidents that took place at Imola were unrelated in so far as causes were concerned.

Ironically, at the time of Ayrton's death former Ferrari ace Niki Lauda was attempting to persuade the Brazilian to spearhead a revival of the drivers' Formula 1 safety lobby. 'The drivers have no role at the moment and they obviously have a very particular view,' said Lauda in the aftermath of Ratzenberger's accident.

'In my time there was a drivers' association which was started by Jackie Stewart and continued by me. In the old days the drivers were part of the process. Now they're nothing.'

◇ ◇ ◇

What was less widely known at the time of his death was the fact that Ayrton Senna was much concerned about the superior performance of

Michael Schumacher's Benetton. Privately he was slightly perplexed. He knew enough about racing car performance to have some suspicions that all was not as it should be in connection with the Benetton B194.

Both to Frank Williams and to Gerhard Berger he expressed those concerns. Although the FIA would subsequently give Benetton a clean bill of health as regards their conformity with the regulations, those close to the Brazilian driver believe that Ayrton Senna went to his death in the knowledge that his key rival in the Championship battle might be using some sort of illegal traction control system.

Privately again, both Williams and Renault shared Senna's burning sense of frustration. They believed that a number of teams were bending the rules, and were disappointed that the FIA didn't seem able to control the situation. Max Mosley had, from the outset, promised dire consequences for anybody found infringing the technical regulations in 1994, but some teams were now questioning the governing body's ability to keep control of this complex situation.

The Williams team contested the Monaco Grand Prix as if on auto-pilot. The pressures were immense, heightening the stark sense of Senna's loss. Ayrton had won a record six times through the streets of the Mediterranean Principality, while Damon had another monkey on his back in the form of his late father Graham's record of five wins. Twelve months earlier, when Senna had driven his McLaren-Ford to the victory that broke Graham's long-standing record, Damon had been the man to finish second on his first Monaco Grand Prix outing for Williams.

This time things were different. The Williams FW16 was short on development and still difficult to drive. Hill found the pressure stifling, not helped by Renault's over-anxious concern as to how Williams proposed to salvage its reputation. Senna may have been dead for barely a fortnight, but the harsh commercial reality of the Formula 1 merry-go-round was already making itself felt. Ayrton was one of the cornerstones on which the team's 1994 effort was built. He had to be replaced. And fast.

Rothmans, as the team's title sponsor, proved more sanguine. They figured that Frank knew the business and demonstrated more resilience than Renault initially displayed. In fact, emissaries from the French company reportedly made an approach to none other than Nigel Mansell within a week of Senna's death. Mansell, who had won the 1993 Indycar championship in historic style at the wheel of his Newman/Haas Lola-Ford, was having a miserable time defending his title against an onslaught from the all-conquering Penske-Ilmors. He was willing to listen to whatever Williams and Renault had to say to him.

At Monaco Hill qualified the lone Williams fourth and was taken out in a first lap collision with Mika Hakkinen's McLaren. Renault made no secret of the fact that they didn't think he was up to it. Frank, meanwhile, privately felt sorry for Damon. He seemed such a lonely figure, suddenly shouldering the team leadership.

As things transpired, the 1994 season would be the making of Damon Hill. He had originally joined the team to take over as test driver in 1991 when Mark Blundell accepted a similar position with the McLaren-Honda squad. There is also little doubt that he was not regarded as the most obviously qualified future Formula 1 talent when he was fighting his way through the ranks of the minor-league single-seater categories.

Damon was born in 1960, just about the eve of his father Graham's Grand Prix ascendancy. He would be too young to recall his parent's emergence as one of the leading Formula 1 forces of the 1960s, and Damon was barely two years old when Graham won the 1962 World Championship at the wheel of a BRM. Later, he admits that he displayed only a passing interest in his father's chosen profession.

'I remember when we were staying in a friend's cottage in Kent and I was playing in the garden with their son and Mum came out and said, "Come and look at Daddy winning the Monaco Grand Prix", and I sort of thought, "Can't I stay out here and play?"' he recalled in 1992 in the run-up to the 1993 Monaco race.

'I must have been eight years old at the time and I remember coming in and watching Dad coming round the old Gasworks hairpin in the red and gold Lotus 49, and sort of finishing the race and that was it. It didn't impress me at all.'

As Graham's Formula 1 career peaked then faded following a terrible accident at Watkins Glen that left him with serious leg injuries, Damon became more aware of his father's celebrity status. Yet it quickly became clear that motorcycles sparked Hill Junior's interest much more decisively than cars.

'My attraction for bikes started when I was about 11 years old and this guy was knocking around with a monkey bike over the weekend of the 1971 International Trophy at Silverstone, which my Dad won in the Brabham,' says Damon. 'I was out the back of the pits and this guy was messing around with this bike and let me have a go. I thought, "This is fantastic, this is what I want to do, I want one of these."

'So I said to my Dad, sheepishly, "What do you think the chances are?", and he got me one for passing my Eleven Plus exam. I was absolutely stunned. A Honda monkey bike! I thought it was the best thing that had happened in my life. I've still got it and from that moment on I was into bikes.

'Dad later got into bikes himself, because we had some land on which we could ride. He got a bike off Bultaco from Spain, and he used to ride that round enthusiastically. I had a go on that 350, which was obviously a lot more powerful than my 50cc monkey bike, and I was a bit surprised when he let me have a go. But he just said wear your helmet, be careful and off you go.'

Damon was just getting to know his father properly on a man-to-man basis as he grew into his teens when Graham was killed in an air crash one foggy night in late November 1975. He had retired from driving earlier that season and was now concentrating on tutoring his young protégé Tony Brise as the lead driver of his own Embassy Hill team.

They had been at the Paul Ricard circuit, near Bandol, doing some preliminary tests on the 1976 Hill GH2 and were returning to England when Graham's Piper Aztec crashed in flames on Arkley golf course about three miles short of the runway at Elstree. Graham Hill, Tony Brise and the other four team members on the plane all perished in the disaster.

Apart from the obvious grief surrounding this dreadful bereavement, what followed was a more than usually testing time for Graham's widow Bette, Damon and his sisters Brigitte and Samantha. They were left in straitened financial circumstances and were forced to move from their beautiful country house in Hertfordshire to a more modest home in St Albans. Damon was brought face to face with life's hardships at a vulnerable age. It put a determined edge on his personality, although he remains understandably reluctant to dwell on the loss.

'Let's just say that perhaps I'm a bit more experienced about life than my contemporaries,' he says firmly. 'I thought, well, I've been very privileged for the first 15 years of my life, but now I'm going to have to get on with it like Dad did. He started from scratch and made his own way. Now I had to do the same.

'At the time he was killed, I was beginning to have more interest in the team. Who knows, if he had lived, the Hill team might well be where Williams is now.'

Damon initially went motorcycle racing on much the same financial shoestring as his father had done back in 1954. He eventually switched to cars, largely through his mother's bidding. 'My first bike race was in late 1979 and I moved to cars in 1982,' he explains.

'I think bike racing is more damaging to your body than motor racing, because while nobody gets to this [Formula 1] level in a racing car without the odd spin and shunt, on a bike you never have a spin – you break something, you go down the road, lose some skin . . . I mean, I broke my collar bone, but that was getting away lightly really. I knocked myself out a few times.

'Then in 1982 I went to the Winfield racing drivers' school at Magny-Cours in France and decided, yes, I would make the switch to cars. My mother was pretty relieved, as there is no doubt bikes can be pretty dangerous.'

Damon duly served the classic British single-seater motor racing apprenticeship. He started in Formula Ford, then graduated to the cut-and-thrust of F3. Along the way he battled with the sort of nerve-racking lack of finance experienced by many of his contemporaries. He was good, but not obviously outstanding. There were others who believed themselves to be better, but never ultimately got quite as far.

It is easy to detect an undercurrent, if not of resentment, then of mild indignation that Damon Hill ended up challenging for the World Championship in 1994 at the wheel of a Williams-Renault. But F3, important though it certainly is, merely represents a yardstick by which to measure young drivers, one against the other.

Outstanding success in this close-fought single-seater nursery is a virtual guarantee that the driver concerned has the credentials necessary for Grand Prix racing. But, as Nigel Mansell and Damon Hill proved, lack of such a consistently high level of success does not, by definition, bar one from going all the way to the sport's highest reaches.

Midway through a rather patchy Formula 3000 career – high on promise, short on results – Hill got the lucky break every driver prays for. He was signed up to drive as official tester for the Williams-Renault team at the time when it was preparing its superbly competitive FW14s and FW14Bs. His career was now poised to take off, although he couldn't have guessed it at the time.

'The first time I drove the FW14 I was like a kid in Santa's grotto,' he remembers. 'It took some minutes for me to come down to earth. I said to myself, "Right, you're here to do a job, so stop dreaming that you're a budding World Champion. Just get in the car and do what you're told." In any case, my illusions didn't last very long. Everyone working with the car – engineers and mechanics alike – brought me very quickly back to reality.

'I was not being asked to drive the best car in Formula 1 [at that time] for my own personal pleasure. In fact, I was not asked to drive the car flat-out anyway. That wouldn't be of use to anyone. My job was to drive at a pace that allowed engineers to do their respective jobs, probably at about 95 per cent of the car's potential. A test session has nothing to do with the excitement or glamour of a Grand Prix. It's just a job to be done like many others. Even so, the work could be immensely fulfilling since I knew I was making my own individual contribution to the progress of the team. Each time a Williams-Renault won, it was my win in a way as well.'

Both Patrick Head and Adrian Newey would quickly come to appreciate Hill's very significant qualities in this role. Moreover, when the opportunity arose for him to race for the Brabham team in 1992, they did not stand in his way. This was a totally separate issue and Damon obviously had his career as a racer in his own right to consider. It would give him additional experience that could only be of benefit to his job as Williams test driver. Moreover, to put it bluntly, the Brabham-Judd BT60s, driven by Damon Hill or anybody else, were not going to pose any sort of threat to the Williams-Renaults!

The team that carried the Brabham name had enjoyed earlier contacts with the Hill dynasty two decades before. Founded by 1959 and '60 World Champion Jack Brabham in 1962, the canny Australian drove a Formula 1 car bearing his own name in a title round for the first time when he contested the German Grand Prix at Nurburgring, a race that marked Graham Hill's second win of the season for BRM.

Brabham won his third World Championship in 1966, thereby achieving the distinction of being the only man ever to do so at the wheel of a car bearing his own name. At the end of 1970 he retired from Formula 1 at the age of 44, selling the team to his long-time partner Ron Tauranac. Little more than a year later, Tauranac in turn sold it to Bernie Ecclestone, the South London car dealer who was to become Formula 1's most dynamic entrepreneur over the next two decades.

Graham Hill joined the Brabham team at the start of 1971, winning both the Silverstone International Trophy meeting in the works BT34 'lobster claw' and the prestigious Easter Monday Thruxton F2 international at the wheel of a BT36 fielded by Rondel Racing, the team established by former Brabham mechanics Ron Dennis and Neil Trundle. Dennis, of course, would continue to scale considerable heights of achievement in the 1980s and beyond in the role of Managing Director – and driving force – behind the McLaren International Formula 1 team.

Graham Hill, now struggling at the age of 43 to keep in touch with the new generation of youngsters, ended up being replaced in the Brabham team at the end of 1972 – the last points-scoring position of his career was a fifth in that year's Italian GP with the Brabham BT37. Yet Brabham would continue to thrive under Ecclestone's stewardship. From 1974 to 1985 the team was firmly established in the front rank, producing the machinery that carried Nelson Piquet to the first two of his three World Championship titles in 1981 and '83.

By 1990, however, the team was fading fast. It had been sold originally to Alfa Romeo, then to Swiss businessman Joachim Luhti and on to the Middlebridge Group in 1991, when Martin Brundle and Mark Blundell competed with the benefit of a works Yamaha engine deal. However, at the end of that season the Yamaha contract was switched to Jordan, leaving Brabham unable to finance the construction of new cars for 1992 and thus forced to re-work the previous year's BT60 chassis to accommodate leased Judd V10 engines.

The team began the season with Belgium's Eric van de Poele partnered with Italian girl Giovanna Amati in the driver line-up, but Amati was replaced after only three races and the vacant seat offered to Damon Hill. Thus it was against a backdrop of the team's acute financial problems that Hill, at 31 years old no spring chicken by the established standards of Formula 1 aspirants, faced the prospect of attempting to qualify for his first Grand Prix. He failed to make the cut in Spain, San Marino and then, finally, Monaco, where he missed making the field by 0.4 seconds on his father's old stamping ground.

Damon retired philosophically to his hotel at nearby Beaulieu. 'When I see Nigel Mansell and Riccardo Patrese passing me out on the circuit, I feel terrible,' he admitted wistfully in an oblique reference to his continuing role as the Williams team's test driver. 'But I like to think there's a bit of me in that Williams FW14B. I've helped with quite a few of its features . . .'

He continued plodding along, more in hope than any firm conviction that Brabham would experience any meaningful upsurge in their performance. He failed to qualify in Canada and at Magny-Cours. Finally, at Silverstone, 34 years after his father's maiden outing for Lotus in the British Grand Prix, Damon Hill put the family name back into the Formula 1 record book again.

The weekend had started on a disappointing note with Damon's engine failing and van de Poele's car springing a water leak. Although the Belgian driver's car was repaired, common sense dictated that Hill should use it for first qualifying, taking into account his experience at the Northamptonshire circuit. Hill was also benefiting from a slightly uprated Judd engine specification and a few aerodynamic modifications, finance for which had somehow been conjured up from within the ever-tightening Brabham team's budget.

Damon managed 26th fastest time to take last place in the provisional grid order on Friday night. Then the weather took a hand and the onset of steady rain prevented anyone from improving their times the following day. Hill was in.

Of course the race turned into a crushing Nigel Mansell benefit and the Williams team leader totally demolished the opposition on his way to his fifth victory in a World Championship qualifying round to be held on British soil. It seemed a minor detail at the time, but Damon at least finished. He took the chequered flag in 16th place, having been lapped for the fourth time shortly before the finish by the car he'd had such a hand in developing. It was also close enough for him to witness 'Mansell mania' at first hand as he cruised the slowing-down lap a few lengths behind the crowd's hero.

'I was right behind Mansell and thought, "We're not going to get out of here alive," because the place was just awash, just swarming with people,' he told *Autosport*. 'I nearly ran over six people. They didn't seem to know that there were other cars on the track; they just saw Nigel and leaped onto the circuit. It was very difficult. They were giving me a great big cheer, even though I was almost last.'

He also expressed the view that Mansell deserved the adulation: 'He's doing a fantastic job and I think that I'd be very pleased to drive that car in a Grand Prix, but I have to say I don't think that I'm capable of doing the sort of job that he's doing. I can't see how he can lose the World Championship now.'

Hill would only qualify the Brabham-Judd once more, in Hungary, before the team went bust. By the time Mansell stood up on race morning at Monza to announce his decision to quit Formula 1, once again Damon's sole employment was his role as Williams test driver. Now started the nerve-racking countdown to see who would take over the vacant Williams seat alongside Alain Prost for 1993.

Hill was obviously in with a chance. His close, well-established contacts

with both Williams and Renault clearly counted in his favour. Against that
had to be set his lack of Formula 1 racing experience, which amounted to
those two races in the arthritic Brabham. Martin Brundle and Mika
Hakkinen were considered and assessed for the job by Williams, then both
rejected for reasons that remain only partly explained to this day. Then the
Ligier team, which also used Renault engines, began to show an interest in
Hill's services for 1993.

However, Hill had powerful and influential supporters within Williams in
the form of both Patrick Head and Adrian Newey. Both men had become
increasingly impressed with the way in which Damon had developed while
operating under their wing.

'In his first year as a test driver, I don't think we were considering him as
a potential race driver,' said Head in an interview with *Autosport*. 'But from
about the middle of 1992 onwards, he started putting in performances which
were looking very impressive.

'He certainly became faster and I'm sure he developed while he was with
us. Within the first year he regarded himself as purely a test driver. But I
think by the middle of 1992, not only was he desperately trying to qualify
the Brabham, but he wasn't thinking of himself being a test driver for 1993.

'So I think it was a mental thing. Maybe his ideal was to drive for us, but
he also wanted to show that he was good enough to have a drive with somebody else. So I think he started pushing himself a lot harder.'

In early December 1992 all that commitment paid off. He was summoned
to Didcot by Frank Williams. Damon, by his own admission, drove down
the M4 with his heart in his mouth. The information waiting to be imparted
in Frank's spacious, airy office was as a dream come true.

Damon Hill was to partner Alain Prost in the Williams-Renault squad for
a full World Championship season in 1993. Another remarkable chapter of
achievement for the Hill family was about to be opened.

In many ways Hill could not have had a more sympathetic team-mate during
his freshman year. Prost might have been a man committed to ploughing his
own furrow, but he was also wedded to the philosophy of running no quicker than was absolutely necessary to win races. Not for him the Senna-style
need to crush his team-mates and the opposition. Alain had learned the old-
est adage of all from his time with Niki Lauda: namely that it's not possible
to win a race on the first corner, but it's certainly possible to lose it.

'It is a professional relationship,' explained Damon, referring to his partnership with Prost in the Williams squad. 'You don't have to be friends with
the people you work with, but you need to get on with them. You must create the right environment whereby you get the most out of yourself and
don't create any animosity – unless that's the way you want to work, but I
don't like working like that. I like Alain, but I wouldn't count him as a

friend of mine – I wouldn't presume to.

'Alain is under no obligation to help me. It's not his job. But if I want to know something, I'll ask him and he'll tell me. But I don't presume that he should help me in any way. Formula 1 is about helping yourself. If I get stuck, I'll ask his advice; I'd be stupid if I didn't try to learn from Alain Prost.

'It is difficult to say what he has specifically taught me; it's just the *way* of working which I've learned from him. His concentration over a race weekend is total and he barely spends a second without thinking what needs to be done, or what can be done, to win the race. That makes it very hard work; he puts in a lot of car work, mental concentration.

'That surprised me. Any moment you relax, you have to think, "Alain's not going to relax now." It's too late when you get into the car, you're five laps into the race and you think, "Oh bugger, I should have done that."'

The bottom line, of course, is that Damon Hill did remarkably well in his first full season for Williams. He may have blotted his copybook in his maiden Grand Prix at Kyalami, but made his first visit to the winner's rostrum with second place at Interlagos. It was only his fourth Formula 1 race.

As an interesting yardstick, even Ayrton Senna took five races before scoring a top three finishing position. Prost didn't manage it at all in his first year in the sport's most senior category, neither did Niki Lauda. Nigel Mansell had to wait until his sixth race before notching up third place in the 1981 Belgian Grand Prix. Jackie Stewart, however, managed second place to Jim Clark's Lotus 16 years earlier in the same race. It was only his third Grand Prix.

Add to this the fact that Hill led his fourth Grand Prix, qualified on pole position for his tenth race, then went on to win his 12th. But if you had to pinpoint the moment when Damon Hill really got the hang of front-line Formula 1, it was the 1993 French Grand Prix at Magny-Cours.

Prost had encountered trouble early on, spinning off during the Friday morning free practice session due to a programming problem with the software controlling his car's anti-lock braking system. As a result he was stranded out on the circuit and never quite pulled back the lost time. Perhaps crucially, when it came to Saturday's second qualifying session he discarded the ABS braking system, but Damon retained it. This may or may not have offered Damon a slight, but nonetheless crucial, edge. After a great battle Hill pipped his team-mate for pole position.

'I have made a big effort to concentrate and drive hard over the last few qualifying sessions,' he said, 'and I rather feel that I have at last come out from behind Alain's shadow.' There was no impertinence intended in such a remark, even though some found it, shall we say, a little premature. The thing was, nobody ever *quite* knew what Prost had got in hand.

Nevertheless, the event turned out to be a two-horse race between the two Williams-Renaults. Hill led all the way to lap 27 when he came in for a 7.1-second tyre change. Alain made a 6.94-second stop two laps later, just getting back onto the circuit ahead of Damon.

'As I came into the pit lane I found myself following Michael Andretti's McLaren,' explained Hill, 'and I got boxed in behind him again as we accelerated out. Then, as we came up to the end of the pit lane at full chat, one of the Saubers was waved out in front of us and there was very nearly a big accident.

'That delayed me enough that Alain was able to rejoin ahead of me. We had a good dice from then on. I gave some serious thought to making a second stop to change tyres, but the risk factor would have been too high. As we didn't have to push too hard, I stayed out.' At the finish Hill was 0.3 seconds behind Prost, rounding off the first Williams 1-2 of the 1993 season.

At Silverstone the following weekend Prost took command again, just pipping Hill for pole position after a great battle. 'That's what it should all be about,' enthused Patrick Head. 'Two guys getting really stuck in and giving each other a bit of stick.' But Damon again made the best start, surging into an immediate lead while Senna's McLaren-Ford boxed Alain into third place – and keeping him there for eight laps of extremely questionable manoeuvring.

As previously recounted Hill retired from the lead with a broken exhaust valve in his Renault engine. But Prost had signalled his true potential by trimming Damon's advantage from 8.2 to 1.3 seconds before the outcome of the race was so abruptly decided in his favour. 'In situations like this, you just feel empty,' noted Hill. 'It's only the second time this year that one of our engines has blown up, and both times it has cost me a race [the first had been at Barcelona]. I feel anger, a furious sense of disbelief. You do everything right and something stops you . . .'

Damon would again be frustrated at Hockenheim when his left rear tyre disintegrated. On the face of it Prost was handed another lucky win. But Alain had been ahead anyway before being on the receiving end of a specious stop-go penalty that dropped him back through the field. Only when Prost made the rare error of stalling on the grid at the Hungaroring was Hill able to speed to his maiden Grand Prix victory, unchallenged and alone.

Of course Hill was absolutely correct when he said that the real pressure had come from within. 'I kept telling myself it's not over until it's over,' he later reflected, 'and I thought of my Dad and what he might have said to me to keep my concentration up. And if you knew my Dad, you know that just imagining him talking to me was enough to make me concentrate!'

As we have seen, Damon would go on to win again at Spa and Monza, then qualified on pole position for the Portuguese Grand Prix at Estoril only to have problems starting his Williams and be late away on the parade lap, as a result of which he was forced to start from the back of the grid. He finished a storming third behind Michael Schumacher's Benetton-Ford and Prost.

'The external starter became dislodged on Damon's car,' explained Patrick Head, 'and we had some difficulty inserting it back into its aperture because of the failure of a little light bulb inside the shaft that is designed to help the mechanics locate the correct position.

'Eventually we got the engine fired up, but it was still quite cold and running rather erratically. In a couple more seconds it would have been revving freely, but Damon flicked it into first gear and it stalled. By the time we reset the automatic gear-change and fired it up for the second time, the rest of the field was setting out on its parade lap.'

Going into the final race of the season in Adelaide, Damon would be only two points ahead of Senna in the battle for second place in the Drivers' Championship behind Prost. However, in his last race for McLaren Ayrton proved to be absolutely in a class of his own, qualifying the Ford HB-engined MP4/8 fastest to take his only pole position of the season, then simply running away with the race once the starting signal was given.

Damon, despite a half-spin in the closing stages of the race, finished third behind Prost. That left him third in the final points reckoning with three wins in a Formula 1 career that had so far included only 18 races. It was worth reflecting that Ayrton Senna took 17 races before scoring his first victory!

The Williams team was unquestionably impressed. 'Damon's outstanding characteristic is a fierce determination,' observed Patrick Head. 'He seems to have great depths of personal resource. Instead of wringing his hands and gnashing his teeth when things go wrong, he will sit down, go through all the available data, work it out and go quicker the next day.

'At Adelaide, for example, he had some problems on the first day of practice, then bounced back to be the fastest car on the second day. That was very impressive, and he did it a number of times. I was also impressed by the fact that only if he was in desperation would he look over at Alain's chassis settings.

'Damon's ability level hasn't stabilised yet. He's learning, learning, learning . . . He's won three Grands Prix, which is more than Michael Schumacher, and in truth could have won twice that number. I really believe that's a pretty impressive performance in a first year.'

It was against this backdrop of solid achievement that Damon Hill entered his second full season of Grand Prix motor racing. It seemed that now he would be cast in the supporting role to the great Ayrton Senna. After 1 May 1994, however, everything was different. All the bets were off and Damon was faced with the prospect of picking up the pieces for the emotionally shattered Williams team.

It was at the '94 Monaco Grand Prix, the lowest point of Damon Hill's Formula 1 season, that the Grand Prix fraternity was suddenly shocked when the FIA announced draconian new changes to the technical regulations as a direct result of the Imola tragedy. Max Mosley may have hoped to resist the pressure for instant change, but within days of the ill-starred San Marino race he knew that he would have to give ground. What he announced, though, did not meet with the unanimous approval of the competing teams.

The FIA was clearly extremely sensitive about the way in which some segments of the media were attempting to forge a link between the decision to ban electronic driver aids at the start of the season and Senna's fatal accident in the Williams. In an effort to quash such speculation before it got out of hand, in the run-up to Monaco, the governing body issued the following *aide memoire* entitled 'Some questions and answers after Imola'. It is reproduced in total below, with the author's comments to each point duly italicised where appropriate.

Q: There have been some rule changes for 1994 – isn't this what has caused the problem?

A: No. The rule changes have merely removed certain devices which one or two teams had in 1992 and most had in 1993. The changes have restored conventional suspension technology. Ten of the twelve years without fatality have been without these electronic devices.
Substantially correct.

Q: But was this not done to 'improve the show'?

A: No. The changes were to eliminate the tendency for computers to take the place of drivers and to reduce the gap between the rich teams which had access to the technology, and poor teams, some of which did not. It is absurd to suggest that a driver of Senna's ability would be troubled when less skilful drivers managed perfectly well without these devices.
The second sentence was unquestionably accurate. But the rationale behind the first was vigorously disputed by many leading teams.

Q: But removing active suspension must make the car more difficult to drive and hence more dangerous?

A: A badly set-up car on conventional suspension is difficult to drive, but this is an everyday problem known to all racing drivers, even beginners. It is not dangerous. By contrast, drivers were constantly complaining that a malfunctioning active system could be extremely dangerous and unpredictable.

There are many examples of this, of which the most obvious was the Berger/Warwick incident at Estoril. (In the previous year's Portuguese GP, Berger had lost control of his Ferrari over a bump as he exited the pits following a tyre stop and speared broadside across the start/finish straight, only just being missed by Warwick's Footwork which was approaching at 190 mph. The incident was attributed to a glitch in the Ferrari's active suspension system.)
These comments were regarded by some teams as the FIA using selective hindsight to justify its actions.

Q: But drivers including Senna were against removing electronic aids?

A: Not so. Indeed Senna led the campaign against them. He said in an interview with *The Times* (London) that he wanted to drive his car himself, and not have it driven by computers. The removal of driver aids was supported by drivers in innumerable interviews.
Broadly correct.

Q: But Senna said he had problems with his car?

A: Yes, conventional problems, particular to his car. Such problems were not shared by other cars and had nothing to do with electronic aids.
Correct. The Williams FW16's early season handling problems were due to lack of testing and the team's need to reacquaint itself with conventional suspension after two years of active technology.

Q: So you think none of the accidents had anything to do with the rule changes?

A: Nothing whatever. The reasons for four of the five accidents are known with reasonable certainty and none had anything to do with electronic aids or active suspension. The precise reasons for Senna's crash are not yet known, but all the cars (including his) were generating over 2.5 g in the relevant corner at a speed when the available cornering force is over 4 g. With nearly 40 per cent of the cornering power unused, a driver of Senna's ability would not need any help, electronic or otherwise, to get round the corner.
Substantially correct.

Q: Why was no shock-absorbing barrier, such as tyres, placed in front of the wall?

A: Because the leading drivers asked us not to. After a number of accidents at that spot without significant injury, the leading drivers and the FIA experts felt that a glancing blow was likely (as had happened before) and that tyres would be dangerous. Whenever leading drivers feel it may be helpful, tyres are installed. This happened at the recent Pacific GP in Japan and on many other occasions. There is now a strong suspicion that Senna was struck by part of the car and that, but for this misfortune, he would have walked away as he had done from many more serious accidents. Piquet's accident (in 1987) at this point was with a more powerful car but without serious injury.
Correct.

Q: Surely it is wrong for drivers to race between concrete walls?

A: Not necessarily. Everything depends on the likely angle of incidence should the car hit the wall. If this is shallow, experience has shown that the car suffers damage but spins harmlessly down the track, dissipating its energy slowly. Only if the angle of incidence is steep does a concrete wall become dangerous. Both the drivers and the FIA were happy with the arrangements at Imola. All oval racing in the United States depends on this principle.

Q: Did the drivers not complain about the Imola circuit before the Grand Prix?

A: No. During testing, some weeks before the race, Senna asked for some work to the road surface at Tamburello. This was done. He then went out and broke the lap record and expressed himself entirely satisfied. A major test was booked for most of the teams after the race. This would not have been done had drivers or teams thought the circuit unsafe.

Q: Why was the race not cancelled after Senna's accident?

A: It is usually impossible to know the extent of someone's injuries until they have had extensive tests in hospital. This would mean either cancelling a race, even if a driver had only minor injuries, or waiting hours for a full report from the hospital before restarting. For this reason, it has never been the practice to cancel a race if a driver is hurt. Perhaps this should change, but officials on the spot had to follow current practice.

Not strictly the case. Professor Watkins, the FIA Medical Delegate, knew that Senna was gravely injured within minutes of arriving at the accident scene. The FIA was also a little shaky on the subject of contemporary motor racing history. The 1975 Spanish Grand Prix was stopped and not restarted following an accident to the German driver Rolf Stommelen. The 1989 Portuguese GP was stopped and not restarted after Aguri Suzuki was injured. The 1987 Austrian GP was stopped twice and restarted. The 1984 British GP was stopped, and the same race two years later was also flagged after a lap, later to be restarted. So there were precedents.

Q: But Senna was dead.

A: No, he was not. He received extensive medical treatment from a large team of doctors, nurses and technicians for several hours. He died at 6.40 pm, long after the race finished. As the director of Bologna Hospital, Dr Giuseppe Guerra, has pointed out, there would have been little point in all this effort had there been no hope.

Q: Was not Ratzenberger dead on the spot, but taken to hospital to avoid problems at the circuit?

A: No. He was in a serious condition. Resuscitation techniques were used to keep him alive pending full tests in hospital. This is standard procedure if the necessary expert medical help is available. Under Italian law the place of death is not relevant, it is the place of the accident which matters. It would have made no difference if he had died on the circuit.

Q: Why was the race not stopped after the pit lane accident?

A: Because if the race had been stopped, there would have been a great confusion, with cars trying to get into the pits followed by thousands of fans. As soon as the incident happened, a pre-arranged plan for a pit emergency was put in place with yellow flags at the pit entrance. This ensured that any driver seeking to enter the pits knew there was an emergency and would drive with extreme care. In this way the emergency services could attend the injured, safe in the knowledge that, with the race continuing, they would not be disturbed by cars or public. If necessary, they could also reach a hospital more quickly before the traffic jam.

Q: What are you going to do to make cars safer?

A: We are constantly working on this, but you must understand that none of the measures which have so far been proposed would have saved either Senna or Ratzenberger. A substantial reduction in engine power and/or aerodynamic downforce would make almost no difference to the speed of the cars at the relevant parts of the Imola circuit. This is because the cars are so far below their limits in Tamburello. With less power, the teams would run less wing (for more speed). If we were to compel the cars to run minimal wing (by drastically curtailing permissible wings) we would simply increase the speed (for a given power) at these points. Loss of grip and loss of power would produce slower lap times, but not lower speeds at the points where the accidents happened.

Q: So you are saying that nothing can be done?

A: Not at all. The cars are too fast and we need to slow them down. But it is very important to understand that any measures to slow the cars, however extreme, would have had only a marginal effect where these accidents happened. Drastic changes to the cars of the kind being advocated by some observers would not have saved either driver. Nevertheless, it is necessary to slow the cars because there are places on a number of other circuits where they would be safer as a result. It is for this reason that further measures to slow the cars were voted last year for 1995. We are now looking at additional changes and at introducing the 1995 changes this season.

Q: Should you not listen to the drivers?

A: We do, and some of them give a lot of input. A recent example is the tyre walls at the Pacific Grand Prix in Japan. However, at present there are no outstanding requests from drivers. Still less has any safety measure been refused. Everyone is seeking to improve safety, but no one – driver, engineer or doctor – has a magic solution.

Q: Are you saying that nothing can be learned from the tragedies at Imola?

A: No. We can probably learn a great deal once we have all the facts. For example, we may be able to bring in changes which make it less likely that the driver will be hit by a wheel or suspension in an accident. We may be able to make it less likely that a critical part of the car will be damaged (and subsequently fail) if a driver goes slightly off the track. Serious work on these and other points can begin as soon as we have all the facts from the teams and from the Italian enquiry.

Q: Is not Formula 1 governed by money alone and not by sporting and safety considerations?

A: This allegation is very easy to make and wholly untrue. First, it is the high quality of our sport which generates money in Formula 1. A good sporting contest attracts the public. Secondly, accidents resulting in injury are very damaging to F1, both economically and from a sporting point of view. In general, if you look after the sport and its safety, the money looks after itself. Following this principle has made the more successful teams and drivers rich. There is nothing wrong with this. But even the richest teams and drivers recognise that without safety there will be no sport, and without the sport, no money. The FIA's commercial arrangements are very similar to those of the International Olympic Committee.

Q: What about refuelling?

A: This was brought in at the unanimous request of the teams to improve the sporting contest by enabling the cars to race for the entire Grand Prix with a strategy instead of having to preserve tyres and run relatively slowly on full tanks at the beginning. The slight increase in danger from a fire in the pits is balanced by the significant decrease in danger from fire now that the cars can refuel and no longer have to carry over 200 litres from the start of a race. If a car crashes carrying 200 litres instead of 60 or 70, the crash energy and fire risk are much higher.

A very questionable piece of reasoning. The very fact that the cars now have to refuel transformed the Grands Prix into a succession of sprint races between pit stops, completely removing any strategy from the driver, at least. Excellent contemporary standards of car construction have made fire risk minimal, even with a full fuel load. Lorenzo Bandini, it should be remembered, suffered fatal burns in the 1967 Monaco Grand Prix when he crashed carrying an estimated 12 gallons of fuel and with only 18 of the race's 100 laps left to run.

Q: What about the pit lane?

A: For several years we have had tyre stops. The danger has always been a collision or car failure in the pit lane. Despite many requests, the teams have failed to come up with proposals and the FIA have had to take the initiative. This is not a new problem, but it must now be solved.

Q: You have stopped Formula 1 cars using ABS brakes and traction control and you have made them run on narrower tyres. All of these changes reduce grip and road holding. Surely this must make them more dangerous?

A: Quite the reverse. With a road car, provided you more or less keep to the speed limits, the more grip you have the safer you are. If, however, each time your car was improved you were to use the extra grip to go faster, you would increase the danger. Apart from the difficulty of avoiding an accident at high speed, the energy of a car goes up as the square of its speed.

Double the speed and you quadruple the energy. This, in turn, quadruples the violence of the crash. With racing cars, every improvement in grip is used by the drivers to the maximum, to go faster. As a result, reducing grip is an effective way to reduce speed and increase safety. Hence the elimination of ABS and traction control. Narrow tyres and constant attempts to limit aerodynamic downforce also help. The more grip a racing car has, the faster it goes through the corners and the greater the danger to the driver.

Q: What will you do if there is another serious accident in the near future?

A: Although great advances have been made in safety, and serious accidents are now very rare, another one may happen at any moment. The only certainty is that it is far less likely than 20 years ago. People look back to the 1950s and '60s as a sort of golden age of motor sport. In fact the casualties were appalling. If governments had made the same progress in the prevention of death and injury on the roads as motor sport has on the race tracks, many thousands of lives would have been saved. But for all the progress we have made, we still can give no guarantees. It would be tragic if, despite our best efforts, the worst should happen again, but it will never be impossible.

Although keenly aware of the mounting pressure from outside motor racing for something to be seen to be done, Mosley nevertheless remained anxious to calm the situation and ensure that no precipitate action was taken on changing the technical regulations. But Grand Prix racing was not yet finished with disaster. In Thursday morning's free practice session at Monaco, Karl Wendlinger lost control of his Sauber-Mercedes under braking for the waterfront chicane and slammed sideways into the protective barrier.

Although the car was only lightly damaged, the Austrian sustained severe cranial contusions and was quickly removed to hospital in Nice where he remained in a critical condition with swelling of the brain for some time. In fact, Wendlinger would remain in a coma for 19 days, thankfully thereafter continuing to make a complete recovery in time to resume his Formula 1 career in 1995.

In the immediate aftermath of the accident, however, pressure intensified for Mosley to be seen to do something – anything – to allay concerns about Formula 1 safety. In the heat of the moment the steadying voices, which pointed out that there was no common thread linking the five accidents that had taken place across the last two races, went unheard. Motor racing's dramatically high television profile was now working against its own interests.

On Friday morning, traditionally a free day at Monaco, Mosley stunned the Formula 1 fraternity by convening a press conference to announce a whole host of technical changes to be phased in over the next few races. Aerodynamic downforce would be slashed in an effort to reduce cornering speeds, and longer-term proposals to trim back engine power were also advanced.

Although changes in the technical regulations theoretically required unanimous agreement from the competing teams under the terms of the Concorde Agreement, Mosley now invoked the provision that permitted the governing body to implement immediate changes on emergency grounds of safety.

'Unfortunately what we wish to put forward does not meet with everyone's approval,' said the FIA President. 'We did not have the agreement of everyone concerned, so we're going to have to do it despite the Concorde Agreement. The time has come, because of the gravity of the situation and the force of public opinion, to push aside such considerations and simply do what is right in the general interests of the sport.'

As from the next race, the Spanish Grand Prix, all teams would be required to reduce the size of their rear diffusers – the aerodynamic ramps under the tail end of the car – raise the front wings by 10 mm and remove any part of the front wing end plate protruding behind the leading edge of the front wheels. The FIA contended that this would yield an immediate 15 per cent reduction in downforce.

As from the Canadian Grand Prix a fortnight later, increased lateral cockpit protection would be demanded in addition to strengthened front suspension components to guard against the possibility of drivers being struck on the head by flying pieces. This was a direct and very specific response to Senna's post mortem, which had established the cause of death as the Williams driver's helmet being punctured by a piece of flying suspension ripped off as the FW16 impacted with the vertical concrete wall. In order to accommodate these changes, the Formula 1 minimum weight limit would be raised by 25 kg.

The ram effect of engine air boxes would also be eliminated and the use of strictly regulated pump fuel made mandatory. Yet the most dramatic decree concerned the introduction of the 50 mm 'stepped undertray' regulations, planned for 1995, being brought forward by six months in time for the '94 German Grand Prix. Although many team owners remained tactfully discreet in their comments on this development, the timing of Mosley's bombshell took them by surprise. Only the previous afternoon had the designers met with the FIA, and the governing body's unilateral announcement did not, in some people's minds, bear much relation to what had been discussed barely 24 hours earlier.

'We're being presented with a *fait accompli*,' shrugged Ferrari R&D Director John Barnard, 'and I doubt the measures would have been announced now had it not been for Wendlinger's accident. It's only a week or so since Max Mosley emphasised the need to avoid a knee-jerk reaction to the events at Imola. Now he has undermined that statement.' Many months later, Mosley would concede that Wendlinger's accident was indeed a further unwelcome development, under pressure from which he felt he had no alternative but to move.

Patrick Head kept his counsel, allowing Adrian Newey to sum up the Williams team's attitude towards the whole affair: 'It's not just a question of whether you're going to reduce downforce considerably,' he said. 'That would be good as long as it's coupled with a reduction in horsepower – but on its own it would be a bad thing. I'd be a little wary if we go to Spain with the regulations as they are being proposed.'

However, Jordan's Chief Engineer Gary Anderson was less diplomatic, and the tone of his reaction perhaps most accurately reflected what many of his colleagues were thinking, but declined to say: 'It was right to do something,' he explained. 'but it was wrong to do what they're doing. I think the proposed rule changes for Germany are absurd and hopefully somebody will realise what we're trying to do before they kill a few more people.

'If we started now, we could be there. But we'd have to work flat out and we wouldn't be building a car which we understood. If you go to a circuit with so much 200 mph running and don't really understand the car, it's not a very good position to be in.'

Privately Mosley understood the problems. Yet he had to move, even though imposing rushed technical changes on competitors in the middle of a season favoured the better-financed teams like Williams. They had the resources and personnel required to deploy on re-designing the cars. The smaller, financially strapped teams – the ones that Mosley had originally sought to help by banning electronic driver aids – did not. And it would show.

Yet questions about the safety of international motorsport were starting to be asked at governmental level, and Mosley had noted the number of political journalists who suddenly applied for media accreditation at Monaco. He had to head off public opinion, and rule changes were the only panacea instantly available.

More aggravation followed in the immediate run-up to the Barcelona race after Benetton boss Flavio Briatore penned a stormy letter to Max Mosley – then made the tactical error of circulating it to the media. In a nutshell his message was that Benetton couldn't guarantee the safety and security of its own cars after the hasty re-design necessary to conform with the changes in the FIA's technical regulations. Briatore was then curtly asked to think again, the FIA Technical Delegate making it clear that neither Michael Schumacher nor J. J. Lehto would be permitted to compete unless the team could guarantee that the cars were OK. Benetton modified its stance and gave the necessary undertakings.

However, that didn't prevent the leading teams from boycotting Friday morning's free practice session while their representatives tried to thrash out an understanding with Mosley during a meeting in the Williams motorhome that, by all contemporary accounts, involved some pretty direct talking from both sides.

Mosley recalled nine months later, 'I was in a peace-making mode, particularly after Imola, so I went to see them and really didn't agree anything. They explained they thought the changes were all too much, and I explained – probably for the tenth time – that the FIA really didn't care what the technical changes to the cars were, as long as they slowed the cars down – and were seen to slow them down – so that public opinion was satisfied.

'In retrospect, I shouldn't have gone to the meeting. I should have said, "We'll talk about it next week." But I remember it being a friendly meeting and we all said we would say [to the media] that we had a frank exchange of views.'

That was emphatically not how some team principals characterised it, however, and the word went round that Mosley was relinquishing most of the FIA's power in the Formula 1 rule-making process; would not come to any more races, and the Formula 1 Technical Working Group would be allowed to get on with it.

However, after Max returned to London and read such fanciful speculation in the following morning's *Sunday Times* he quickly moved to disabuse everybody concerned of this particular notion.

In the meantime, what became crystal clear from the outset at Barcelona was that the Benetton B194 remained the car to beat, rule changes or not. In the Williams camp Damon Hill was making steady progress with the FW16's chassis settings, and was partnered at this race by Formula 1 debutant David Coulthard, the 23-year-old Scot who had finished runner-up to Rubens Barrichello in the 1992 British F3 Championship and had gone on to contest the International F3000 series the following year.

Hailing from Twynholm, a village near Kirkcudbright, Coulthard was brought up surrounded by machinery. His father Duncan was a successful haulage contractor who encouraged his early competition career in kart racing and helped bankroll his progress all the way through to F3 and F3000 when he drove for the Milton Keynes-based Paul Stewart Racing team and benefited from the tutelage of triple World Champion Jackie Stewart.

'Above all David is a good racer,' said Jackie to Hugh McIlvanney of the *Sunday Times* towards the end of 1994. 'Sometimes you get good drivers, sometimes guys with plenty of natural talent and good intelligence, but unless they are genuine racers those other assets won't be enough in the end. There are people who can drive very well, but don't have the spark which, for example, in the first three laps of a race will enable them to carve their way up through the field, up through the traffic.

'If David has not qualified particularly well, he has the ability to improve his position very quickly after leaving the grid, to take advantage of the tentativeness of other drivers on the first lap. Great natural talent doesn't always have that positive edge. David has it. He still has much to prove about himself but, on what we have seen so far, he has every chance of becoming a serious player in Grand Prix racing.'

Adrian Newey had already been impressed by Coulthard's similarity to Hill in the role of test driver. Both men, noted the Williams designer, had the ability to run consistently quickly without forgetting to carry out any in-car adjustments that might be required of them during the course of a run. He felt that the degree of focus and restraint, key qualities that had helped Damon to make such a worthwhile contribution to the team's development programme, were also evident in this latest new boy.

Hill eventually wound up second on the grid behind Schumacher. 'I think that the FW16 is a good car,' he said, as if to boost his own confidence. 'In first qualifying it felt a bit like walking a tightrope, but it was certainly a lot better on Saturday. So I think we're making ground on the Benettons.'

Coulthard, meanwhile, didn't drive the FW16 until Friday morning practice at Barcelona, as a scheduled acclimatisation run at the Jerez circuit, scheduled for the previous Tuesday, had been rained off. But the young Scot shouldered the pressure of front-line Formula 1 with absolutely no problems, qualifying a very respectable ninth for his maiden Grand Prix outing.

Although you wouldn't have noticed it from his outward demeanour, Hill was under quite considerable pressure at Barcelona. The Renault Sport management was doing a very poor job when it came to demonstrating much in the way of confidence in his role as team leader, and, very much behind the scenes, preliminary contacts had been made with Nigel Mansell to see whether he would be available for a restricted programme of Formula 1 races during the course of the season.

At the start Hill duly ran second behind Schumacher, just ahead of Mika Hakkinen's McLaren-Peugeot and Jean Alesi's Ferrari, while Coulthard made a simply storming start, making up three places on the opening lap to come through sixth behind Lehto's Benetton. In the early stages it didn't seem as though Damon could do much about Schumacher, who moved 6.5 seconds ahead by the end of the fourth lap. Moreover, Hill had opted for a strategy encompassing two refuelling stops, and was under pressure from Hakkinen who, planning to stop three times, was benefiting from a lighter fuel load in the opening phase of the race.

By the time Schumacher had made his first refuelling stop on lap 22, Coulthard was already in trouble. On lap 17 he had come into the pits, and an electrical problem twice caused his engine to stall at low revs. He resumed in a distant 20th place and hauled back to 12th by lap 32 when he was called into the pits again and his car retired after Williams engineers discerned from the telemetry readings that the electronic problem was now affecting the car's semi-automatic gear-change system. It was better to be safe than sorry under the circumstances.

Coulthard was understandably disappointed. 'I felt relaxed and competitive,' he said, 'and I thought I might finish my first Grand Prix in the points. It was comfortable learning how they run in Formula 1.'

Just when it looked as though the best Damon could hope for was second place, Schumacher began to show signs of slowing up. The Benetton's transmission had stuck in fifth gear and the engineers radioed to him that he would just have to live with the problem. There was nothing he could do.

At the end of lap 20 Hill made his first refuelling stop and Hakkinen went ahead from lap 22 after Schumacher stopped for the first time. When the McLaren came in at the end of lap 31, Damon took the lead for the first time, briefly dropping to third from lap 41 to 46 after making his second refuelling stop. Thereafter he went back into the lead, reeling off the laps to win by just over 24 seconds from Schumacher's hobbled Benetton. Psychologically it was just the boost that he and the Williams team needed.

'This is better than any of the wins last year, much harder under the circumstances,' he said jubilantly. 'In the opening stages Mika was giving me pressure and I lost a bit of time in traffic when I came into the pits. It was difficult to know what fuel load he was running, and that makes it difficult to know how to drive if you're not on the same footing as the next guy!'

Coulthard would continue to partner Hill at Montreal, but by the time the teams arrived in Canada rumours of Mansell's impending return to the Williams ranks were running at full blast. The week after the Indianapolis 500, during which he'd been eliminated by novice Dennis Vitolo, Mansell competed in the Milwaukee Indycar race where representatives of Renault, Elf and Rothmans made a special trip to meet him in company with Williams team director Richard West.

Students of motor racing semantics drew their own conclusions about what might be going through Mansell's mind from his comments in the wake of the Indy 500, which he used to slam both the race organisers and the hapless Vitolo. He delivered his remarks with all the force of a man who had a fair idea that he would not be contesting America's most famous motor race again.

'I've got to say that this is the most disgraceful display I've ever witnessed,' he said in reference to Vitolo's driving. 'Everyone in Formula 1 has to have a Super Licence and you have to have won races or a championship. To have people just hire cars for a race with the magnitude of Indianapolis, it's a disgrace for the body which allows it.'

In fact, Hill and Coulthard went into the Canadian Grand Prix knowing that Mansell was almost certainly returning for the French GP at Magny-Cours three weeks later. This may have seemed like something of a vote of no confidence in Damon, but it left Coulthard in a potentially desperate situation.

The young Scot had passed up the opportunity to drive a Formula 3000 car at Pau on the weekend of the Spanish Grand Prix, but still owed around £30,000 to the team concerned. In addition he was in debt to the tune of around £250,000 to Paul Stewart Racing for finance owing on his 1993 F3000 programme. So he needed to make his mark as a Grand Prix driver as a matter of some urgency. He was also being paid only £5,000 per race by Williams, who already had long-term options on his services. With that in mind, Mansell's reappearance on the scene was something he very definitely could do without.

During qualifying at Montreal the Scot put Hill under considerable pressure. As was becoming usual, Schumacher qualified his Benetton on pole position ahead of the much-improved Ferraris of Jean Alesi and Gerhard Berger. Damon squeezed onto the second row by 0.1 second from Coulthard, still unhappy with the knife-edge handling of the Williams FW16.

'We're not making a big breakthrough,' he confirmed. 'In fact, you begin to wonder whether that's possible. We're not producing the lap times, but I certainly feel a lot more confident than I did before Barcelona.'

Hill's mood was not improved when Coulthard lived up to his fast-starting reputation and jostled ahead to take an immediate fourth place on the opening lap. Once safely ensconced behind the Ferrari, David stayed there until cramp in his right foot caused his driving to become a little ragged, much to the detriment of his tyre wear and lap times. Williams eventually signalled that he should let Hill past, allowing Damon to get down to the serious business of chasing Berger, who was now in second place.

'I understand the competitive nature of Formula 1 and the fact that there's no love lost between team-mates,' said Hill afterwards by way of mild admonishment, 'but it is, after all, supposed to be a team sport. I was getting a bit cheesed off sitting behind him, because I knew I could go quicker, but even if I'd have passed him earlier I don't believe I could have caught Michael.' In the end Hill finished second to Schumacher and ahead of Berger.

There was inevitably a great deal of anticipation and speculation surrounding Mansell's return to the Williams squad. Immediately after contesting the Indycar race at Portland, Oregon, on 26 July, the '92 World Champion flew back across the Atlantic for a day's intensive testing at Brands Hatch before joining the Williams team at Magny-Cours. On the face of it this rather deflected the attention from Hill's robust efforts to mount a World Championship challenge. In reality, many Formula 1 insiders believed that the next fortnight turned out to be the making of Damon as an Formula 1 front-liner.

For second qualifying in France, Renault produced two examples of its new high-revving RS6B V10, which the team would use only in the quest for pole position. As things transpired Schumacher had a few off-course excursions and the battle for fastest time on the grid developed into an exclusive Williams affair. Nigel was frustrated slightly when he lost one of his weekend's allocation of seven sets of tyres, one of which picked up a deep cut. That left him one short of three fresh sets for second qualifying, while Hill had his intact.

Mansell went ahead with a 1 minute 16.987 second lap only 11 minutes into the final session. After the session was briefly interrupted by a red flag period to retrieve Jos Verstappen's damaged Benetton, which had slammed into the pit wall almost at Hill's feet, Damon went out to stop the clocks at 1 minute 16.609 seconds. Then Mansell did 1 minute 16.359 seconds before Hill settled the matter for good with a 1 minute 16.282 seconds. He had forced his way through a crucial psychological barrier.

Hill, however, had no worries about Mansell's return from a pure comparative performance viewpoint, although he hinted at private worries that Williams and Renault might be about to ease up on their commitment to the Drivers' Championship – a realistic concern bearing in mind the fact that Renault had pledged itself to winning the Constructors' title in the wake of Senna's death at Imola. Under the circumstances it would have been surprising had Damon not been slightly concerned.

'A lot has happened this year which has been difficult to comprehend and it requires quite a while to consider the implications,' said Hill thoughtfully after first qualifying in France. 'Nigel Mansell coming to the team I view as a positive, another opportunity to compare myself against another great driver.

'[But] I would be very disappointed if Williams and Renault were to quit on the Drivers' Championship. I've done a lot more miles [than Mansell] and Nigel is bound to feel a little more circumspect, but, having said that, nine times out of ten if a driver gets in a car they're not familiar with, they are on the pace straight away if they are any good.

'Ayrton Senna was the first driver at Williams, but I'm now second in the Championship and I don't know if I am the first driver at Williams. Nigel is superior to me in terms of experience, and the fact that he's won a World Championship, so it would be difficult to say I'm number one in the team in this situation, but we're being given equal equipment – and I feel strongly that my championship hopes should be given serious priority.'

Even so, one could detect that Hill felt ever so slightly wary about the situation. 'Put it this way,' he said. 'I feel it's not really my place to tell the team how to do their business. I've played my hand, saying what I said, which is that if we're going to go ahead and win the championship, then I think it should best be done by putting everything behind the resources you have and beating Benetton by hard work, but the business of Formula 1 is more than just driving racing cars – it's marketing, as much as anything.

'That's not to say I think Nigel can't offer a lot. I understand that. But I feel I could get the results this season, now I have an opportunity to prove myself. It [success] doesn't come quickly. Nigel was driving a number of seasons before he won a race. He has a wealth of experience, is a World Champion, and is very valuable to any team.'

Yet did Damon regard Nigel as something of a monkey on his back from the psychological standpoint? 'You could look at it like that,' he conceded, 'but you could also say that I wouldn't be driving for Williams if it wasn't for Nigel, for the fact that he retired [in 1992] at the right time for me to be in the right place, and that, in many ways, he has been in the vanguard of British drivers in terms of producing interest in the sport. He has an enormous following, so I wouldn't say he's been a monkey on my back.'

However, Hill did also hint that he wished Williams would show more acknowledgement of his technical input when it came to suggesting modifications to the FW16. 'Things only really move forward if drivers insist on certain things being done,' he explained, 'and, of course, Ayrton was the guy to get things moving, so we're missing that factor.

'I'm not saying that they don't listen to me, but they were more inclined to listen to Ayrton Senna, naturally, and were more inclined to act on it. And that's not something I've managed yet.'

Come the French Grand Prix race, Hill's Williams was almost a match for Schumacher's Benetton in the early stage, the German star scorching through to take an immediate lead from the second row of the grid with an alacrity that rang warning bells in the minds of those uncharitable enough to continue in the belief that perhaps the Ford-engined car might not be totally legal. However, in stopping to refuel three times to Hill's twice, Schumacher eked out a decisive 12-second advantage at the chequered flag. 'No question, they beat us with a better strategy,' conceded Damon.

Mansell, meanwhile, fought a battle against unpredictable handling from the start, perhaps unwisely having made adjustments to his chassis set-up after the race-morning warm-up. He ran third in the opening phase, grappling with excessive oversteer, and, at his first fuel stop, asked for differently pressured tyres to be fitted and the tail flaps to be removed from the nose wings in an effort to improve the situation.

Thereafter Mansell found himself briefly back in sixth place, now coping with too much understeer. It wasn't long before he pitted again for fresh tyres, without bothering to refuel, a strategy that went some way towards rectifying the handling imbalance, but not completely. While he was running, however, Nigel seemed to have luck on his side.

He profited from a collision between Jean Alesi's Ferrari and the Jordan of Rubens Barrichello to pick up a couple of places after his second tyre stop dropped him back to fifth, then just managed to slip ahead of Berger's Ferrari on lap 45 as the Austrian emerged from the pits. However, Nigel's third place lasted barely two corners before his Williams rolled to a halt with the failure of its gearbox hydraulic pump drive. He was already in his private jet, heading back to England, before the race had finished.

The following Thursday, from the moment when Damon Hill strode into the team's pit-lane garage at Silverstone, Adrian Newey detected a transformation in his attitude. 'Nigel's biggest contribution at Magny-Cours was that he gave the team a morale-boost,' he remembers. 'Damon thought, "I'm blowed if I'm going to be blown off by Nigel," and this had the effect of kick-starting the programme again.'

Patrick Head agreed. 'I do think Mansell's presence at Magny-Cours helped in that, while I don't think for one moment that he pinpointed any particular problems with the car, his views were similar to Damon's at a time when I think Damon was wondering whether it was the car, or him or whatever.'

Coulthard was back at the wheel of the second Williams-Renault for Silverstone, where Damon's weekend kicked off with a heart-stopping moment in the first free practice session when his FW16 skittered to a halt in the middle of the circuit at Becketts, its front suspension arms flailing wildly above the monocoque.

Detailed examination revealed that the rearward legs of the top wishbones had only been done up finger-tight, so the moment Hill went onto the brakes, they twisted upwards and the car shuddered to a halt. This was just what Damon didn't need. With his race car stranded out on the circuit and the 1994 regulations forbidding the use of a spare car, he was forced to sit out the first free practice session. It wasn't quite the way he had been hoping to kick off a race weekend on his home turf.

Stunned with disbelief, he climbed out to begin the long walk back to the paddock. By coincidence, his path converged on Patrick Head who was also just strolling into the paddock, his arrival having been delayed by heavy traffic on the local roads. Meeting a pumped-up Damon in such embarrassing circumstances to be informed of such an unlikely technical glitch was also hardly calculated to improve the Williams team's Technical Director's mood.

However, with admirable confidence and loyalty, Hill moved quickly to reassert his confidence in the Williams team's high standards of operational efficiency. 'I was shocked, and also saddened as well,' he admitted, 'because it's not the sort of thing you expect to have happen. I know it's not good for the team to have something like this happen, and it's certainly not good for the confidence of the driver.

'Although this was a bit of a glitch, I've done a lot of miles for Williams and have absolute 100 per cent confidence in the team and their workmanship. And I think I proved my belief in everybody at Williams by getting in and going as fast as I did immediately afterwards.'

Damon was referring to his fourth fastest time in first qualifying, a session in which he found himself over-driving slightly in an attempt to make up for the ground lost during the morning. He finished the day confident that he could make the front row the following day. Coulthard, meanwhile, remained remarkably phlegmatic in the aftermath of a 170 mph spin at the Bridge right-hander.

'I went into Bridge almost flat out,' explained the Scot, 'but when I hit the bumps the car sat down at the rear, dug in at the front, and I was going backwards almost before I realised I'd got it wrong. I had time to think that I was going to end up pretty sore, but thankfully I didn't hit anything. It's an uncomfortable feeling when you're going backwards, not in control of the car. It all happened so quickly that I thought "What went wrong?" rather than "Am I scared?"'

On Saturday Damon was embroiled in a four-way fight for pole with Schumacher and the two Ferraris. For a while it looked as though Berger might get the job done for Maranello, but the Austrian inexplicably slid into the retaining wall as he accelerated out of the pit for his final run, damaging the left front wheel rim so badly that the tyre deflated before he could make it back to the pits. So it was down to Schumacher versus Hill at the end of the day, and Damon got the job done superbly, offering further evidence of a psychological breakthrough after Magny-Cours.

'Nigel Mansell claimed that being on your home ground lifts you,' said Hill, 'and it's worth a second a lap. I don't think he's far wrong. Believe me, it was very, very emotional in the car. My heart was in my mouth watching the others – although not as much as when I was out on my best lap.'

Damon also chose this weekend to launch a further robust defence of his position within the Williams team. For once he cast aside his familiar diplomatic tone to speak out on race morning at Silverstone.

'Last weekend I beat Nigel Mansell for pole position at the French Grand Prix, and the year before I beat Alain Prost to it,' he reminded his audience. 'Last Sunday I led the race and came closer to beating Schumacher than anyone, other than Ayrton Senna, has come to beating him all year.

'Yet all I seem to read is that my bloody job is in jeopardy – and it is not in jeopardy. I am second in the World Championship. [But] I don't get any credit for being polite and diplomatic, so I'm to ditch that tack because it's not getting me anywhere.

'I am fighting a battle here with a car which is clearly not as good as the Schumacher-Benetton combination. I need the 100 per cent backing of Williams to do the job properly and I have asked for it. After last weekend I should think I've proved I'm getting the best out of the equipment.

'It has taken me ten years to get to this position in Formula 1 and I am not going to relinquish it or give it up without a serious fight.'

Whether Damon was simply hyping himself up for a massive effort on home ground was not clear. Yet Williams's response to this outburst was so cool as to be almost interpreted as equivocal.

'I'm not quite certain what Damon means by this,' said Frank Williams, knowing full well in reality. 'Of course we support Damon. His pole position here at Silverstone was absolutely outstanding. Just when you are thinking that he has reached a certain level, he moves forward to find a new one. He was most impressive.'

Yet it was a remark by Renault Sport's Patrick Faure that offered the most obvious hint towards the source of Hill's thinly veiled concern. He made it clear that he saw no problem in Damon remaining in the Williams-Renault squad, even if Mansell should be of a mind to make a full-time return to Formula 1 in 1995. In retrospect this was the first public signal that Nigel's Williams deal was not a one-off arrangement for Magny-Cours, but a contract that incorporated the final three races of 1995 once his Indycar commitments were at an end.

'I have been particularly impressed with the way Damon has coped since the death of Ayrton Senna,' said Faure at Silverstone. 'If Nigel was to return, I see no reason why the two men couldn't race together. There would be no problem for us at Renault with them both being British. We don't go on nationality, just ability.'

Cometh the day, cometh the race, cometh the man. On that summer Sunday at Silverstone, Damon Hill delivered the victory that his celebrated father had never quite managed to pin down in 17 years of Formula 1 effort. Pumped up with adrenalin after out-qualifying Schumacher by 0.003 seconds in that gripping second timed session, Hill out-ran the Benetton from the start to reach Copse Corner in the lead.

'I was almost craning my neck to see where Michael was as we went into the first corner,' said Hill, 'because I thought he might be tucked in my blind spot. But I turned in anyway and found that I was ahead!'

Coulthard, meanwhile, had twice stalled his Williams on the grid, causing the start to be aborted on the first occasion, then being moved to the back of the grid after failing to get away prior to the second parade lap. The young Scot them overtook four cars before the first corner only to spin, drop to the tail of the field, then begin his recovery all over again.

Hill led superbly through to his first refuelling stop at the end of lap 15, resuming third behind Berger and Schumacher. Unbeknown to everybody outside the Benetton team, Schumacher had been informed of a 5-second penalty for breaching the rules by twice getting out of position on the parade laps.

The German driver had accelerated away into Copse corner at the start of the first parade lap, overtaking Hill as he did so. But Schumacher pressed on doggedly, believing the penalty would be added to his overall race time, even in the face of an official black flag being shown, together with his race number, at the start/finish line at the end of laps 21 and 22.

After much debate between the Benetton team management and race officials, Schumacher was eventually told to come in for a 10-second stop-go penalty, finally doing so at the end of lap 27. This dropped the Benetton to second place over 20 seconds behind Hill's Williams.

Hill and Schumacher made their second refuelling stops at the end of lap 38, resuming 17 seconds apart at the head of the field. From then on Damon braced himself for a counter-attack from the Championship points leader, but Schumacher was troubled with a gear-change malfunction that was causing him to lock his rear tyres under hard braking, so Hill was able to run out an emotional winner by 18.7 seconds.

'I feel it's absolutely superb,' said Damon after receiving his trophy from the Princess of Wales on the winner's rostrum. 'It's the best day of my life, like a dream. I feel like every part of my life has come together at this point. If you believe in destiny, I was destined to win this race.

'I got a lot of motivation to win here – not least because my father never won it. I feel a dream has come true and I have completed a little hole my father left in his record. He would be delighted.'

Benetton and Schumacher might well have counted themselves fortunate to have escaped with a $25,000 dollar fine for not being properly versed with the rules. But that was only the start of things. The German driver would be summoned before a special meeting of the FIA World Council to find that the penalties were to be increased quite dramatically. Now the team would be given a $500,000 fine, Schumacher would be disqualified from Silverstone and face a two-race suspension. It was a decision on the part of the sport's governing body that served to inject a degree of dramatic unpredictability into the balance of the Championship season.

Schumacher appealed against the ban, at least enabling him to race in front of his home crowd at Hockenheim. This was just as well, because a hardcore of German fans had threatened to torch the tinder-dry pine forests surrounding the track near Heidelberg and death threats were made on Hill, which contributed to an extremely worrying weekend indeed.

Hockenheim was also the race at which the new stepped undertray regulations came in, although the FIA had compromised to accept a 10 mm 'step' formed by a wooden composite plank, rather than the full 50 mm step that would be required from the start of 1995.

Ever since the FIA had imposed those wing limitations in time for the Spanish Grand Prix, the teams had been struggling to control the vortex developed by the front wings. Shorn of the cone-like vortex controllers that had previously extended rearward from the front wing end plates, Williams, like all their rivals, were left to deflect this flow with unsightly vertical deflectors, popularly known as 'barge boards'.

'In turn, we felt this pushed us towards a shorter side pod, so we could have a less aggressive plan profile for the "barge boards",' explained Adrian Newey. 'That meant cutting back the leading edge of the side pod, which, although it was moulded into the chassis, was not a structural area.' This revised aerodynamic package, together with the more powerful Renault RS6B engine, was used by both the team's cars, now dubbed Williams FW16Bs, from Hockenheim onwards.

Schumacher suffered a rare Ford V8 engine failure in the German race on a day that Hill could have capitalised on his misfortune with a likely win. Unfortunately, after a poor start, he bent one of his Williams's steering arms in a silly collision with Ukyo Katayama's Tyrrell-Yamaha. He wound up eighth after a pit stop for repairs, and Berger won for Ferrari.

Speaking at Spa the following month, Patrick Head would reflect on Damon's German GP misfortune. 'Hockenheim was a disaster when he really needed to keep the ball rolling,' he said firmly. 'In fact, if you look at Damon's performance, the only weakness that stands out particularly is that he's had three first lap accidents this year.

'Without those [Imola, Monaco and Hockenheim] he would be looking pretty good and they are something he needs to keep out of.

'I think you can get away with one a year, but not three, and particularly not one like Hockenheim. He could have overtaken Katayama at any time. To try dipping inside him at the third chicane on the opening lap – and then to say that he moved over for Schumacher, so I thought he was going to move over for me – is not good.'

However, Head also made some generous observations about Hill as a man. 'He is capable of giving absolutely outstanding performances, but as a Grand Prix driver you've got to get yourself into a state when you can do that 16 times a year.

'The trouble is that people who get into that position tend to be moody and selfish. Maybe they become that way because they have to work themselves up into that level of aggression 16 times a year. Or it may be it's natural to them and they are like that the whole time, which makes them such uncomfortable people to be with. Whereas, with Damon, you'd be quite happy to spend a week off with him and end up thinking what a hell of a good bloke he is.'

Damon finished second in the Hungarian Grand Prix at Budapest, pondering that the Williams team's strategy of two fuel stops might have been less effective than Schumacher's three for Benetton. In fact, although Patrick Head later expressed the view that the strategy was fine in theory, the tight nature of the Hungaroring circuit saw Damon getting some bad breaks in traffic where Schumacher seemed to slice past the slower cars in more decisive style.

Of course, to look at it from another viewpoint, Schumacher spent more time on fresher tyres and a lighter fuel load, so it could be argued that the Benetton was more nimble and had better grip for a larger percentage of the race than had Hill's Williams. Either way, it was slightly disappointing.

Coulthard, meanwhile, had a less successful time, spinning off twice in practice, then crashing in the race when running third. Hill now went into the Belgian Grand Prix at Spa 31 points behind Schumacher. The German driver's appeal against his two-race suspension was due to be heard the week after the Belgian race and, as few observers could see Benetton's man getting the FIA Court of Appeal to overturn the initial judgement, Damon also steeled himself for the task of winning the Italian and Portuguese races. If, as it correctly transpired, these were the two races that Schumacher would be forced to sit out, Hill had no choice but to take them both if he was to retain a realistic opportunity of winning the title.

As it turned out Schumacher was in for even more trouble at Spa. He ran away with the race only to be disqualified when his stepped undertray was found to have sustained more than the 10 per cent wear rate permissible under the regulations. Benetton claimed that the wear was accident damage, caused when Schumacher spun over a kerb during the race, but that contention was rejected. He was disqualified, lost the appeal, then faced his two-race suspension. Hill, who finished the day slightly at odds with the Williams management over their reluctance to signal Coulthard aside during the early stages of the race, wound up inheriting the status of surprised winner.

By lap 22 Schumacher had been running just over 17 seconds ahead of Coulthard, and Damon was right on his tail, hustling to get by. The Scot kept his slender advantage through their second refuelling stops, but then started to drop away from Schumacher. But there was no way he was going to defer to Hill unless instructed to do so by the Williams management.

The matter never quite came to a head out on the circuit as David was signalled into the pits with only seven laps to go after the Williams crew noticed his FW16B's rear wing seemed to be wobbling slightly. As Coulthard pulled in, Patrick Head ducked under the rear wing to discover that the right-hand wing support on the gearbox casing had broken. Taking an instant decision, Head judged that the aerodynamic downforce generated when the car was running would keep the mounting in place satisfactorily and David was waved back into the race. Patrick later admitted that he had made what was, in truth, a marginal decision.

After the race, and before he realised he had inherited the win, Damon made his thoughts quite clear. 'In my view the team should have acted sooner,' he said firmly. 'I let them know my feeling over the radio and they replied, yes, they understood what I was saying. But nothing happened.

'Once I got past him [Coulthard] I was able to run much quicker because I was not in dirty air. But ultimately it's Frank and Patrick's team and they are quite entitled to run it their way.' Once again it was possible to sense Damon's inner feelings that the team couldn't quite bring itself to offer him the unreserved support he had been so obviously seeking since that glorious day he beat Mansell to pole position in France.

Patrick Head explained to Damon that he didn't believe he had been quite close enough to his team-mate. 'If he had been really hassling him, then there would have been no question, we would have asked David to let him by,' he said. 'But Frank and I discussed it and we really didn't think Damon was.'

Coulthard suffered from overheating electrics, which caused his transmission to jam in fourth gear over the final few laps, depriving him of sufficient engine braking to prevent him from nudging Mark Blundell's Tyrrell into a spin. He wound up fourth, on amended results, behind Hakkinen's McLaren and Jos Verstappen's Benetton, and immediately apologised to Blundell for the incident once the race was over.

During the interval separating the Belgian and Italian Grands Prix, Schumacher's appeal against the two-race suspension was duly presented to the FIA Court of Appeal. As expected it was rejected and the original penalty upheld. He would now miss both the Italian and Portuguese Grands Prix. To have even a sniff of the World Championship, Hill had to win both in his absence. Just as in Hungary the previous year, Damon was faced with the nerve-racking pressure of no obvious pressure.

At Monza Hill's car would be tended by Williams's senior engineer David Brown rather than his colleague John Russell. Damon made a totally pragmatic decision in requesting this change; Brown was much more experienced, having worked with Mansell, Prost and Senna, and he needed to plug into that experience at a crucial moment. It was explained away as an internal matter, but some Williams insiders felt that Hill could have perhaps handled the matter more sensitively and explained his decision in person to Russell prior to the race weekend.

Jean Alesi's Ferrari set fastest time in both qualifying sessions to clinch pole position ahead of his team-mate Gerhard Berger, but Hill felt confident that his third place on the grid was a more accurate measure of pre-race form. After all, the Ferraris had benefited from a programme of intensive testing at their home circuit in the run-up to the team's most important race of the year. 'Given that Ferrari have been testing here for three days, I'd say we were going to spoil their party,' he predicted correctly.

Coulthard qualified fifth behind Johnny Herbert's impressive Lotus, which was using a brand-new Mugen Honda V10 engine for the first time. Unfortunately, as he sprinted for the first corner in second place behind the two Ferraris, Herbert was hit from behind by an over-zealous Eddie Irvine's Jordan. This coming together triggered off a multiple collision that left the circuit blocked and the organisers with no alternative but to red-flag the race to a halt.

For the restart Hill took over the spare FW16 after his race car developed an oil leak that the mechanics had to quench with some haste, as Coulthard needed to take Damon's discarded machine after his own had been damaged in the first corner shunt. At the restart Alesi, running with a light fuel load and planning to refuel twice, sprinted away from the pack with Berger hanging on to second in front of Hill and Coulthard.

The Austrian driver was not exactly feeling at his best in the opening stages of the race. During the race-morning warm-up he had crashed heavily enough to require a hospital check-up before he was permitted to start the race in the spare Ferrari, the engine of which wasn't quite as powerful as the one he'd hoped to use. Nevertheless, Gerhard hung on doggedly at the head of the pack and, when Alesi came in for his first stop on lap 14, surged through to lead by just over a second from Hill's Williams.

'In the early stages I had been worried about Jean going away so much,' admitted Damon later, 'but it seemed to stabilise a bit and I had the feeling he was going for a two-stop race, although I couldn't guarantee it.

'Also, when I was running behind Gerhard I noticed he was leaving a little trail of oil. I don't know what sort of goo they put in those engines, but they just eat helmet visors!'

Alesi didn't emerge from his first refuelling stop, scrambling the dog-rings of his Ferrari's semi-automatic gearbox as he tried to restart, then leaping from the cockpit in an hysterical rage. Hill then managed to dodge ahead of Berger by making a faster – single – refuelling stop, but Coulthard got the better of them both to lead briefly before dutifully dropping in behind Damon and touring round in his wake for the rest of the afternoon.

Unfortunately, as Damon came storming out of Parabolica on the very last lap to take the chequered flag, Coulthard wasn't riding along in his slip-stream. On the run down to the final corner, the Scot's Williams ran short of fuel and spluttered to a halt, eventually to be classified sixth.

With all the confusion involved in both drivers switching cars immediately before the race, Renault seemed to have lost track of how many warm-up laps Hill's original race car had completed, with the result that their fuel load calculations were thrown out by a single lap. It was a bitter pill for David to have to swallow. 'I tried short-shifting [changing up early] to save things all the way down to Parabolica, but at the last corner it just cut out altogether,' he shrugged.

Hill was now 11 points behind Schumacher in the drivers' table, and another win at Estoril, in the Portuguese Grand Prix, would reduce that deficit to a single point with only three races of the season to go. It was almost too much to hope that the Championship battle could be set up for such a dramatic grandstand finish, but that's just how events would unfold.

Despite rolling his Williams dramatically in practice after clipping a rear wheel of Eddie Irvine's spinning Jordan, Hill produced just what was needed of him at Estoril. Even so, in the early stages of the race it looked as though Damon would be facing a tough battle after Coulthard beat him to the draw at the start, bursting through to run second behind Berger's Ferrari in the opening laps. When the Austrian retired with gearbox failure after seven laps, Coulthard took over at the head of the field as Hill faded slightly, unhappy with the balance of his Williams's handling on its first set of tyres.

Damon felt much happier on his second set of tyres, energetically pressing in on to Coulthard's tail and nipping through into the lead going into a very tight hairpin that had been incorporated into the Estoril circuit this year for the first time.

'He got stuck behind some slower cars,' grinned Damon, 'so I thought, well, I'm coming through – I just hope I have enough steering lock to get round.' Coulthard frankly conceded that he'd been caught on the hop. 'Damon took me totally by surprise,' he admitted. 'He pulled a terrific over-taking manoeuvre and caught me asleep. But had it been anybody else, I would have felt free to defend my position.'

Thereafter the two Williams-Renaults stroked it home to the team's first 1-2 success of the season, the first such result by British drivers since Damon's father won the 1969 Monaco Grand Prix for Lotus ahead of Frank Williams's Brabham driven by Piers Courage. It was a statistic that brought a smile of satisfaction to Frank's face, although he is not usually a man to reflect on the historic perspective of motorsport, very much preferring to look forward to the next race.

For Damon it was just the result he needed. Now he was a single point behind Schumacher on the eve of the German driver's return for the European Grand Prix at Jerez. For Coulthard the future must have seemed slightly less certain. He'd finished second in only his eighth Grand Prix, but his joy was tempered by the knowledge that he would have to relinquish his Williams cockpit to Nigel Mansell for the remainder of the season.

Precisely what the future held for him remained clouded in uncertainty. It was an unnerving situation for any wide-eyed and ambitious young racing driver to cope with.

During testing at Estoril prior to the European Grand Prix at Jerez, Michael Schumacher launched an uncharacteristic verbal assault on Damon Hill. 'Certain people felt our punishment [Benetton's suspension] was too hard. Very few people, one or two little men, felt the decision was right,' said Michael, obviously aiming his comments at his rival.

'He [Damon] has been thrown into the job of being a number one driver. He was never a number one driver. I would not have been in this position [leading the Championship] if Ayrton Senna was still around. He would have driven circles round me. That does not say much for Hill.'

Schumacher was also scathing about Hill's performance relative to Coulthard, pointing out that the younger driver had relinquished the lead both at Monza and Estoril, and rounded off by expressing the view that Nigel Mansell wasn't returning to the team to make life easy for Damon. It was a very harsh, ill-judged critique.

Not for the last time Damon handled himself well in the face of an assault that, although suggesting a degree of immaturity on Schumacher's part, in fact mirrored the understandable tension building between the two men.

'I think it's a half-baked attempt to destabilise me and he'll have to try better than that if he wants to do it,' responded Damon briskly. 'I'd rather not drag the championship down in that way by trying to diminish the reputation of the opposition. And I think it's sad that Formula 1 for too long has arrived in that [sort of] situation with the two protagonists seemingly hating each other's guts.

'That's sad for the sport, sad for Formula 1, and particularly so in a season where we've lost a great champion in Ayrton. I would prefer a clean fight and a sporting fight.

'I feel it's ill-conceived and immature, but there isn't any animosity. He's a young man and he's not been in this position before. Neither have I, but I hope I can carry myself through this with some dignity and not resort to undermining the reputation of fellow competitors. I'm pretty relaxed, feel comfortable and am enjoying the situation.'

In qualifying at Jerez, Schumacher quickly demonstrated that his enforced lay-off had in no way blunted his finely honed competitive edge. He qualified on pole 0.8 seconds ahead of Hill, with Mansell, making his return to the Williams-Renault cockpit, a strong third ahead of the Sauber-Mercedes of Heinz-Harald Frentzen.

In the warm-up on race morning, Hill lapped 0.9 seconds faster than Schumacher's Benetton and went on to make an absolutely storming start to lead into the first corner. Behind, Mansell got bogged down with wheelspin, being passed on all sides to complete the opening lap in sixth place behind Frentzen, Barrichello's Jordan and Berger's Ferrari.

With just three laps completed Hill and Schumacher were over 6 seconds ahead of Frentzen, the Sauber driver weighed down by a substantial fuel load and aiming for just a single pit stop. With 15 of the race's 69 laps completed, Schumacher came in for a 6.8-second refuelling stop. Three laps later Hill followed suit and things began to go wrong. He resumed in second place and, by the end of lap 19, was 4.8 seconds down.

The Williams began to drift back from its key rival, but Damon figured that – with a two-stop strategy – as long as he kept within 20 seconds of Schumacher he would still have a strong chance of winning because the Benetton would lose that time, possibly more, as its driver had chosen to make three refuelling stops.

Schumacher stopped again on lap 33, allowing Hill through into the lead, but Damon couldn't quite believe it when he was signalled into the pits again only two laps later. To the Williams team's frustration, there had been a glitch with the refuelling rig whereby Hill's car had been under-fuelled by 13 litres at the first stop. An additional 14 litres were added on top of the planned amount, in order to compensate for this earlier than expected second stop, and off Damon went.

Damon now had 95 litres of fuel in his Williams as opposed to the 50 being carried by Schumacher's Benetton. As a result, not only did he have a car weighing around 50 kg more than his rival's, but he was also now in a position where he would have to run the balance of the race on one set of tyres. Schumacher, of course, benefited from another set of fresh rubber at his final stop.

In fact, the odds stacked against Hill were even more overwhelming. At his first fuel stop the 13 litres in question *had* been loaded aboard the Williams – the wrong assumption had been reached on the basis of a faulty gauge – so he ran the rest of the race carrying this surplus, plus the additional 14 litres to compensate for its supposed absence. He was 25 seconds down at the chequered flag, frustrated, bewildered and slightly annoyed.

Mansell, meanwhile, spun off the road into retirement. The Williams team, which had gone into the Jerez race nursing a two-point advantage over Benetton in the Constructors' Championship, emerged from it two points behind. Clearly the outcome of this contest was destined to be as nail-bitingly close as that for the drivers' title.

Hill was now five points behind Schumacher going into the Japanese Grand Prix at Suzuka. Again the Benetton driver qualified on pole position but, come the race, Damon dramatically kick-started his faltering title prospects with a sensational, tactically astute victory in conditions so appalling that, at one point, the event was red-flagged to a halt after a spate of accidents during a particularly intense torrential downpour.

Schumacher led away from the start in conditions that were so atrocious that, after only eight laps, the race officials were prompted to deploy the Safety Car to slow the field. The pack slowly filed round behind it for six laps before the racing proper resumed, but then Martin Brundle's McLaren spun off and hit a marshal, breaking his leg, and the race was brought to a halt in order that an ambulance could be despatched.

When the race was restarted once more, Schumacher again took the lead, but relinquished it when he made his second refuelling stop with ten of the 50 laps left to run. That was the moment at which the Benetton team realised that Hill was going through without a second stop, and the Englishman duly never made a slip, winning by just over 3 seconds in an aggregate result calculated on the outcome of each of the two parts.

'This is the first time that Michael has been beaten fair and square all season,' reflected the understandably jubilant Damon. 'I put myself under a lot of pressure this weekend and, for that reason, I think this result is even more satisfying than when I won the British Grand Prix.

'It's a tall order to beat Michael because this year he's been the class driver of the field, and especially with the conditions the way they were. I just think it was a shame that Michael and I were not racing each other on the same part of the track at the end, but it was a tremendously exciting race watching the gap.' Williams were additionally satisfied that Mansell's great race to fourth place pushed them back into a five-point Constructors' title lead.

Going into the final race at Adelaide the following week, Hill then shook the paddock by making an uncharacteristically robust call for a pay hike the moment he arrived in Australia. In many ways it seemed like an echo of his pre-Silverstone demands for more recognition and support from the team. Now, however, it was framed in financial terms that carried with them faint echoes of Nigel Mansell's complaints at Monza in 1992, although one could see his point at a time when he was driving for a retainer of around £300,000 while Nigel was receiving over £500,000 per race.

'I am pretty disgusted with some of the things that have gone on,' he said firmly. 'I feel that they [Williams] have not contributed to making me feel that the team is behind me to win the Championship.

'I have been in negotiation with the team about my contract; they have taken up their option on my services for next year, but I reckon I am a lot better than my contract says I am. The dispute is about the team recognising what you feel yourself to be worth.

'I have won nine Grands Prix. This year I have had to carry the role of number one driver in only my second season in Formula 1. I'm only one point off the Championship lead with one race to go.'

It was an intemperate observation, but one that had been prompted by a harsh exchange of words with the Williams team management in the pit lane during practice at Suzuka the previous weekend. Yet, to his credit, he quickly appreciated that he'd handled things tactlessly and, the following day, moved to soften his stance.

'I think a lot more has been printed than I actually said,' he confessed. 'What I tried to get across was that, throughout the period since my option was taken up – and even before that – I have been trying to get some sort of reassurance that Williams have got the faith in me to do the job.

'What I want to know is whether I am going to get the financial recognition for the job that I think I'm doing. It's a question of endorsement, a show of faith, and I feel sometimes I have been left not too certain about where I stand. Maybe I am wrong, maybe I have misinterpreted the signals, but this is all new territory to me.'

Coincidentally, as if to endorse Hill's viewpoint, on the eve of the 1994 Australian Grand Prix Jackie Stewart put Damon's career achievements thus far into a very sharp perspective.

'I'm really thrilled for Damon, because I think he has had one of the toughest rides that I know of,' said Graham Hill's old friend and team-mate. 'I have known him since he was a little wee boy and Graham was my number one driver at BRM. There were complications about the insurance on Graham's plane after the accident and his financial affairs were not left in the best condition. Bette had to move out of a beautiful country estate to a very modest living with three children who had to be taken out of their fee-paying schools because they could not afford it.

'Damon left school at 15. He found a very nice girlfriend and they got married; their first baby had Down's Syndrome, a terrible shock to anyone. Damon worked as a brickie, a motorcycle courier, scratching around to get into Formula Ford and, because his Dad was Graham Hill, he could get some small benefits and some little sponsored rides. But he struggled to get those – and he didn't have his Dad to give him advice like I did to Paul.

'So he tried to go through F3 successfully – and struggled. He tried to go through Formula 3000, and didn't make it because of the finances required. Then a magic wand came along in the form of Frank Williams with a testing contract. And Damon Hill went about that task in a very thorough, workmanlike and dedicated fashion. He showed himself to the mechanics and the team to be a really serious racing driver.

'Then Nigel Mansell retired – a fairy tale! But Damon took over the drive and delivered. Immediately delivered. OK, he may have had the best car in the world, but you've got to drive it. You know, in 1994, Jos Verstappen had one of the best cars in the world. And look at his results. So you have to give the boy [Damon] an immense amount of credit, bearing in mind he has had not nearly the same level of experience as Michael Schumacher, and probably many of the other drivers.'

Stewart did admit that Damon, in the run-up to the Australian race, had perhaps got a little too wound up over what he clearly regarded as the Williams team's failure to recognise his true status as team leader.

'I think he's become a little bit sensitive about that,' continued Jackie. 'Nobody likes not to be appreciated for their endeavours, and Damon is not fully appreciated – and I'm not talking about simply within his own team. I'm saying it generally. And keep in mind that Damon is not the most experienced man when it comes to dealing with the media either. He has been suddenly thrust from being a nonentity to the status of a world leader in motorsport.

'So if you take all those things into account, you've really got to appreciate what he has achieved with very little knowledge or experience. I'm not saying for one moment that Damon Hill has deserved anything more or less than he's got; I think he's done one hell of a job. Anybody who says he would not make a worthy World Champion is talking absolute rubbish.

'I've never seen an unworthy World Champion, believe me. For example, Denny Hulme only won one title in 1967, and there were people who said that Jim Clark should have really won it that season. But there was never a time that I did not regard Denny Hulme as one of the best drivers in the world. And the same now goes for Damon.'

Mansell qualified superbly on pole position for the final race of the season with Schumacher second, despite crashing heavily in practice, and Hill a rather disappointed third. But with both Michael and Damon planning identical race strategies encompassing three refuelling stops, it was a two-horse race between the two title contenders from the start.

At the end of the opening lap Schumacher was 2.1 seconds ahead of Hill, but Damon closed up next time round and from then on there was nothing between them. On lap 18 they came in for their first refuelling stops together, by which stage they were half a minute ahead of Mika Hakkinen's McLaren in third place.

Perhaps it was inevitable that a season already tarnished by tragedy and controversy should end with what many people would deem as more than a hint of disreputable driving. After battling it out head to head for 36 of the scheduled 81 laps, Schumacher, who had gambled just before the start and taken off some wing angle to retain maximum straight-line speed, made a slight mistake, hit a wall and damaged his suspension. At that instant the World Championship opened up for Damon Hill.

Seconds later it slammed closed again as Hill attempted to drive through inside the Benetton. Schumacher appeared to cut across him, the two cars collided and the Benetton was momentarily pitched on to two wheels before slamming into a protective barrier. Hill drove slowly back to the pits to find that his Williams's left front upper wishbone had been damaged beyond repair. Schumacher was champion by a single point.

Hill reacted with admirable dignity, although he must have been simmering beneath the surface. 'It's a bit of an empty feeling,' he shrugged, 'but I think I gave him a good run for his money. He was certainly feeling the pressure because he ended up falling off the road.

'I saw the opportunity and thought I had to go for it, but it didn't happen. I'm afraid that's motor racing. Going into the last race with a one-point deficit to Michael was always going to put me in a position where I had everything to lose.

'I didn't see him hit the wall, but I thought, "Hello, you've slipped up there." In retrospect I should have let him go.'

Schumacher could sense the tension in the aftermath of this controversial race and diplomatically moved to defuse the situation by dedicating his championship to Senna and apologising to Hill for the remarks he had made prior to the Jerez race.

'My car was difficult to drive throughout the race because I was suffering from a lot of oversteer,' he admitted, referring to the consequences of that last-minute change of set-up. 'But somehow I kept Damon behind me and found a way to increase the gap. After that I got caught out on a bump when the car stepped out and went sideways, and I caught it. Then I went over the grass and touched the wall, but continued.

'Then I just wanted to run into the corner and suddenly I saw Damon next to me and we just hit each other. I went up in the air and was a bit afraid that the car would roll over, but it came back.'

Then, in a voice almost trembling with emotion, he added: 'I have to say that I did make some comments this year about Damon that I didn't have the kind of respect for him that I might have had for some. But I have to admit that I was wrong. He has been a great rival and I must say sorry for what I maybe have said.'

Meanwhile, Mansell went on to win the race and ensure that the Constructors' title was kept out of Benetton's grasp by the healthy margin of 15 points.

It was a success that prompted Patrick Faure, the Deputy Chairman of Renault Sport, to claim that Mansell's return was entirely positive for the Williams team. 'I don't think it's a secret that Renault played a major role in recruiting Nigel Mansell, firstly for the French Grand Prix and then for the last three races of the season.

'Given the objective we had set ourselves – which was to win the 1994 Constructors' title – it was our belief that, after what happened at Imola, Williams and Renault needed an electric shock to help them find their feet again. We saw the return of Nigel at the French Grand Prix as an effective way to re-motivate the team and encourage it to perform well during the second half of the season. I believe we have been proved right.

'Even though Nigel didn't finish at Magny-Cours, he was the star of the race and his performance in qualifying was quite remarkable. His presence re-motivated Damon, who has himself recognised as much in a number of interviews. I believe we were entirely right in our strategy to recruit him, both from the psychological and sporting points of view.'

Of course, despite persuasive evidence to the contrary, a hardcore of grizzled old cynics found it difficult to believe that the FIA hadn't made sure Schumacher's two-race suspension stuck firm in order that fresh life be breathed into a Championship contest that had turned into a one-horse race. Max Mosley responded to the notion with a degree of amusement, pointing out that the governing body obviously had no way of anticipating how events would develop.

'What you say makes complete sense,' he grinned, 'but I think when you're actually sitting there [at the Court of Appeal hearing] you tend to concentrate on the narrow issue and, if it had been the other way round, you would still have disqualified the driver.

'I think as far as Schumacher's behaviour at Silverstone was concerned, the reaction of those not directly involved was that somebody had been shown the red card, had told the referee to "Sod off", and the trainer had stood on the edge of the field saying "Don't take any notice".'

'We had a situation where the whole authority of the sport seemed to have been called into question. At that stage, halfway through the season, nobody could have predicted that Hill would win the races where Schumacher was absent, that Schumacher's engineers would mess up the settings in Belgium which led to his disqualification, or that Hill would actually blow Schumacher off fair and square in the penultimate race.

'The unpredictability of Formula 1 is one of its greatest qualities. It's a funny old game!'

Some weeks after the season ended, Frank Williams reflected a considerable amount of warmth and satisfaction over the way in which Damon Hill had handled himself throughout the year. Speaking to Nigel Roebuck of *Autosport*, he said: 'Damon's a very unusual man in some ways; a remarkable man, I should say. I've said this time and again, and I still say it; he never stops surprising one with his performances.

'You go to Silverstone – Patrick will tell you – and you go round and round getting nowhere, and think "what a terrible test". That happened several times. What are you *doing*, Damon?

'Then in Adelaide, a second off Nigel in practice, I remember Patrick and I looking at each other, rolling our eyes. No way for the Championship! Next day – where did that come from? It was a quite remarkable performance.

'He is a straightforward soul. Not malicious, not avaricious. OK, all drivers push for more money, of course, because their earning time is finite. But he's not really avaricious. He's a remarkable person.'

The last word should go, appropriately enough, to Damon Hill: 'I think everyone in the Williams team deserves some sort of medal this year, because we've been through a hell of a tough time, and to be here for the last race fighting to win the Championship was quite an achievement.

'We will be back next year . . .'

Chapter 5

The return of the not-so-prodigal

'Every man is wanted, and no man is wanted much'

Ralph Waldo Emerson,
American philosopher and poet

Nigel Mansell's switch to the Indycar World Series was confirmed a couple of weeks after the 1992 Italian Grand Prix at Monza. Most observers believed that, with a £3 million contract in place to make him the highest-paid driver of all time in the North American domestic series, Mansell would be turning his back on Formula 1 for good. He would be taking a place alongside Mario Andretti in the Newman/Haas Lola-Ford team and gave every sign of not being able to wait.

'It is a wonderful new challenge for me,' said Mansell. 'I have seen a number of [Indycar] races on television and they look good and competitive. Indianapolis and the other ovals will obviously be a new experience and I am ready to give it a go.'

Team-owner Carl Haas was also cock-a-hoop with delight over plucking the reigning Formula 1 World Champion from the Grand Prix stage. 'Both Paul Newman and myself are very excited about signing Nigel,' he admitted. 'It's obviously a great challenge, good for the sport as a whole and a real shot in the arm for Indycar racing.' Later, during Mansell's pre-season testing in the new Lola-Ford, Haas would remark thoughtfully, 'Why did they let this guy go? If I'd been Frank Williams, I'd have killed to keep him!'

Born in Germany and raised in Chicago's underprivileged South Side, 63-year-old Haas is one of the pivotal personalities on the American motor racing scene. A somewhat reclusive, superstitious man who blesses his cars before each race, his trademark has become an endless supply of huge Honduran cigars, which he chews incessantly at the tracks.

In addition to his achievements as a racing team operator, he is one of the five voting directors on the Indycar board, the body that controls the way in which this racing category is administered. He is also a shareholder in the Road America circuit and a promoter of races at the Milwaukee Mile, where Mansell would score his first oval track victory in the summer of 1992.

Haas's strategy to sign Mansell was calculated with the precision of a military campaign. In the late summer of 1992 Michael Andretti, the reigning Indycar champion, told Haas that he would be switching to Formula 1 with McLaren for the following season.

'Carl has a tremendous amount of experience and is very good at letting the people he's hired do the job,' said Andretti junior. 'He also knows when to get involved, and when to stay out of it. I think that's the biggest key – something that almost every other racing team owner doesn't understand.'

Haas admitted that he had talked to Mansell before the Englishman announced his decision to retire from Formula 1 at Monza. 'I had some conversations with Nigel prior to that,' he agreed. 'Then after his announcement at Monza, I followed up on it fairly strong. But at that point we didn't have anything in place but an outline framework.'

The PPG Indycar World Series for 1993 effectively mirrored the Formula 1 championship across a 16-race schedule beginning with a street race at Surfers' Paradise, Australia, in March, and running through to the final round at California's Laguna Seca Raceway in October. The schedule included purpose-built race tracks, street circuits such as Long Beach, Toronto and Vancouver, as well as the daunting banked ovals like Indianapolis, Michigan and Nazareth.

Initially much concern was expressed about Mansell transferring to Indycars, particularly in view of the severe leg injuries sustained by his one-time Williams-Honda team-mate Nelson Piquet during practice for the 1992 Indy 500. With lap speeds averaging over 200 mph against the backdrop of an unyielding brick wall – a stark contrast to the gravel run-off areas waiting to catch the unwary Formula 1 competitors – some critics cast doubt as to whether Mansell would be able to adapt to a specialised new driving style. Yet his new team-mate, for one, believed that this would pose him no problem at all.

'A lot of people have been short-changing Nigel Mansell's abilities with their critical comments,' said Mario Andretti. 'For a driver of his calibre, the ovals will be no problem, believe me.'

In purely historic terms, Mansell's defection to Indycar racing was as momentous a development as the arrival of the great Jim Clark at Indianapolis in 1963 with Colin Chapman's compact rear-engined Lotus-Ford. The arrival of this spindly little F1-derived machine sounded the death knell for the traditional front-engined Indy roadsters and, by the time Clark won the race two years later, everybody in the business was following the Lotus design lead. Two decades later British-built cars would completely dominate the entire Indycar grid thanks to the efforts of March, Lola and Penske.

A hardcore of British fans were aghast at Mansell's defection. Letters objecting to Frank Williams's perceived treatment of the new World Champion were published in *The Times*, while the *Sun* took a more direct approach by launching a 'Save our Nige' campaign, which involved promoting a plan to picket the Williams factory. It duly published maps of how to get to the Didcot premises and laid on coaches from London which, presumably, that august organ believed would be packed with indignantly nationalistic enthusiasts whose sheer weight of numbers would leave Frank Williams with no alternative but to beg Mansell to stay. As things transpired only a handful of fans took up the paper's most generous offer.

As an amusing aside, the *Sun*'s promotion earned Mansell's Formula 1 cause a few column inches. But those on the inside of the Williams team knew the sort of damage this could do. Frank made little secret of the fact that he'd had quite enough Mansell-mania to last him a long time, and the danger of such well-meaning displays of xenophobia was that it might prejudice the team chief from ever selecting another British driver. This was a matter of some obvious concern to those within the team who hoped that Damon Hill would eventually get the drive as Mansell's successor, a development that, thankfully, duly came to pass.

Early in January 1993 Mansell had his first run at the wheel of a Lola-Ford Indycar on an oval track at Phoenix, Arizona, after some preliminary runs on the nearby Firebird Raceway road course. The new World Champion set a shattering lap time and was called into the pits by circuit officials who thought that he was going too fast too soon after lapping within half a second of Michael Andretti's outright record.

'I am not fit and I don't feel great,' said Mansell, referring to the after-effects of a recent operation on his right foot. 'I am overweight and need to go on a diet. Then I can go even quicker, but at least I have shown what I can do.

'You've got to have new challenges and I'm under no illusions that on some circuits I'm going to be struggling, I'm going to be slow. But I think that I have the ability to learn reasonably quickly and we'll get there in the end.'

Mario Andretti, meanwhile, stated that he was expecting total honesty and no politics in his relationship with Mansell. 'This is a selfish business, and we all know it,' he warned. 'So the only thing that can sometimes create problems between team-mates is a lack of honesty between them as far as their rapport is concerned.

'I think he will find it easy to adjust to the racing here. I expect him to beat me a few times. He is a force to be reckoned with in any race car. I am sure we will enjoy racing together and I am looking forward to it, but he cannot expect me to hold his hand for long.'

Yet even at this early stage in Mansell's relationship with the

Indycar world, some cautionary notes were being sounded. The new World Champion may have seemed set for an extended honeymoon in his new environment, but the acid test would obviously be his behaviour once the racing began and whether he could control the raw edge of an ambition honed in the ruthless, self-serving Formula 1 jungle. Although peopled by many highly competitive drivers, the Indycar ethos is characterised by an overall concern for the series as a whole, even to the point of subjugating personal desire to the wider benefit of pursuing the title.

There were several key personnel close to the Newman/Haas team who questioned whether Mansell could embrace such sentiments. One team member was reported to have told Carl Haas: 'You have no idea what you have done bringing Mansell into the team, Carl. He has the capacity to rip it apart from a political standpoint.'

However, Mansell declined to be ruffled by these rumours and continued to say all the right things in the run-up to the title battle: 'I am glad to be racing in North America and looking forward to competing with the likes of Bobby Rahal and my team-mate Mario. They are great ambassadors, great champions. They don't think they are bigger than the sport. Some guys in Formula 1 think they are.'

Interestingly, Frank Williams obviously thought that Mansell belonged to the ranks of those he so criticised. 'I think Mansell and Senna and, to a lesser degree, Prost have done the sport a great disservice,' he noted at about the same time. 'I think they've grown a bit drunk on their own power, and it's done Formula 1 no good at all.'

The cynics who believed that Mansell was too impetuous to come to terms with the tactical demands of Indycar racing were forced to eat their words. Nigel won his first Indycar race at Surfers' Paradise and bounced back from a bruising 170 mph accident at Phoenix, prompting the need for complex micro-surgery on damaged muscles, to take third place in his first try at the Indianapolis 500. In fact, had it not been for his inexperience at rolling starts, which allowed Emerson Fittipaldi and Arie Luyendyk to jump him at the restart from the final yellow flag period, he might well have won on his debut outing.

Even more impressive were his victories on the high-speed Milwaukee, Michigan and Nazareth ovals, duly clinching the Championship with one race of the season left to run. Mansell seemed totally at ease with the American way of life, completely integrated into the Indycar world, and finished the season toying with a £10 million pound offer from Newman/Haas, which would secure his services until the end of 1995.

Sports coverage of Mansell's achievements from the English tabloid media was understandably lavish and approving. Nigel, moreover, seemed to take every opportunity to snipe at the Williams Formula 1 team and the Grand Prix circus he had left behind.

'The thing I get satisfaction from is that Prost and Hill have had very little contribution to their success this year technically,' he told Steve Atchison of *Today*. 'The Williams team, Riccardo Patrese and myself were the key players of the last three years from the driving point of view. They are reaping the benefit of it and I get satisfaction from seeing their cars winning because that's a little bit of me out there.'

'Whether they want to admit it or not is something else, but I get satisfaction seeing the Williams success continuing, especially with Damon, because I know I did a lot to make it what it is.

'Damon's had the opportunity people dream of this year. Williams have had absolutely no competition. He was very fortunate with me having problems with Williams and Riccardo switching teams instead of being a bit more patient, because Riccardo could probably have stayed.'

This was not a standpoint that found much sympathy with *Today* reader P. May of Tiverton, who wrote: 'I am surprised by the way your motor racing writer rubbished Alain Prost – the second finest F1 driver after Ayrton Senna – particularly when he writes such sickly reports on Nigel Mansell, whose behaviour on the track is sometimes appalling.'

Ted McCauley quoted Mansell in the *Daily Mirror* as saying, 'What I will say is that the case for my staying on racing in America is looking very strong and the case for coming back to Europe very weak.

'I love my country, but I'm focused on winning another title, the Indycar title. I got a great kick out of winning the Formula 1 title. I never believed anything to be so exciting until I raced in the Indy 500. It's impossible to explain its sensational feeling, but it was the most stunning event of my life. I want to be back next year, for sure.

'I have a lovely home, a settled lifestyle, great peace and quiet. My wife and kids are happy and the racing is just great. It's all a fantastic new adventure for us – why should I want to change it?'

In June 1993 Mansell returned to London to receive the Segrave Trophy at the RAC headquarters in Pall Mall, and continued his same theme: 'At the moment I'm very happy not to be involved in Formula 1. My popularity in America is growing all the time, the image is getting stronger. Indycar racing is growing too. It's an exciting formula and they seem to have got it right. Six races have produced five different winners. That's what the fans want to see.'

Then he couldn't resist another dig at his successor in the Williams team: 'I tell you this, if I was still racing in the Williams, Prost wouldn't have won any races at all!'

This yielded a robust response from *Mirror* reader M. Gallei from Oxford. Published under the heading 'Belt up Nigel', he commented, 'Will somebody tell Nigel Mansell to stop belly-aching. We're fed up hearing him say Formula 1 shouldn't have let him go and it was all political. Where would he be today if it wasn't for Frank Williams and his team? Prost, Senna and Co are pulling in the crowds without you!'

However, at the end of the day Carl Haas was delighted with Mansell's performance. 'Sure he can be tough to deal with,' said the American, 'but that's exactly what I would expect from a man who is operating at this sort of level.'

Yet the 1994 Indycar season would be every bit as disappointing as the previous year had been joyously successful. The Newman/Haas Lola-Ford, and the rest of the field come to that, were crushed by the Penske-Ilmor steamroller. Now Mansell was up against it and not a happy man.

Frank Williams and Patrick Head never expected Nigel Mansell to cross their paths again. But in the aftermath of the Senna tragedy there were some harsh realities to be confronted. Rothmans and Renault had paid top dollar for a superstar driver in the Williams squad, and suddenly there wasn't one. Within days of Ayrton's death preliminary discussions were opened at Renault's behest to investigate the possibility of Nigel driving for Williams in a programme of selected races when there was no conflict with his Indycar commitments.

This was not the work of a moment. Negotiating a deal whereby Mansell would race a Renault-engined car running on Elf fuel and oil when his Indycar commitments were to a Ford-engined team running on Texaco was obviously set to pose some problems. Frank Williams privately felt that Mansell had said some hurtful things about his team, but was shrewd enough to appreciate that a small specialist company like his own sometimes has to be able to turn the other cheek. The world could survive quite easily without Formula 1, but not without motor cars. Even so, he was surprised that Renault was prepared to be so resilient after what had gone before.

Patrick Head was absolutely against having Mansell back from the outset. 'I think it is fairly well known that I wasn't greatly in favour of his employment,' admitted the Williams Technical Director early in 1995. 'That was a commercially driven decision mainly from Renault and Bernie Ecclestone.'

It was an expensive option. Mansell wanted £900,000 for a one-off race in the French Grand Prix, and the same again for each of the last three races of the year, once his Indycar commitments were completed. Later he modified his requests, saying that he wanted a £7 million deal for a full season in 1995. At this point Patrick Head absolutely opposed the idea of committing to Mansell beyond the end of 1994. So Nigel reputedly asked for a £2 million compensation clause to be written into his contract in the event of his not being employed in 1995. Williams was hesitant, but Renault seemed willing to bankroll the deal and eventually gave it the nod.

Considering he was no longer F1-sharp, Mansell didn't do badly at

Magny-Cours. It seemed clear from his subtly changed attitude to the Indycar scene that he was not totally certain that he wanted to remain racing in America into 1995. The taste of a Williams-Renault had obviously revived his appetite for the spicy tang of Formula 1. Yet with his options now apparently covered on both fronts, he could certainly afford to be relaxed about his future, as he explained to *Autosport*:

'How do I view the future? I view it year-by-year. This year is no different to any other. I wouldn't think there will be any change on that view until probably about September. Then we'll see how the land lies.

'I'm a lot more laid back than I was, a lot more patient. All these things will fit into place, whereby I don't have to make much of a decision about what might or might not happen.

'On the Indycar front, Penske is doing an absolutely outstanding job, which it's got to be congratulated on. But the Newman-Haas team – no disrespect to Mario, but he's in his retirement year, he's having parties at every race . . . At times some of the team feel as if they are retiring as well!

'I turn up at the circuit and the motivation isn't there sometimes, because you can sense it around you. It's very difficult to compete against a top team when you're not working as you should do as a team.'

These remarks incensed Carl Haas and Mario Andretti. In retrospect Mansell's outing for Williams at Magny-Cours could be seen as the beginning of the end of his relationship with the Indycar team. True, the 1994 Lola-Ford combination wasn't quite up to the mark, but after the French Grand Prix Mansell lost interest in testing and the mood in the Newman/Haas enclave became more than a little strained. Haas, for one, could see the way the land lay and began making plans for 1995 on the assumption that Mansell might be preparing to absent himself from the equation.

On the face of it one might have expected British fans to be unreserved in their enthusiasm to have Mansell back in the Formula 1 fold. However, as Sarah Edworthy noted in the *Daily Telegraph*, letters supportive of the former World Champion were outnumbered two-to-one in the correspondence received by *Autosport* in the weeks following his histrionics at Indianapolis.

Edworthy commented, 'This is not because of his notorious whingeing and self-importance, but because of the fans he attracts. A significant number of "Mansell Maniacs" – as the more extreme branch of his followers are known – come from the less desirable fringes of the sport's activist parties.' After laying out her misgivings about Mansell's return to Formula 1, she concluded, '. . . which is why Mansell's apparent money-motivated bid to return is repellant. It comes at a sensitive time when fans are in the delicate business of re-calibrating their scale of heroes . . .'

By September, with another few weeks to go before his second guest outing for Williams, Mansell had not received any indication from the team as to their plans for 1995. This was largely because Frank Williams had privately decided to pair David Coulthard with Damon Hill, but wanted to keep his cards close to his chest as it was clear that Renault was keen on a Mansell/Hill alliance at Williams for 1995.

'Frank has a choice of the drivers,' acknowledged Patrick Faure. 'He usually discusses with us the names, but the final word belongs to him. I think he has already had discussions with Nigel. I hope he can reach an agreement for next year.'

Despite speculation from some sources that the Williams-Renault partnership was slightly shaky, the French car company had reaffirmed its faith in Frank's operation during the summer of '94 by extending its engine supply contract with the team, originally due to expire after the '95 season, until the end of 1997. This news came a fortnight before Renault's much-speculated partnership with Benetton was confirmed, guaranteeing the rival British team parity of engine specification with Williams.

Williams was known to be concerned over Renault's impending deal with Benetton, as they felt that their contract guaranteed them a position as the French car-maker's sole works-supported representative in Formula 1. Yet Frank and Patrick were realistic enough to appreciate the level of support the team had received from Renault over the years, and were understandably anxious to accommodate their ambitions. As things transpired, the revised contract was positive for both parties and the strength of Williams's relationship with Renault was further emphasised when Williams Touring Car Engineering was established to field works-backed Laguna saloons in the 1995 British Touring Car Championship.

'I couldn't wish for a more honest, direct, friendly partner,' said Williams of Renault in the summer of 1993. 'It's a pleasure to work with all of them, from the top down. One Saturday morning I was sitting behind one of the cars, pushing round the shop, as I often do – I think this was in '91, and I was very proud of FW14, showing everybody the way with a new concept – and Patrick said, "Frank, I know what you're thinking, but let me tell you the technology in the Renault engine is *way* ahead of the Williams technology!'

Meanwhile, clearly anxious to retain his high profile at a time when his Indycar career was coming to an end, through mutual agreement, and his Formula 1 prospects were less than certain, Nigel Mansell expressed his irrepressible confidence about his future potential to Oliver Holt of *The Times*:

'I will not hang on in motor racing past my time, and my time is while I am competing at the highest level,' he insisted. 'As I sit here talking to you, my motivation is knowing that I am still one of the best in the world. If some people want to believe I am overweight and unfit then let them do so, because it is pathetic. If that were true, why would there be all this manoeuvring to try and get me back.

'Given the opportunity, the motivation, the encouragement, I can go on and win another Formula 1 World Championship without batting an eye. I can beat Schumacher, I can beat anyone.' Nevertheless, Frank Williams wanted David Coulthard.

At the Belgian Grand Prix the young Scot agreed with Williams to extend the option on his services, at Frank's request, until two days after Adelaide. At Spa, Monza and Estoril, Coulthard really began to shine and McLaren boss Ron Dennis suddenly appeared on the scene to make him an offer.

Then in mid-October Frank's secretary walked into his office carrying a letter from IMG, the management company representing Coulthard, which expressed the view that his Williams contract was unenforceable. Frank summoned Coulthard immediately and he came round about three hours later, accompanied by Tim Wright, the IMG executive who looked after his interests. A frank exchange of views followed.

'Subsequently I told him that I was taking up the option, but he told me that he wasn't driving for me,' recalls Williams. 'How do you get out of that situation? I say "I will" and he says "I won't". You have to go to court – the Contracts Recognition Board. To do that you need a conflicting contract. This went on for some time, and in Japan I said, "You have to sign another contract. The only way this will get settled is in front of the CRB."'

The FIA's Contracts Recognition Board is made up of a panel of three international lawyers who meet in Switzerland to adjudicate purely on the legal aspects of any conflicting contracts. There is no way in which they are empowered to give a verdict on an individual contract in isolation, hence the need for Coulthard to sign with McLaren in order that the matter could be examined.

It was a tricky time for Williams. He hadn't wanted to tell Coulthard he was going to take up his option because, by the very nature of Formula 1, the news would get out. Mansell still had two more races to drive for the team and they wanted to get the best out of him. But Frank did give David his assurance that he was very likely to be in the second Williams alongside Hill for 1995. At this stage keeping Mansell happy was the name of the game.

After spinning off at Jerez, Mansell drove a storming race to finish fourth in the pouring rain at Suzuka, underlining his terrific commitment by racing wheel-to-wheel with Jean Alesi's Ferrari in a battle that produced some of the best Formula 1 television coverage of the year. He then won in Adelaide, despite going off the track on the third corner and ending up as the somewhat fortunate beneficiary of a slight error from Gerhard Berger in the closing stages, which cost the Austrian driver his second win of the season.

'One thing I would say about Nigel in those last races,' said Frank, 'is that, yes, he obviously wanted to drive next year, so he went out of his way to be co-operative, but it was a pleasure to have him around. Nothing was too much trouble for him. Of course, he tends to be rather different when he's got his feet under the table. If we take him next year, I know what's going to happen; it will be wall-to-wall aggravation between him and Damon.'

In the event the Contracts Recognition Board decreed that Williams's option on David Coulthard's services was valid. With good grace McLaren bowed out of the contest for the Scot's services, and there followed a few nerve-racking weeks over Christmas 1994 as Williams sat down and finalised what David willingly accepted was a much more realistic deal. Just as he had done, a few weeks earlier, to address Damon Hill's complaints in Adelaide.

'I am delighted that we've been able to come to an agreement,' said Coulthard, 'and I hope now I can carry on where I left off last year, because it seems such a long time since I last raced.

'I've always been a big fan of Nigel's ever since I raced karts; he's always given total commitment, always 110 per cent, and I'd like to think that's something I can display as well. It's very difficult to put it into words, because that [beating Nigel] was not the main focus. I just think I've got a great opportunity after competing in only eight races.'

Coulthard admitted that he felt quite inhibited during those early Formula 1 outings. 'Definitely more than at any other time in my career,' he said thoughtfully. 'If I crashed the car I wasn't sure I would be driving in the next race. The low point was at Hungary when I crashed the car twice in the weekend, but now all bets are off from the start of next season and I'm looking forward to learning a lot from Damon.

'Of course the McLaren business will always be there, even though they may forgive and forget, but it's always there. But I'm sure it won't affect my relationship with Williams and I'll be out to secure my long-term career in 1995.'

The bottom line, of course, was that Williams would not be paying much more than £2 million in driver fees for 1995 – a great deal less than they would have committed themselves to had they opted to pursue a long-term deal with Mansell. Having turned his back on Florida and returned to rent a home in the Isle of Man as he concentrated on developing his newly acquired golf club at Woodbury, near Exeter, it was now clear that Mansell was at a bit of a loose end and, perhaps inevitably, got together to strike a deal with McLaren-Mercedes for 1995. For those commentators who recalled some of Ron Dennis's comments about Mansell in the past, it seemed an unlikely alliance. But no less formidable for that.

Meanwhile, for Williams, the grind continued. A totally new car, the FW17, was completed to conform with the much-changed technical regulations that came into force for the 1995 season. The team also announced plans to move from its present 6.5-acre factory site to a 28-acre facility about six miles from Didcot, at Grove, near Wantage. Frenchman Jean-Christophe Boullion, the 1994 International Formula 3000 champion, was signed up as the team's official test driver, following the profitable and successful route pursued to such fine effect by Hill and Coulthard.

It had been a remarkable 26-month period in the team's history. Nigel Mansell, Riccardo Patrese, Alain Prost, Damon Hill, Ayrton Senna, David Coulthard and Nigel Mansell again had all come forward to carry the team's banner into battle, yielding two Drivers' Championships and three

Constructors' titles. Yet the tragedy of Ayrton Senna's death, and the still unresolved investigation into the cause of his fatal accident, would continue to hang over Williams Grand Prix Engineering as it prepared for 1995.

Now it was time to go forward again. The tears had been shed, the tributes written, reflected on and duly consigned to the archives. Ayrton's brief spell at Williams was now settling into a wider perspective as but one glorious moment in the multi-hued patchwork of the team's history.

There were more races to be won, titles to be secured. Within weeks Damon Hill and David Coulthard would be embroiled amidst the rough and tumble of another frantic battle for the 1995 World Championship. The scream of the engines, the vivid colour, the intensity of the settings and the frenzy of competition would serve to dull the pain of what had gone before and sharpen the anticipation of what could be achieved in the future.

Endpiece

A s the remainder of the 1994 World Championship Grand Prix season unfolded, an investigating magistrate, Maurizio Passarini, was appointed to carry out a detailed investigation into Senna's fatal accident. Reporting to him was a committee of experts including former Ferrari engineers Mauro Forghieri and Tomasso Carletti, Roberto Nosetto, former F1 driver Emanuele Pirro, and Professor Dalmonte, one of Italy's leading authorities on sports medicine, who was based at the University of Bologna.

As previously recounted, much nagging interest initially centred on press photographs of the wrecked Williams FW16 which clearly showed the car's steering wheel, still attached to a section of its shaft, lying in the debris alongside the car. It wasn't simply the fact that this fuelled speculation that Ayrton might have suffered a breakage of the steering column. It was more fundamental than that. From the outset many outsiders — including several Grand Prix drivers well acquainted with Imola — believed it was the *only* reasonable explanation behind apparent failure to negotiate the Tamburello left-hander and the reason why he braked so hard at the last moment.

However, the investigation proceded painfully slowly, with the result that by the time the F1 teams returned to Imola on the first anniversary of Senna's death, nothing had been officially resolved. Even more frustratingly, Passarini requested that he be given another six months to complete his work. Thus at the time of writing (May 1995), it seemed that no decision on whether or not to proceed with possible charges was likely to be made public prior to September 1995.

All this was at odds with optimistic predictions at the Japanese Grand Prix in November 1994 when Passarini was tipped to be on the point of making a decision about possible manslaughter charges against key Williams team personnel.

According to Roberto Causo, the FIA lawyer appointed to represent both Williams and Simtek, a worse case scenario could see Frank Williams, Patrick Head and several others receiving a four month jail sentence, suspended for five years. Yet at the same time when Causo spoke at Suzuka, it seemed that the complex jigsaw of events surrounding Senna's accident was still missing several key pieces.

It appeared that top metallurgists who examined components from the FW16's steering column had found both fatigue and impact traces on sections of the shaft and could not reach a definitive conclusion. However, there was some indication from the FOCA television transmission, which was terminated a second or so before the impact, that Senna had looked down in the cockpit, raising inevitable speculation that this was the moment he realised something was wrong.

It was also firmly established that Senna had mentioned to his team-mate Damon Hill not to run on the tight inside line round Tamburello because the bumps were too severe. Yet photographic evidence from the Williams on-board camera revealed that Ayrton took what might best be described as a conventional line through the corner.

In attempting to establish definitively what caused the accident, Williams was frustrated by being unable to examine the wrecked car. Patrick Head was permitted to view the car only briefly. This left the team attempting to piece together whatever information they could from such telemetry data which survived the impact.

The Williams team's contribution to the investigation was extremely limited. Patrick Head was permitted only brief access to the crashed car during a couple of fleeting occasions in the months following the accident. Steering input remained a key area of consideration, and Williams submitted a comprehensive report which supported the view that it would have been impossible to produce any of the telemetry data involved without the wheel being attached to the column at the moment of the accident.

It was also suggested that Senna's Williams FW16 might have picked up debris on the circuit from the startline multiple collision which had promoted deployment of the safety car.

"Something that surprised myself and Patrick Head came from reviewing the film of the cars following the safety vehicle," explained Causo. "Ayrton was following it directly, while Michael Schumacher was close to the pit wall. I think that is where Ayrton took some debris.

"When I saw the accident my immediate reaction was a tyre failure from the debris. But it doesn't appear to have been, because the telemetry shows that the car was level. It was running a little low, but not much."

So there was no concrete evidence pointing towards a technical failure, yet by the same token it seemed inconveivable that Senna would have made a mistake at Tamburello. However, there was some slender evidence to suggest that he was looking down into the cockpit just before he plunged off the road.

Causo explained to *Autosport*: "On the in-car video, you normally see the 'Nacional' decal on the lower part of his crash helmet (reflected) in the mirror, but this time you see his visor — as if he was looking down. He could have been looking down at the steering wheel, or he could have been checking the whereabouts of Michael Schumacher behind him. Who knows?"

Who indeed. The only thing that was certain beyond belief was the reality that, 12 months after the disaster and with all the high technology available to the inquiry, no firm conclusion had been reached. On the face of it, this was quite unacceptable. Not only were there possible legal implications involved, but also worries amongst rival F1 teams about the whole question of racing in Italy.

Yet the investigation ground on through the summer of 1995. It was ironic to reflect that, 26 years before Senna's death, when the legendary Jim Clark crashed to his death in a minor-league Formula 2 race at Hockenheim, the moment of impact — on the long straight through the pine forests — was not witnessed by a single individual.

A generation later, the sport's acknowledged leader would be killed on live, prime-time television. Yet a year after this numbing catastrophe, the bottom line was that nobody knew *precisely* why Ayrton Senna plunged to his death in the spring sunshine any more than they knew why Clark slithered off that rain-soaked German circuit to oblivion.

Meanwhile, Williams continued its preparation for the 1995 F1 World Championship season and the new 3-litre regulations. Adrian Newey pencilled a distinctive high-nosed new F1 challenger, the FW17, powered by the latest Renault RS7 V10, a unit developed from the previous season's highly successful 3.5-litre unit. The pressure was on the team as never before with Renault expanding its engine supply deals to include arch-rivals Benetton, but all the signs from the start of the season pointed to the new Williams being a quite outstanding machine which was more than capable of dealing with its immediate opposition.

Hill opened the season by qualifying on pole position for the Brazilian GP at Interlagos, and although Schumacher led the opening stages, Damon dodged ahead after his first refuelling stop and was edgeing away at the head of the field when his FW17 suddenly snapped into a spin at the ess-bend immediately after the start/finish line. It was the initial conclusion that the spin had been caused by a gearbox failure — Damon had reported a problem over the radio the previous lap — but close scrutiny revealed that the left rear suspension push-rod had broken, causing the car to sit down on that corner and pirouette out of control.

Schumacher was thus left with an easy run to victory from a slightly under-the-weather David Coulthard who'd been suffering from a fever in the run-up to the first race of the season and paced himself sensibly to run just behind the leaders as a result. However, the Brazilian race was fraught with controversy as, just before the start, both Benetton and Williams were advised by the race stewards that fuel samples taken from Schumacher's and Coulthard's cars during practice did not match the officially 'registered' samples lodged with the FIA prior to the race.

As a consequence, the cars would be taking part in the race on a provisional basis, and the teams would be fined. After the race, more fuel samples were taken and, since Elf only took a single fuel specification to Brazil, it was hardly surprising that the samples again failed to match. The matter was reported to the stewards of the meeting and both cars were disqualified, promoting Gerhard Berger's third placed Ferrari to an apparent victory.

However, the FIA Court of Appeal subsequently took the rather odd step of reinstating Schumacher and Coulthard to first and second places at Interlagos, but at the same time disallowed the two teams' Constructors' Championship points from this event, and fined each entrant $200,000. The convoluted logic behind this was that Elf had not deliberately infringed the rules — it was a case of inadvertent muddling — and, either way, the drivers could not be held responsible.

By this time Hill had won a convincing victory in the Argentine GP at Buenos Aires, the second round of the title chase where Coulthard had started from his first pole position and led convincingly from the start. Unfortunately he was slowed by sudden electrical trouble, dropping to third, but fought back into contention before his engine abruptly cut out, stranding him on the circuit for good.

Three weeks later Hill avoided every pitfall and dodged every hazard to win the San Marino GP at Imola, an emotional success coming just 12 months after the bleak misery surrounding Senna's death. There were four cars in with a shout at Imola — Schumacher's Benetton, Berger's Ferrari, Hill, and Coulthard.

Michael crashed the Benetton after switching from wet tyres to slicks on a still damp track surface, Coulthard had a spin and a stop-go penalty for speeding in the pits — and Berger stalled his engine at his first refuelling stop. Damon never put a wheel wrong, emerging from the race at the head of the Drivers' Championship points table.

With Williams sharing the Constructors' points lead with Ferrari, it was almost as if the race represented a symbolic exorcising of too many painful memories. Williams had come through the eye of the storm and survived. Arguably, they looked stronger than ever.

Index